Decentralizing City Government

Decentralizing City Government

An Evaluation of the New York City District Manager Experiment

Allen H. Barton
Norman I. Fainstein
Susan S. Fainstein
Nathalie S. Friedman
Stanley J. Heginbotham
Joel D. Koblentz
Theresa F. Rogers
John M. Boyle
Ronald Brumback

Columbia University

Lexington Books
D.C. Heath and Company
Lexington, Massachusetts
Toronto

Library of Congress Cataloging in Publication Data

Main entry under title:
Decentralizing city government.

Report by Columbia University's Bureau of Applied Social Research on the results of a project conducted by New York City's Office of Neighborhood Government.
Includes index.
1. Decentralization in government—New York (City). 2. Municipal services—New York (City). 3. New York (City)—Politics and government—1951-   I. Barton, Allen H., 1924-   II. Columbia University. Bureau of Applied Social Research. III. New York (City). Office of Neighborhood Government.
JS1234.A15D423   352'.002'097471   76-43600
ISBN 0-669-01098-7

NSF/RA-770006

Published simultaneously in Canada.

Printed in the United States of America.

International Standard Book Number: 0-669-01098-7

Library of Congress Catalog Card Number: 76-43600

Contents

Foreword

For some time now, Americans have poked and prodded their municipal governments looking for better ways to run neighborhood affairs within the huge confines of the American city. The common complaints giving rise to these experiments are feelings on the part of citizens of helplessness, of remoteness of the city officials and of neglect. Beginning in the 1960s, reform efforts were stepped up and took various shapes and directions. Some were efforts by cities themselves—little city halls and storefront service centers. Others were federally funded under the Poverty Program and Model Cities Program. Mixed into all of these were experimental programs designed to see what could be done to ease what was generally recognized to be a decline in the quality of urban life.

During the two and one-half years I served as Secretary of Health, Education and Welfare, a number of programs, studies and experiments were set in motion aimed at solutions to the urban condition and at the just complaints of minority groups. One of them was the Office of Neighborhood Government demonstration in New York City. The results of that experimental program are contained in this volume. The idea was to create a small urban unit of government with a devolution of power to the neighborhood level to provide better delivery of wide ranges of city services and to encourage citizen participation.

It will become quickly apparent to readers of this volume that this is not a routinely optimistic report of breakthroughs in the New York program. Instead, it is a review of a program with high ideals that foundered on inadequate finances, resistance from city officials, and politics. Yet the study is, for all of this, an optimistic one for those of us convinced that people want a sense of autonomy and want a government that is more responsive and accessible. The potential, this report makes clear, is still there.

As for the failures of this program, any effort of an experimental nature is, by definition, designed for a short period of time—two years in this case—and, therefore, is bound to have the sort of trouble that the Office of Neighborhood Government had. Politicians are apt to look on such efforts as temporary irritants that invade and upset the status quo. City administrators, accustomed to shifting tides as one administration gives way to the next, will ride along until the water settles again but are seldom seen rowing hard unless there is a clear and permanent commitment from city hall. These reactions are understandable. Citizens themselves are likely to be cynical about investing their trust in such ephemeral organizations. This, too, is understandable.

What I am suggesting is that this may have been one of those classic sociological cases in which the presence of the sociologist himself distorts the social patterns he is studying. In this case, the experimental nature of the program distorted the results. Certainly the experiment itself was quickly distorted, as Stanley J. Heginbotham points out in Chapter 2, with initial goals and intentions differing strongly from the actual patterns of organization and activity which evolved. In what seems to me understatement, he pointed to one of the pitfalls that all these changes brought about: "When social scientists design base-line survey research to measure the effects of a particular set of stimuli, they are disconcerted when they discover that those stimuli have been changed even before the first questionnaires reach the field."

Despite this, I continue to hold fast to the intuitive belief that there is a correlation between participation and political efficacy on the one hand, and between powerlessness and alienation on the other. Citizens' participation is the essential fabric of our form of government. And where government has grown too remote, it must be decentralized and dispersed to the levels where the citizen instinctively knows that playing his part does make a difference.

The question then becomes whether this concept can be "proved" in a test tube or a demonstration program. I am inclined, now, to think that it cannot, given the very forces that distorted this program. If this is true, then perhaps the wisest next step is to study the contemporary scene in America's big cities, measuring them against the assumptions that underlaid this very program.

For example, take a heavy industrial city on one of the Great Lakes, such as Milwaukee, and compare it to another—Cleveland or Buffalo. Is there a difference in citizens' feelings about their lives and their cities? If there is, is it traceable to better service delivery in one than another? Is there a pattern that corresponds in these cities to the district managers efforts? Do minority community demands have a positive effect on services in ghetto areas? Is some form of devolution a fact in those cities where people perceive their lives to be better and their political institutions more responsive?

I suspect that many of these questions have already been asked and the answers are in a report on a dusty library shelf somewhere. Certainly the Rand Corporation Study published in 1974 and titled *Street-Level Governments: Assessing Decentralization and Urban Services* confirmed my feelings about the need to make government more responsive and accessible. Another Rand study, published in 1973 and titled *Citizen Organizations: Increasing Client Control Over Services* pointed in the opposite direction.

Aside from these considerations, the frankness and honesty of this report, assembled under the direction of Allen H. Barton at Columbia University's Bureau of Applied Social Research, makes it a valuable and thoughtful addition to our knowledge and a guide to future plans.

Elliot L. Richardson
Secretary of Commerce

Acknowledgments

The New York City neighborhood government study grew out of the interests of the Office of the Mayor in the City of New York, the Office of the Secretary in the Department of Health, Education and Welfare, staff members in the Department of Housing and Urban Development, and social scientists at Columbia University, in evaluating a unique program of broad-gauge administrative decentralization in a number of New York City's sixty-two Community Planning Districts. The city decentralization program itself was partially supported by a grant from the Department of Health, Education and Welfare program of Services Integration Research and Development. The Columbia research team obtained support from the brand-new program of Research Applied to National Needs of the National Science Foundation for a three-year study, with four major research components involving sociologists, political scientists, and economists.

Urban problems and their remedies run the gamut from engineering problems of street cleaning to human services problems in helping people out of poverty. No one city department, no one state or federal department, and no one social science discipline can deal with the whole range of problems. The New York City "neighborhood government experiment" crossed all these lines. It was therefore fortunate that a program such as NSF's Research Applied to National Needs existed and could support an interdisciplinary study of this broad-gauge effort, which otherwise would have fallen under nobody's jurisdiction because it fell into too many areas.

The Bureau of Applied Social Research grew up at Columbia University during World War II as an institution in which newly developed social research methods could be tried out by faculty, students, and research personnel on a wide range of problems. The Bureau is an interdisciplinary research institute drawing on all the social science departments of Columbia and where necessary on its professional schools. The New York neighborhood government study drew on faculty and students from sociology, political science, and urban planning.

As a university research institute, the Bureau had several responsibilities in this study. As a study of an applied problem, the research had to be designed to provide answers to questions of importance to policymakers on urban problems, in New York, in Washington, in state capitals, and in cities generally besides New York. As a study carried out by social scientists committed to their disciplines, it had to contribute to the expansion of knowledge in their several fields. As a study of several highly organized and active communities and as one requiring repeated interviews with community leaders, it had to provide useful information to the communities themselves. As a study in a university setting, it had to provide opportunities for apprentice work to advanced graduate students.

This volume is the first, overall summary of the findings of the study.

Additional monographs and articles that will be appearing deal with special topics, including the problem of stability of city neighborhoods, the beliefs of community leaders about community control, and the experiences of particular neighborhoods and agencies. Over a dozen doctoral dissertations now in progress at Columbia and Rutgers will provide additional scholarly analysis of the results.

The first contact between New York City and Columbia, which led to this project, was initiated in the spring of 1971—when the city was actively planning its decentralization program—by E.S. Savas, then Deputy City Administrator, with Professor Amitai Etzioni, then chairman of the Department of Sociology. In the early stages of developing the research plan, the senior author received helpful advice from many people, of whom the late Professor Wallace Sayre was one of the most important. Professors Donald Haider and Sam Sieber assisted in drafting the proposal.

The project benefited at all stages from the concern and advice of its NSF project manager, Dr. George W. Baker, and other members of the NSF staff.

The NSF grant made explicit provision for a project advisory committee consisting of both scholars and of governmental practitioners with local and federal experience relating to urban problems. Members from outside Columbia were:

Dennis Allee, Executive Director, State Charter Revision Commission for New York City

George W. Baker, Program Manager, Research Applied to National Needs Directorate, National Science Foundation

Alan K. Campbell, Maxwell School of Citizenship and Public Affairs, Syracuse University

Wyndham Clarke, Director, Office of Research and Technology, Department of Housing and Urban Development

Thomas Coyle, Director, Office of Intergovernmental Systems, Department of Health, Education and Welfare

Richard Langendorf, Department of Housing and Urban Development (now Center for Urban Studies, University of Miami)

Arthur Naftalin, School of Public Affairs, University of Minnesota

Peter Rossi, Department of Sociology, University of Massachusetts

Columbia faculty members of the Advisory Committee were:

Herbert Gans, Department of Sociology
Charles Hamilton, Department of Political Science
James Jones, Graduate School of Social Work
Eugene Litwak, Department of Sociology
Donna Shalala, Teachers College
Bruce L.R. Smith, Department of Political Science
William Vickrey, Department of Economics

Additional advice was given by the panelists at the Workshop on Urban Decentralization and Neighborhood Government held at Columbia in January 1975 to review the project findings:

Alan Altshuler, Massachusetts Institute of Technology
Wayne Anderson, Advisory Commission on Intergovernmental Relations
Herman Badillo, Congressman, 21st Congressional District
William Boyd, Associate Director, National Municipal League
Terry Clark, University of Chicago
James Davis, National Opinion Research Center
Scott Fosler, Committee for Economic Development
Howard K. Hallman, Center for Governmental Studies
Harry Hatry, The Urban Institute
Herbert Kaufman, The Brookings Institution
Kirk O'Donnell, Special Assistant to the Mayor, Boston
Elinor Ostrom, Indiana University
Harriet Saperstein, Detroit Planning Office
Stanley Speirs, Regional Office, HUD
James Vanecko, Brown University
Donald Wortman, Department of DHEW

To the respondents in our public, leadership, and city official samples who gave their time and thought to answering so many questions, the project is deeply indebted; social research cannot be done without help from the people being studied. The district managers of the Office of Neighborhood Government, and its directors, first Lewis Feldstein and then John Mudd, were extremely helpful. City officials from the police, sanitation, parks and recreation, housing and development, human resources, health services, transportation, and addiction services departments and administrations were most cooperative in providing access to great amounts of data for the resource allocation analysis.

Two research organizations worked under subcontract to Columbia University to help gather data for the study. The National Opinion Research Center did an extraordinary job in fielding the first wave of the public surveys from its New York office under the supervision of Pearl Zinner and Esther Fleischman. The Administrative and Management Research Association of New York managed the first two years' work of extracting city data for the analysis of resource allocation and service delivery.

The first wave of the public survey was skilfully organized by Dr. John Michael, while Drs. Ronald Lawson and Wen Kuo managed the first wave of the leadership survey. Dr. Astrid Merget carried out a useful survey of current thinking on urban decentralization among academic, professional, citizen, and governmental groups which helped to focus our analysis on policy-relevant issues.

The direction of the four main components of the project was carried out by Stanley Heginbotham (administrative analysis), Joel Koblentz (service delivery and cost analysis), Norman and Susan Fainstein (leadership study), and Nathalie Friedman and Terry Rogers (public survey). In addition Nathalie Friedman served as overall project coordinator. The work of this group of professionals speaks for itself.

Finally, no project of this size can operate without a devoted staff of research assistants, administrators, technicians, and secretarial workers. Research assistants for the administrative analysis included Geraldine Alpert, Stephen Barton, John Boyle, Marianne Chawluk, David Hom, Howard Katz and Robin Maas; for the leadership study, Gary Barrett, Larry Bennett, Robert Blank, Neil Bomberg, Fran LaSpina Clark, John McLoughlin, Peter Roggemann, Sam Seiffer and Mary Jane Wilson; for the public survey, Kenneth Andrews, Laurie Bauman, Deborah Bell, Flora Davidson, and Naomi Golding; and for special community studies, Paul Ballard, Michael Bucuvalas, Perry Davis, Jeanette Michelson, Dale Nelson and Candelario Saenz.

Excellent clerical and technical assistance was provided by Estelle Cooper, Carol Dulaney, Susan Erichsen, Pnina Grinberg, Nora Litwak, Laurie Mengrone and Sharon Neumann. Madeline Simonson performed miracles as publication production coordinator for dozens of interim reports, staff papers, and drafts of this book. The Bureau's Administrator, Phyllis Sheridan, kept the whole operation on the road from beginning to end with her skillful handling of personnel, budgets, conferences and administrative relationships within and outside the University. All those who worked on the project over its four years can be proud of their participation.

The basic data from the public and leadership surveys can be obtained by scholars interested in further analysis through the Data Archivist, Bureau of Applied Social Research, Columbia University, at the cost of reproduction of computer tapes, codebooks, and questionnaires, or from the Roper Center for Public Opinion Research, Williamstown, Massachusetts.

The Research Plan, Major Findings, and Implications for Public Policy

Introduction

The study reported in the chapters that follow looked at the experience of New York City's Office of Neighborhood Government to find evidence bearing on the question:

Will decentralization of big-city government help solve urban problems by improving service delivery to the public and by improving the public's relationships with city government?

The specific form of decentralization studied was the creation of district managers for areas of about 130,000 people within New York City. Each manager presided over a district cabinet consisting of local service administrators (police precinct commanders, district parks foremen, district sanitation superintendents, and representatives of health, housing, human resources, addiction services, and transportation) and met with advisory groups of community leaders. The managers tried to get better coordination between departments at the neighborhood level, better adaptation of services to local needs, and greater responsiveness to citizen requests. Starting in January 1972, the managers and cabinets were set up experimentally in eight of the city's sixty-two Community Planning Districts; a weaker version involving cabinets without full-time managers was installed in sixteen more districts in 1973.

At the request of the mayor's office, Columbia University's Bureau of Applied Social Research developed a research plan to evaluate the experimental program and to make findings available to all interested governmental and citizen bodies, locally and nationally. Because of the broad interest of the problem of administrative decentralization and its interdepartmental and interdisciplinary nature, support was obtained from the newly created program of Research Applied to National Needs of the National Science Foundation.

The Research

The research was carried out over the period February 1972 through the fall of 1974 and was written up during the 1974-75 time period. The project was organized in four main components:

1. The administrative analysis component examined the organizational

structure and actual implementation of the district manager-district cabinet experiment in the first five districts where it was tried out by using observation and informal interviewing techniques. In 1974 this component also interviewed one-hundred and five local officials in ten districts—four with district managers, three with cabinets only, and three with neither. This component was directed by a political scientist, Stanley J. Heginbotham.

2. The service delivery and cost analysis component did three things. It recorded the results of sixty-five "projects" of interdepartmental cooperation initiated by the district managers and cabinets and tried to assess the obstacles encountered, resources used, and accomplishments of each; it measured the costs of operating the district manager offices and the central Office of Neighborhood Government, which coordinated them; and it gathered data from eight city departments on allocation of resources to all sixty-two Community Planning Districts to check on whether resources were being diverted to experimental districts from other districts, and to study the determinants of resource allocation to districts within a large city. This component was directed by an economist, Joel D. Koblentz.

3. The leadership study component surveyed three-hundred and fifty community leaders in 1972, interviewed selected community leaders and local officials participating in district cabinets in 1973, and resurveyed community leaders in 1974. The interviewees were asked about their contacts with city agencies, perceptions of local problems, satisfaction with city services, and attitudes toward decentralization of city government. The observers sat in at meetings of community organizations and sessions of the district cabinets. This component was directed by two urban sociologist-political scientists, Susan and Norman Fainstein.

4. The public survey component interviewed 1683 residents of seven Community Planning Districts in 1972, four with a District Manager and three without one, about 4 months after the start of the experiment. It asked about problems of living in the neighborhood actually experienced by respondents, satisfaction with city services, participation in community activities, contact with city agencies, and plans to stay or move. In 1974, 973 of the original respondents living at the same locations and 124 who had moved elsewhere were reinterviewed, as well as 252 people who had moved into dwelling units from which original respondents had moved out. The earlier questions were repeated along with some new ones, to measure changes in satisfactions, activities, and experiences with government in experimental and nonexperimental districts. This component was directed by a sociologist, Dr. Nathalie S. Friedman.

Summary of the Major Findings

1. *The program changed during its planning phase from one emphasizing community representation and outreach to citizens to one emphasizing the strengthening of local administrative capacity.* The final plan involved:

Appointment of a district manager, without line authority but with mayoral backing, to promote interdepartmental coordination within experimental Community Planning Districts (averaging 130,000 population);

Creation of a district cabinet of local line administrators of city agencies operating in these Community Planning Districts;

Delegation of greater authority to these local line administrators from their respective departmental superiors at borough and city levels;

Shifting service district boundaries of the various departments toward coterminality, so that each would eventually use the Community Planning Districts as the basis of their service administration.

The deemphasis on community representation resulted from the political, racial, and union confrontation over community control of schools in the Ocean Hill-Brownsville district in 1968-69, as well as the realization that a local administrative capacity was a necessary condition for any further political decentralization.

2. *The program was modified in actual implementation*, since most city departments did not delegate additional authority to their field administrators and did not redraw district service boundaries to make them coterminous. The extent of mayoral backing in dealing with the departments was less than planned, and the City Council blocked allocation of small supplemental funds for locally initiated projects and service modifications. District managers and cabinets were left to work with whatever local discretion and resources were available. Managers turned to mobilizing community leaders and groups to support service changes proposed by the cabinets.

3. *The program actively involved most local operating officials and community leaders*, who worked together to initiate a wide range of service modifications and community projects to solve specific local problems. Most community leaders in the experimental districts reported contact with the manager and his staff.

4. *Departments with clear line authority and district organization—such as police and sanitation—were able to cooperate most easily* with the managers and the cabinets. Departments with highly centralized functionally specialized components (e.g., health) had the most difficulty in relating themselves to a district-level coordinating effort.

5. *Most service modifications initiated by the managers and cabinets involved creating procedures for local cooperation between field administrators of different departments* where no procedures or only very cumbersome ones had previously existed. Other manager-cabinet projects involved identifying strategic points at which small additional resources for services or equipment would eliminate recurring problems previously left unsolved. A few projects attempted to secure major funds from federal, state, or private sources for community improvement programs, with interdepartmental coordination and community support organized through the district manager and cabinet.

6. A little over *one-third of the locally initiated projects were fully*

implemented, and another one-third were partially implemented. Obstacles generally were the failures to obtain authority for changes in service delivery from higher levels (borough or city) of the departments involved or approval from the city councilman for minor discretionary funds budgeted for local use. The few large projects depending on federal funds found that these were not forthcoming as a result of the Nixon administration's cutback of urban programs.

7. After two years of operation, *the field administrators of city agencies in experimental districts reported essentially the same levels of interdepartmental contact and cooperation* as did those in nonexperimental districts. A moderate level of cooperation existed with or without the manager or a cabinet. *More interagency conflict was reported in experimental than in nonexperimental* districts. In spite of the success of a number of specific cooperative projects, the overall level of contact and cooperation reported by local administrators did not appear to be affected.

8. *The field administrators of city agencies in experimental districts (line officials of police, sanitation, parks, and other agencies) had strongly favorable attitudes*, toward the district managers and cabinets after two years of experience, and desired to have them continued. These administrators saw the program as having valuable potential.

9. After two years of operation, *the community leaders in experimental districts had the same degree of dissatisfaction with city services* overall and department by department as those in nonexperimental districts.

10. *The great majority of community leaders in experimental districts*, virtually all of whom were familiar with and had direct contact with their local Offices of Neighborhood Government, *had strongly favorable attitudes* toward the district managers and cabinets and wanted the program continued. Some opposition came from the traditional political clubs who felt competition from the program in their role as intermediaries with city agencies, although other local politicians found the program a useful channel for their own efforts.

11. *The overwhelming majority of local residents of experimental districts did not become aware* of their local Offices of Neighborhood Government by the time of the second public survey in 1974, after over two years of the local operations. This lack of awareness was largely because the offices concentrated on administrative coordination and working with community leaders rather than on serving as public complaint or service centers. Those citizens who were most active in community affairs were most aware of the experiment.

12. The local residents of experimental districts started out essentially identical with those of nonexperimental districts in satisfaction and attitudes in the 1972 baseline survey. After two years of the experiment, local residents of both sets of districts were more dissatisfied with city services, felt they had more problems, and felt more powerless and distrustful toward city government. *The decline was essentially the same in districts with and without district managers.*

13. The amount of contact with city agencies was about the same in both experimental and nonexperimental districts. However, among the minority of residents (about 20 percent) who did have contact with a city agency about some problem, *those living in experimental districts reported about 10 percent higher satisfaction with the city's response to their contacts* in the second survey, compared either to those who had contacts in 1972 or to the residents of nonexperimental districts on either survey.

14. In all districts surveyed, *the majority of the public said they favored increased local decision making*, both within city departments and through an elected community board that can influence city services.

15. The cost of the district manager and his staff of about half a dozen was about $100,000 a year for a district of about 130,000 people. Participation of departmental officials and expense of the central office can be roughly estimated for a citywide program, so that *the overall cost would be about $125,000 per district of 130,000 people*—about $1 per inhabitant.

16. *The experimental districts did not appear to be favored in the allocation of departmental resources*, when their 1973 manpower and funds were analyzed in relation to population characteristics, except in two services, parks maintenance and highways repair, where the experimental program apparently created pressure to shift resources from nonexperimental districts. Unlike Model Cities and Community Action programs, the experiment was intended to improve services *without* bringing in large additional funds, so it was essential to ascertain that no large-scale shifting of resources took place.

17. The researchers found that *budgets of city departments can practically be broken down on a common district basis* in order to aid district managers or local citizen bodies in keeping track of the resources available in the district and in proposing reallocations according to local priorities. The researchers were able to recombine records of manpower, equipment, and expenses kept by the city agencies for small subdivisions—and for some central operations, to assign "client" home addresses to Community Planning Districts—in order to create district budgets covering about two-thirds of the city expenditures (the rest of the expenditures were mainly central services that could not be allocated to districts).

Policy Implications

What are the policy implications of these findings for city governments or citizen groups considering means of improving service delivery and citizen-government relationships? What do they imply for state and federal government agencies that are concerned with human services, housing, urban planning, crime, health?

The results of the experiment are rather contradictory. On the one hand, the project-by-project analysis shows some specific successes in improving services by achieving better cooperation between departments; local officials and community leaders directly involved in the experiment felt strongly favorable to it and wanted it continued. On the other hand, during its two years of experimental operation the program did not change the satisfaction with the services of the various departments, with the community, or with city government, of the average resident or of the community leaders. A crucial question is whether such changes in satisfaction could realistically be expected from this kind of administrative restructuring in a two-year period.

One can conclude that the experiment showed evidence of *potentialities* for service improvement through district-level coordination of departments and community inputs, by means of district managers, district cabinets, and community advisory groups. But we have no evidence of how much public and community leader satisfaction with services and with city government might be improved—if at all—if the program were implemented citywide, over a period of years, as a normal part of city government.

The experiment also suggests the value of a local administrative coordinating center for the planning and implementation of community improvement efforts using federal, state or private funds; however, projects of this type went through the planning phase, but never reached the operating stage during the course of the experiment due to the freezing of federal urban programs.

The policymaker who is seeking to improve urban service delivery will therefore not find conclusive evidence of what he should or should not do in the results of the New York district manager and cabinet experiment. However, he can learn some things from the New York experience:

1. The program will not create major immediate problems of resistance or conflict involving either local officials or community leaders, if it is handled as carefully as the New York program was, but rather should result in favorable attitudes toward the chance to participate.
2. The program will be able to show some specific improvements in service delivery, such as those documented by the project analysis of the New York City experiment: better procedures for cooperation between field administrators of different departments, identification of gaps in services that create recurring and expensive problems, and improved local capacity to effectively use outside community-improvement funds.
3. The program should not be expected to produce a rapid, noticeable improvement in service delivery from the viewpoint of the public—at least within its first two years of operation—although it may result in somewhat greater satisfaction among the minority who have direct dealings with city departments.
4. The program will be of modest cost—of the order of $1 per capita—and will mainly function through redirecting existing resources at the local level.

In the chapters that follow we have tried to present detailed descriptions of what happened in the New York experiment so that the policymaker, citizen, or student of public administration can draw his or her own conclusions about the overall, long-term potentiality of decentralization and local coordination of service management within large governmental units. We have also tried to present fully the limitations in the city's implementation of the experimental program, as well as the hitches in carrying out the research as designed, both of which have to be taken into consideration in drawing policy implications from the results presented here.

**Decentralizing City
Government**

1

The Problem of Urban Decentralization and the Research Design of the New York City Neighborhood Government Study

Allen H. Barton

The Goals of Urban Decentralization

Urban decentralization has been advocated for three reasons.

First, most big cities are suffering from a crisis in the quality of life—in the physical environment and in the social problems that center around unemployment, poverty, racial conflict, and crime. The majority of big-city residents, regardless or race, tell pollsters that they would rather live in suburbs, small towns, or rural areas. Since World War II, the middle classes have been moving out and the poor moving in—partially as a result of federal programs. Any method that might improve city services and influence the quality of life in the cities demands careful examination. Some governmental experts argue that a reallocation of functions and authority between "tiers" of government would improve service delivery. They favor decentralized, locally coordinated management of some services at the level of subcity districts, at the same time as they advocate regionalization of other functions. Thus, the Advisory Commission on Intergovernmental Relations and the Committee for Economic Developmemt have endorsed the three-tier system of local community, city, and regional governments.[1] Both housing and human services specialists consider the local coordination of services to be especially urgent in dealing with such multiply-caused conditions as neighborhood deterioration, the complex of youth problems such as underachievement and delinquency, or the accumulation of "social pathologies" in a neighborhood.

Second, the black and Hispanic minorities in most cities, finding themselves lacking in political and economic power, developed during the 1960s a demand for "community control" over city services in the ghettos as a form of Black Power (or Puerto Rican or Chicano power).[2] Community control was demanded for varied and conflicting motivations: to improve education and other public services for ghetto people, to take over the local jobs held mainly by whites living outside the area, to secure a political base for minority group leaders, to develop educational programs emphasizing ethnic culture and pride (and in some cases revolutionary or separatist doctrines). The community control movement ran immediately into conflicts with established political, bureaucratic, professional, and labor union forces and was usually defeated. However, the ideas and motivations that created the movement are not dead—only frustrated for the moment. And they have quietly spread to white ethnic groups and middle-class neighborhoods as well.

1

Third, there is the long-standing American tradition of *small units* of government as a means of securing citizen participation in politics and voluntary activity for community improvement. The belief that the big-city neighborhood or community can be revitalized as a basis for participation and social improvement goes back before World War I, when some settlement houses had this goal and community organizing movements in Chicago, Cleveland, and elsewhere tried to create a popular demand for community units of government as an alternative to both the traditional patronage-dominated political machine and the reformer's centralized, professionalized model of city government. These early efforts failed in the face of the machines on the one hand and the centralist reforms on the other. But the last dozen years have seen a revival of interest in "bringing government closer to the people" in the cities.[3] Some argue that localizing city government would bring new life to the political process in cities by stimulating public participation in local problems people care about and can understand and by rendering the bureaucracies and the professionals accountable to those they are supposed to serve. Some believe that the nature of city politics can be transformed in this way.

What cities might consider creating a new tier of community or district governments? Certainly the 26 cities in the United States with a half a million or more population, could create districts of 50,000 to 200,000. Perhaps the 107 cities from 100,000 to 500,000 might also consider smaller "neighborhood governments" for districts of 10,000 to 50,000. And the counties that have 50,000 people or more, of whom many are not organized into self-governing towns and villages might well consider such community governments. This type of reorganization would be particularly important for rapidly growing counties that are taking on many complex services on a centralized basis and are facing problems of coordinating them at the local level.

Who favors developing district governments within large cities or counties? We have already mentioned minority groups and the advocates of democratic small units. White ethnic groups and middle-class groups generally have also been looking for ways of maintaining the quality of life and government services in their neighborhoods. And external groups also have an interest in creating local bodies to help them implement programs in city districts.

In the 1960s the federal government required "community participation" in a host of programs, and citizen advisory groups proliferated with no connection with one another and no clear relationship with either their constituencies or the orthodox political leadership. Despite the cutback in federal social programs and the move toward general revenue sharing and block grants, many of these requirements still apply to health, mental health, community development, and similar programs. If cities and counties could formally organize a tier of district governments within themselves, these activities could be tied together and given a legitimate community base.

State officials who manage state-funded services and work with the governments of cities and large counties might also find such district units a useful locus for integration of services and community relations.[4]

Private groups dealing with urban districts have had severe difficulties in relating to communities that have no legitimately organized representation. "Take me to your leaders" becomes a cry of despair and frustration for a university dealing with conflicting self-appointed "community representatives" or for a financial institution trying to work out a program of investment in the reconstruction or maintenance of a city neighborhood. Voluntary associations and private charitable agencies may find better possibilities for community mobilization and service delivery in district governments. Political parties and organizations may find a new training ground for their active members in filling positions on local councils and committees dealing with service delivery.

The labor movement has had a very mixed reaction to the possibility of district governments. On the one hand, the "specter of community control" is the threat of community boards to the job-control and the established bargaining relationships that public service unions have developed with centralized city governments. On the other hand, in working-class districts community governments would be in a sense "labor governments" that could form models of good public employer-union relationships.

Like all reforms, urban decentralization carries with it controversial possibilities for gain or loss by organized interest groups, as well as the antiseptic potentials of rationalizing services and public representation.[5]

The Limits of Local Action

To a considerable extent, both the problems and the constituencies of the big cities are regional and national. The biggest cities are the cultural and organizational capitals of the major regions and of national industries. They have also been the promised land to which poor and minority migrants from the most backward rural areas have come and the home of the second and third generations of urban poor. Meanwhile the white middle class and better-paid working class find their promised land in the suburbs, thereby leaving the cities with a declining tax base. (Minority-group residents too want to leave, but the combination of discrimination and lack of skills prevents them from finding jobs or housing to do so.) The cities have thus fallen heir to the unsolved social problems of the whole nation.

These social problems plainly cannot be solved by any resources available to city governments—although New York City has been accused of bankrupting itself in trying. In the 1960s, a major federal effort was made to deal with the social problems of poverty, racial discrimination, and failure of the poor to achieve normal employment in the then-expanding economy through job training, compensatory education, antidiscrimination programs, community action programs, and the like. Although the social problems have proved much more intractible than had been hoped, national efforts still go on, both as limited experiments and major programs, involving income supplements, rent supplements, child care and development programs, job creation, reduction of barriers to suburban migration, and increased access to higher education, as well as continued attempts to make job training, compensatory education and social services work. While these programs are or aspire to be national, the cities would be among the major locations for them and the city residents, the major immediate beneficiaries.

But the time horizon for "solving" the problems of poverty and race relations, especially as they are concentrated in the black and Hispanic slums of the big cities, must now be seen as a very long-term one. City governments and school systems must still provide their services and try to make life tolerable for the middle classes and the poor, the urban dwellers and the commuting labor force, and the important organizations that are still city-based, under these difficult social conditions. Policing, fire protection, street cleaning, park and recreation services, housing code enforcement, education, social services, and public transportation must be carried on in the face of slum conditions—as well as the antisocial behavior that springs from them—and tensions that arise from processes of "invasion" and "defense" of ethnic and class territories. Moreover, the services must be provided under conditions of inflation, erosion of tax bases, out-migration of middle-class population, militant public employee unionism, and conflict with noncity political forces over who should pay for what.

The job of city leaders and of all those who deal with urban problems is thus a twofold one: to achieve *national programs* that would resolve the drastic social problems linked to poverty and racial hostility and that would be supported by state and national tax bases, and to work on local programs that would improve *delivery of city services* in the presence of unsolved social and economic problems. These two approaches in fact intersect in poor city neighborhoods and the urban job market, and there may be advantages in linking federal, state, and local programs at these levels. Specialists in public administration currently offer city leaders new technologies, including computers and information systems, and new management techniques, including methods for measuring service performance and motivating public employees. The question of interest to city leaders is whether decentralizing the operation of some city services and coordinating them at a community level will be a help or a hindrance in getting these difficult jobs done. That is what this study is about.

Types of Decentralization

Decentralization means many different things. In the major review of research on the topic sponsored by the National Science Foundation, Yin and Yates examined 269 studies. They distinguished seven major strategies of decentralization (see Table 1-1) that are characterized by their territorial focus and the degree of client involvement in administration of service.[6]

The citywide mechanisms of *community relations* activities and of *grievance-reporting systems* (such as an ombudsman) are intended to promote two-way flows of information between the city government and its clients; they are in fact alternatives to territorial decentralization in serving these purposes.

Among the decentralization strategies at the "neighborhood" or district level, *physical redeployment* places service agency staff in local offices, but does not necessarily involve other changes in agency operation. *Administrative decentralization* is defined by Yin and Yates as "the attempt by a service agency to grant its own district officials greater discretionary authority to be more responsive to neighborhood needs." The *resident employment* strategy involves hiring local residents to work in the service delivery agencies themselves to provide a form of internal representation of the clientele, or "representative bureaucracy." *New neighborhood institutions* are defined as "the development of separate institutions outside the existing service bureaucracy to fulfil neighborhood needs." These have typically involved federal funding. Finally, *political decentralization* is "the attempt to give clients direct governing control over a service being delivered to a specific neighborhood."

New York City's neighborhood government program did not fit into any of these categories as Yin and Yates defined them. It involved administrative decentralization, but of a wide range of departments rather than of a single service. It therefore adds the idea of *coordination of services* at the district level.

Table 1-1
Decentralization Strategies Placed along Territorial and Client-Oriented Dimensions

Territorial Focus	Client Role in Administration of Service		
	Negligible	Informed	Dominant
Citywide	Community relations	Grievance mechanisms	
Neighborhood	Physical redeployment	Employment of neighborhood residents	Political decentralization
	Administrative decentralization	New neighborhood institutions	

Source: Robert K. Yin and Douglas Yates, *Street-Level Governments: Assessing Decentralization and Urban Services,* Lexington, Massachusetts: D.C. Heath and Company (1975), p. 29.

The program also involved "client input" in that leaders of community organizations were frequently consulted about local needs. The Office of Neighborhood Government (ONG) was thus a unique case, for the United States, of *general-purpose* administrative decentralization at the district level within a large city, with some community input.

To compare the ONG program with other decentralization efforts, three dimensions must be added to the typology. Most important is the *range of services* involved. Yin and Yates generally assume that decentralization involves a single agency. However, one should distinguish one-agency political decentralization, as of the schools in New York City, from general-purpose local governments like the county boroughs of Greater London. Administrative decentralization likewise may involve one agency, several related agencies (as in a "multi-service center" for social services), or most or all city services (as in the Office of Neighborhood Government).

A second important dimension is the extent of *command decentralization* or "devolution of authority" to local officials. District offices are often set up for one agency, or for several agencies in common, and are staffed with clerks who have little or no more discretion than those in a central office. This pattern provides convenience of access for clients needing routine services, but does little to promote adaptation of policies to local needs.

A third significant dimension—the extent of *coordination of services* or "service integration"—emerges when several services are decentralized at the same level. Devolution of authority to district officials, and even co-location of their offices in a "little city hall," may take place without any requirement for coordination of their activities at the district level. The distinctive feature of the Office of Neighborhood Government experiment was the effort to combine command decentralization with local coordination of a number of city services.

Leaving out the "citywide" operations discussed by Yin and Yates and adding these three dimensions to the degree of client control produces a complex-looking but basically simple typology of urban decentralization programs (Table 1-2).

Into the categories of this classification can be entered most of the efforts at decentralization described in the literature. The scheme also sets requirements for adequate description of these programs. Little city halls exist in a number of cities, for instance, but they are not all the same kind of animal.[7] Some are simply local field offices providing "one-stop service" for clients of several agencies (the physical redeployment strategy applied to several agencies—type F or M in the classification). Others are staffed with officials having authority to adapt their agencies' programs to local conditions; these are local offices with command decentralization (type G or N). Still others aspire to coordinate the management of several agencies' services, as did the Office of Neighborhood Government (which shifted between types O and R).

The most extensive form of decentralization is political decentralization, including a wide range of public services (type S). This form is not found in any

Table 1-2
Types of District-Level Decentralization of City Services

Range of Services	Command Decentralization	Integration	District Residents' Influence		
			No Formal Influence	Advisory Mechanisms	Political Authority
One agency	Little	—	A. Local field office (physical redeployment of one agency)	C. Local field office with community input	
	Much	—	B. Command decentralization in one agency	D. Command decentralization with community input in one agency	E. Community control of one agency (e.g., community school board)
Cluster of agencies	Little	Little	F. Common field office for multiple services (multiservice center)	I. Common field office with community input for multiple services	
	Much	Little	G. Common field office for several decentralized agencies	J. Common field office for decentralized agencies with community input	
	Much	Much	H. Field coordinator for several agencies	K. Field coordinator for several agencies with community input	L. Coordinated community control for several agencies
Most agencies	Little	Little	M. Common field office for most agencies	P. Common field office for most agencies with community input	
	Much	Little	N. Common field office for many decentralized agencies	Q. Common field office for many decentralized agencies with community input	
	Much	Much	O. District coordinator for most agencies	R. District coordinator for most agencies with community input	S. District government (political decentralization)

large American city, but has been implemented in the Greater London decentralization of the mid-1960s. The London plan created 32 general-purpose borough governments administering a number of services for populations averaging 250,000.[8] Of course, the suburban areas adjacent to most American big cities have "political decentralization" in an extreme form, with dozens or hundreds of small and middle-sized town and city governments, to say nothing of special-purpose districts.[9] The small towns of America have exemplified political decentralization since the Mayflower Compact.

The most publicized "experiment" in political decentralization in an American big city so far has been the New York City school decentralization, which started with three experimental districts, reached a crisis in the confrontation between the Ocean Hill-Brownsville school board and the city teachers' union, and was modified into a system of elective school boards throughout the city that are now criticized as union dominated.[10] The plan is a clear example of single-agency decentralization (type E) and may reveal the difficulty of mobilizing public interest in a one-agency elective board, even one significant to as many people as a school board.

The Office of Neighborhood Government
Program as Planned

Early in 1970, within the New York City mayor's office, the Office of Neighborhood Government was created to work out plans for decentralizing city government that would meet demands from both minority groups and white ethnic areas and would avoid the shattering confrontations between "community control" militants and equally militant public employee unions that occurred in the experimental school decentralization in Ocean Hill-Brownsville.[11] In its first plan put forward for public discussion in June 1970, the ONG plan combined the ideas of a local service office for the public, citizen representation in community boards, and administrative decentralization and coordination through a district office.[12] However, the resistance of the borough political organizations and the City Council, combined with the memories of Ocean Hill-Brownsville, lead to the elimination of citizen representation and public contact as a goal. The second plan published in December 1971 called only for administrative decentralization, involving most city agencies that had district-level organizations, to be set up in several "experimental" districts.[13]

The Office of Neighborhood Government program was to set up an *administrative coordinating mechanism* at the district level within New York City for a wide range of city departments including protective, environmental, and human services. The program was based on Community Planning Districts, which average 130,000 population. The local offices were also called Offices of

Neighborhood Government—although the size of each district was such that it encompassed a large number of "neighborhoods" in the usual sense. The plan intended to use the mayor's authority to secure from top departmental administrators a considerable *devolution of authority* to local service managers. Service districts boundaries were to be redrawn to achieve common boundaries wherever practical ("coterminality"), since existing departmental districts corresponded neither to one another nor to Community Planning District lines.

The administrative coordinating mechanism consisted of a district manager, without line authority but with high civil service rank and experience, and a district cabinet to bring together the local service managers of various departments to raise problems and develop cooperative means of improving services. Eight agencies were initially brought in: police, sanitation, health, housing, human resources, addiction services, parks and recreation, and highways. Other services were added later in most experimental districts, notably the schools, which are under elected community school boards.

What the program did *not* attempt to do is important and should be noted here. It did not try to create elective councils of local residents. It did not provide jobs or direct services for local residents, or bring in large amounts of new money for services or construction, as did the antipoverty Community Corporations and Model Cities programs.[a] It did not make a major effort to inform the public where to go with problems or to handle public complaints as did Boston's Little City Halls or the British Citizens Advice Bureaus, although some district offices did a little of these things. It did not give the district manager line authority over local service managers. The ONG program essentially created a weak city manager for districts within a large city to improve service delivery by encouraging cooperation between local officials of existing departments within existing budgets.

The original formulation of the New York City neighborhood government program drew on all three rationales: administrative decentralization and coordination to improve service delivery, provision of some measure of "community control" for aggrieved ethnic groups, and creation of a local level of government to enhance citizen participation in governmental and self-help activities. As the plan evolved, it emphasized administrative decentralization and service integration, to avoid political controversy and as a necessary first step toward possible community participation. In trying to put the program into practice, most district managers soon found themselves communicating with community leaders to find out their needs and priorities and then mobilizing them to help get cooperation from the departmental bureaucracies and the elected politicians.

---

[a]However, small capital-item sums of a few hundred thousand dollars for equipment and supplies were supposed to be available to be allocated by district managers and cabinets, subject to approval of the city councilmen of the borough in which the district was located.

The Research Questions

Initially, the main question the research set out to answer was:

1. Will decentralization of big-city government help solve urban problems by improving service delivery to the public and by improving the public's relationships with city government?

    Practically, we came to realize that we could only test the impact of whatever the politicians and bureaucrats actually implemented, which might be far less than an optimal version of "decentralization" as theoretically conceived. Therefore, the research was designed not only to measure the ultimate impact of "decentralization" on service delivery and public orientation to government, but also to answer a whole series of questions about what happened to "decentralization" along the way. In the most realistic sense, therefore, the general question the research set for itself was:

2. What happened when New York City set up the neighborhood government program of district managers and district cabinets in the years 1972 and 1973?

    "What happened" thus came to include a whole set of events:

3. How did the proposals for the program change in the process of being formulated and approved?
4. To what extent was devolution of authority and local coordination of services actually implemented by the mayor and the heads of city departments?
5. How did the district managers develop their roles, given the extent of actual implementation of decentralization by higher levels and the responses of local operating officials and community leaders? Did different styles of district management emerge?
6. What did local neighborhood government offices actually do? What kinds of projects did they initiate, and how far did they get with them?
7. What were the reactions of local community leaders to the district manager-district cabinet program? Did reactions differ between types of local leaders?
8. What were the reactions of local agency officials to the district manager-district cabinet programs? Did the presence of these institutions make a difference for interagency relations and agency-community relations, as seen by local officials?
9. How did the public respond to the program? Did it make any difference in their satisfaction with services, problems experienced, or contacts with

government? Were they aware of the program? Were they in favor of administrative or political decentralization?

10. What did the program cost to operate? To what extent did it simply reallocate resources to demonstration districts from less-favored districts?

The research thus was aimed at following the process of structural change in city administration as far as it would actually go and at finding out as much as possible about the reactions of those involved to each stage, as well as at measuring the ultimate impact on delivery of services to the public. In this way we could learn something useful about the process of decentralizing city government, even if the implementation were weakened or aborted so that we could not assess the ultimate effects of decentralization.

Put in a more formal way, the plans of the Office of Neighborhood Government envisaged a chain of events that is summarized in Figure 1-1. Accordingly, adoption of the ONG plan in the demonstration districts should have led to three structural changes: creation of the district manager and the district cabinet, devolution of authority to line officials of departments in those districts, and revision of service district lines to achieve common boundaries. The district manager in turn should have implemented regular interagency contacts through the cabinet and regular contacts with the community leadership (the forms of which were not specified as the plan backed away from earlier ideas of using the Community Planning Boards as formal advisory bodies). The interagency contacts through the cabinet, under conditions of devolution of authority to the line officials and inputs on community problems and priorities from the community leadership, were expected to generate improvements in service delivery and increased responsiveness to individual citizen requests for help. These changes in the behavior of the service agencies should have reduced the neighborhood problems of residents, increased their satisfaction with services, increased public contact with government agencies and satisfaction with those contacts, and ultimately led to more satisfaction with the quality of life in the district, greater citizen trust in government, more civic participation, and more willingness to stay in the neighborhood.

The research was designed to measure most of these variables, in one way or another. In this way, we hoped to find out not only whether the program had the ultimate effects intended on the public, but to what extent it had realized each of the intervening stages. If the program did not deliver some or all of the intended effects, we hoped to find out where the chain of intervening processes had failed to work as planned, and why.

The Research Plan

Measuring the actual impact of decentralization on service delivery is extraordinarily difficult, in part because service delivery is difficult to measure under any

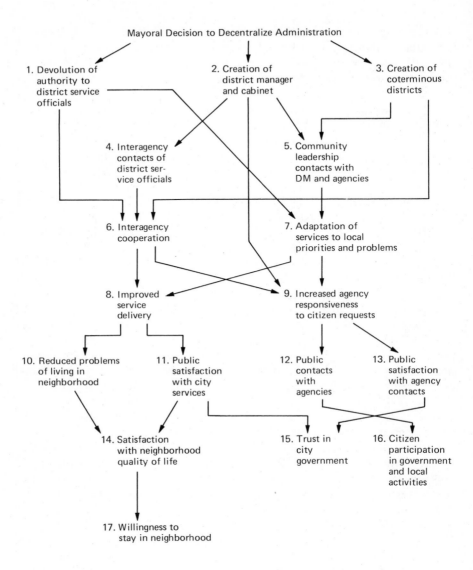

Figure 1-1. Intended Effects of the Office of Neighborhood Government Program.

circumstances. Some aspects of service delivery are best measured by getting reports from the beneficiaries themselves (for instance, surveys of citizens' victimization by criminals, or housing conditions); others by official measurements and observations on those being treated by government services (reading scores of school pupils, rehabilitation rates of addicts or criminals); still others by direct observations of physical conditions (street cleanliness ratings, number of potholes, condition of playgrounds). The basic methods of measuring impact on service delivery in the present study were surveys of the public and of community leaders, supplemented by direct observations and by whatever data we could obtain from official sources.

A second problem in impact measurement is the difficulty of attaining a fully experimental design in evaluating programs under the control of politicians and bureaucrats. Clearly, the term *experiment* has been applied to the Office of Neighborhood Government program in the loose sense rather than the strict sense defined by advocates of social experimentation. Riecken and Boruch write:

Our usage does not encompass "demonstration" programs, which are organized try-outs of social mechanisms to test the feasibility, for example, of a different means of delivering social services or a different incentive structure for providers. Nor do we count as experiments those pilot or prototype projects undertaken to test detailed program procedures so that erroneous assumptions and mistaken notions about how to administer a program can be eliminated. Such studies are useful, although their purpose is also served by well-designed experiments. Unless provision is made for measurement of outcomes, for controls, and, above all, for random assignment of subjects, we do not count demonstrations and prototypes as experiments.

When randomization cannot be achieved, or when a control group is not feasible, a variety of quasi-experimental designs may be substituted—with greater ambiguity in the interpretation of results but still considerably more dependable information than is ordinarily obtained from analysis of nonexperimental data. Quasi-experiments correspond to certain natural social settings in which the experimenter can approximate experimental procedures for collecting data even though he lacks full control over the delivery of the treatment.[14]

To some extent the Office of Neighborhood Government was indeed a "demonstration program" to test the feasibility of decentralization and local coordination of services as well as a "pilot project" to disclose whether the assumptions about how to administer the program were realistic. Since the selection of districts for "treatment" was not random, but dictated by political goals and administrative convenience of the city administration, the research could at best be "quasi-experimental." And at worst it might not be experimental at all, since the researchers had no way of insuring that the proposed treatment would actually be delivered in the "experimental" districts. To test the effects of administrative decentralization on service delivery and citizen-government relations, the city had to actually implement administrative decentralization in the places where it said it would.

The research design was therefore multifaceted. It included a quasi-experimental design involving before-and-after comparisons of public and community leader ratings of services and problems and reports of their own attitudes and behavior in "experimental" and "control" areas. But it also included a major effort to describe in detail to what extent administrative decentralization actually took place in the experimental districts: A group of political scientists closely followed the work of the district managers and district cabinets, and a team of economists produced detailed descriptions of a set of projects initiated by the district managers with information on the extent to which they had been implemented and, where they had not been fully implemented, the reasons why not. Furthermore, the research included a survey of administrative behavior in both experimental and control districts. Finally, city manpower and expenditure data were gathered for all sixty-two Community Planning Districts to ascertain whether resources were being diverted into "experimental" districts by the activities of the ONG and their community allies, and to find out more about the social determinants of service costs and outputs.

Choice of Districts

As "experimental" districts, all five of the original district manager districts were originally chosen; however, one district was dropped for budgetary reasons as the high cost of conducting surveys in New York City became apparent. The least "typical" district—one that was remote from the main part of the city and built around a former summer beach colony—was dropped from the surveys, although it was kept in the administrative analysis and the analysis of resource allocations. The district manager-district cabinet program was later installed in another five districts, but these were not included in the study.

As "control" districts, three Community Planning Districts, in which no district manager-district cabinet program was planned, were selected. These were matched, as a set of three pairs, with three of the experimental districts in terms of income levels, ethnic composition, and home ownership. The fourth experimental district was unusual: It was about three-quarters black, but not poor, and contained a highly active Jewish minority. Similar black and white population groups could be found scattered in the control districts, but there was no precise match at the district level.

The class and ethnic composition of the experimental and control districts, and the distribution of all New York City Community Planning Districts, is shown in Table 1-3. As the table shows, the experiment was carried out in districts that ranged from poor to middle class in socioeconomic makeup and that were of relatively mixed ethnic composition, excluding the overwhelmingly white and overwhelmingly black districts. Results of the public surveys thus should not be generalized to the whole population of New York City, but refer to this range of districts, which was of mixed ethnic character and below the upper-middle-class economic level.

The question is always asked whether experiences in New York City are generalizable to other cities of the United States. Certainly districts of these types can be found in every city. Whether something unique to lower-middle-

Table 1-3
Typology of NYC Community Planning Districts

(Number of districts of each type and names of study districts)

Percent White Non-Puerto Rican (1969)	Shevky-Bell Index of Socioeconomic Status (1960)				Total Districts
	Low SES Less than 50	50-59	60-69	High SES 70 or More	
90 % or more	3	10	7	8	28
70-89%	3	5 *WAKEFIELD-EDENWALD (33% owners)	7 *Jackson Heights (31% owners) **WASHINGTON HTS. (2% owners) **Grand Concourse (4% owners)	1	16
30-69%	6 †BUSHWICK (18% owners) †East New York (27% owners)	2 CROWN HTS. (13% owners)	3	0	10
Under 30%	7	0	0	0	7
Total Districts	19	17	17	9	62

Notes: The Shevky-Bell Index is described in E. Shevky and W. Bell, *Social Area Analysis* (Stanford: Stanford University Press, 1955). Low scores indicate a large proportion of blue-collar workers and grade-school educated people in an area; high scores a large proportion of white-collar and higher occupations and people with more than grade school educations.

Names of experimental districts are in capital letters; control districts are in lower case. Matching symbols show matched experimental and control pairs.

Far Rockaway was one of the five original ONG districts but was omitted from the public surveys. It falls in the same category as Jackson Heights, Washington Heights, and Grand Concourse; its homeowner percentage is 38 percent.

class, ethnically mixed districts in New York differentiates them from such districts in other cities cannot be tested with the data of this study. We leave this issue for the readers themselves to judge.

Time Period Covered

The New York City Neighborhood Project at Columbia University's Bureau of Applied Social Research studied the ONG experimental program from its beginning in January 1972, under the Lindsay administration, through mid-1974, by which time the Beame administration had begun to make substantial changes in the program. The research applies essentially to the program as carried on in the two years 1972 and 1973 under the Lindsay administration.

The Research Operations

The administrative analysis component of the project was designed to ascertain the extent to which the mayoral program was implemented. A staff of political science graduate students under the direction of Professor Stanley Heginbotham observed both the central Office of Neighborhood Government and five district Offices of Neighborhood Government, held a great number of informal conversations and open-ended interviews with their staffs, and collected documents. On this basis a series of qualitative reports was written to describe the degree of implementation of the three main aspects of administrative decentralization: (1) devolution of authority to district service officials; (2) creation of the district manager role and getting local officials to function as a district cabinet; and (3) creation of coterminous districts.

These reports also described the achievement of the next processes in the chain: the response of the various city departments and their local officials to their involvement in the district cabinet and with the district manager (variables 4 and 6),[b] and the interactions between the district manager and the community leadership (variable 5). Detailed analyses of particular agency responses are being written up in monograph form.

Finally, during 1974 a quantitative survey of local line officials was made in four experimental districts, three districts that had recently created district cabinets without any manager (which included two of the originally designated "control" districts), and three districts with neither cabinet nor manager (including the remaining original "control" district). These officials were asked to report the extent of interagency contacts (variable 4) and cooperation (variable 6), of contacts with community leaders (variable 5), and their attitudes toward these forms of interagency and community cooperation. This

[b]Variable numbers in this section refer to those in the flow chart shown in Figure 1-1.

survey was specifically designed to measure the extent to which cooperative behavior and attitudes that the district manager-district cabinet program was designed to produce were on the one hand actually found in the experimental districts and on the other hand spontaneously developed in districts without these coordinating mechanisms. Done on an "after-only" basis, this comparison could not be absolutely insulated from possible spillover effects of the experimental program into "nonexperimental" districts, but questions were asked of the local officials concerning their knowledge of the ONG experiments so that such "emulation effects" could be detected.

The service delivery and cost analysis component of the project had two major purposes. One was to measure the extent to which the stimulus of "decentralization" might be contaminated by the transfer of additional resources into demonstration districts from other districts or from newly tapped sources—which would produce a favorable local response, but not as the effect of decentralization. Data was obtained from such agencies as fire, police, sanitation, parks, highways, and schools on the allocation of manpower and expenditures by their smallest local units (fire station, police patrol route, sanitation pickup or street cleaning route, park, street segments, school districts). Data on location of clients and expenditures on them were obtained from the Human Resources Administration and Health Services Administration. A nonprofit research agency closely associated with the city government (Administrative and Management Research Association of New York, or AMRA) was retained on subcontract to extract these data from city agencies, and generally the researchers obtained what they requested, subject to the fact that the city itself was unable to provide certain kinds of information. These "disaggregated" data were then recombined into totals for the Community Planning Districts of the city, which were also the district boundaries used by the ONG experiment.

The service delivery component intended to have both before-and-after data (1971 and 1973) for the five original experimental districts and the three control districts, and after-only data (1973) for all sixty-two Community Planning Districts. However, since the quality of the 1971 data, which were the first collected, was not as good as that of the 1973 data, the before-and-after comparisons were dropped and replaced by comparative analysis of the 1973 data in which an "expected value" of manpower and expenditures was computed from regressions using social characteristics and service burden data from the full sixty-two districts. The actual expenditures were compared with this expected value.

In addition to checking for possible contamination of the experiment by resource shifting, the service expenditure and performance data have been used for detailed analysis of two services: sanitation and police.

The second main effort of the service delivery component was to record in a standard manner the origins and progress of a sample of sixty-five "projects" initiated by the district managers and cabinets in the experimental districts, to

qualitatively characterize their outcomes (not implemented, partially implemented, fully implemented), to indicate the main obstacles to full implementation, and to provide rough estimates on a project-by-project basis of the actual
value of benefits produced and, where the project was not implemented, the
value that might have been produced. Each project was described in a standard
case-study format that included:

Specific purpose of project;
Reason for project (condition it dealt with);
Client group;
Location of benefit (within and between districts);
Agencies involved;
ONG role;
Nature of change in service production;
Results and sources of benefits;
Resources used;
Implementation problems;
Effect of noncoterminality;
Probability of accomplishment without program;
Status as of December 31, 1973.

The third effort of this component was to measure the cost of the operation
of the ONG offices in the experimental districts, their share of the central ONG
office cost, and the cost of departmental participation in cabinet activities. This
analysis was done for an initial start-up period from August 1971 through June
1972 (the central office had existed since 1970; the district offices were created
around January 1972) and for an eighteen-month period of full operation,
July 1972 through December 1973.

The project analysis therefore provided countable qualitative ratings of
projects that indicated the extent of devolution of authority versus having to
secure higher level permission for the project (variable 1), the activities of the
manager and cabinet (variable 2), and the extent of interagency cooperation or
noncooperation (variable 6) and of adaptation of services to local priorities and
problems (variable 7). This statistical data supplemented the qualitative descriptions obtained by the administrative analysis component and also the survey
data from the local line officials that measured first- and second-level effects of
the program on city agency operations. Each project was also rated in terms of
whether service delivery was improved or not (variable 8), and a very rough
estimate was made of the dollar value of the improvement, in terms of a
percentage range to be applied to the overall cost of the service that was
improved. In general, "improved service delivery" is difficult to measure
directly, without detailed surveys of the changes in condition of the clients
(patients, students, potential crime victims, and so forth) or in the physical

condition of the area affected by environmental services (cleanliness or smoothness of streets, housing conditions, and so forth). The project analysis provided essentially qualitative judgments of changes in service delivery aimed for and achieved by the sixty-five projects studied.

The leadership study component first used informant interviews and documentary sources to identify a population of "community leaders" in each of the seven districts under study. Informants were given the definition of leaders as "individuals who represent different groups of citizens and/or have influence and get things done." They were then asked to give the names and major organizational affiliations of the major community leaders in the district, which was referred to by its common name. A second question asked for the names of leaders in a wide range of categories of associations:

Heads of social action groups;
Voluntary associations;
Religious organizations;
Business groups;
Local newspapers;
Influential politicians;
Planning board leaders and members;
Community corporation leaders;
School heads;
Ethnic or racial group leaders or spokesmen;
Youth groups;
Groups for the aged;
Men's groups;
Women's groups;
Neighborhood associations;
Tenant associations;
Influential block associations.

The interviewer was instructed to use the list flexibly and to fill in "obvious gaps" in the list given in answer to the first question.

"First-choice" leaders were those mentioned by two or more informants in answering the open-ended questions, or by one on the first question and by one or more on the checklist question. "Second-choice leaders" were those receiving only one mention on the first question and none on the second. City employees were eliminated from the list since we wanted to distinguish "community leaders" from those whose local reputation rested on their roles as city officials. The resulting population list consisted of 402 first-choice leaders and 306 second-choice leaders; seventy-four city officials were eliminated.

A target of fifty leader interviews in each of the seven districts was set. Priority was given to "first-choice" leaders, with the second-choice list to be called upon only if not enough first-choice leaders were available in the district (one district had only thirty-eight first-choice leaders, and another forty-four; the rest had at least fifty on the list, and one had seventy-five).

The leader sample of 350 was interviewed early in the fall of 1972 in personal interviews of an hour or more. The leaders were asked a wide range of questions about their contacts with city agencies and officials, cooperation with other organizations, membership and activities of their own organizations, and their attitudes toward the idea of decision-making influence or advisory "community control" over certain city services. They were also asked the same questions asked in the public survey interviews that concerned the most important problems facing the district, attitudes toward city government in general, and ratings of fifteen services.

After this survey, intensive case studies were undertaken to describe how community organizations and leaders interacted with the ONG and city agencies in three of the experimental districts. Voluntary organizations, protest groups, quasi-governmental agencies and political clubs were observed. Cases were written up in detail, as were qualitative reports on each of the districts.

On the basis of the case-study work, a new list of active leaders for these three districts was constructed, and semistructured interviews were conducted with 114 of them in the summer of 1973. Chosen by different procedures, these leaders overlapped very considerably with the original population lists of leaders from which the 1972 sample was drawn. At the same time, all 78 city bureaucrats who sat on the five original ONG cabinets were interviewed concerning their reactions to the program. Finally, a follow-up, mailed survey in 1974 obtained 201 returns, including 151 of the 350 respondents from the 1972 leadership survey along with 50 additional leaders identified in the 1973 intensive study.

The community leadership study therefore obtained both qualitative and statistical information on one of the intermediate links in the intended effects—the community leaders' contacts with ONG and other city agencies (variable 5), and also their attitudes toward the ONG program, which presumably determine their cooperativeness with it. Furthermore, the leaders were asked for the perception of the quality of city services. Since they were more actively involved with both city agencies and with citizens who were clients of those agencies, their perceptions provided at least an estimate of the quality of service delivery (variable 8) and in any case constituted a significant part of the "public" whose satisfaction with city services (variable 11) was one of the goals of the program. Finally, the community leaders were one component of the citizenry whose participation in government (variable 16) might have been influenced by the presence of the program.

The public survey component was intended to provide measures of some of the final outputs of the experiment: whether the program had effects on the problems of living in the neighborhood (variable 10), public satisfaction with city services (variable 11), public contacts with agencies (variable 12), public satisfaction with agency contacts (variable 13) and thereby changes in satisfaction with the neighborhood quality of life (variable 14), trust in city government (variable 15), participation in government and local activities (variable 16), and willingness to stay in the neighborhood rather than migrate elsewhere (variable 17).

The base-line survey ideally should have been done before the district manager experiment was initiated. Due to the well-known problems of obtaining large sums of money required for surveys quickly, the uncertainties of the actual starting of the program, and the time required to launch a survey once funds were in hand, the "base-line" public survey was not fielded until about five months after the district managers were appointed. By this time most of the community leaders already knew about the experiment, but very few of the public had heard of it; and in view of the time lag in carrying out actual improvements in city services, we believe that the ONG program had not had time to influence public attitudes by the summer of 1972 when the district residents were first surveyed.

A target of 240 interviews in each of the seven districts was set, to consist of 10 interviews in each of 24 blocks selected randomly with probability proportional to their number of households. Due to problems of budget and timing, we decided to use the "block quota" method on three-quarters of the sample blocks and to attempt a probability sample of households within the block on only one-quarter of the blocks. The National Opinion Research Center carried out the 1972 interviewing, and 1,683 interviews were obtained. In the block quota method, each household on the block was visited in turn from a random starting point until the desired quotas (of men under and over forty, and of working and nonworking women) were actually interviewed. The quotas were set from census data for the tract in which the block was located. Giving a "completion rate" for the block quota sample is not possible, since households were substituted (following a strict sequence around the block) for those in which nobody was at home, the interview was refused, or nobody present met the remaining parts of that block's quotas.

In the probability sample of households, the rate of completion can be estimated. Typically for New York surveys, it was below the desirable target of 80 to 85 percent—only 73 percent of the sample households were interviewed. Selection within the household was made on a quota basis in both parts of the sample.

We originally planned to reinterview the public sample twice at one-year intervals. The idea of a resurvey after only one year was dropped in favor of coming back only once, after two years, as a result of the slow development of the program, its avoidance of efforts to involve the general public, and the need to concentrate more resources on the other components to insure that we had a good description of what was actually being implemented by the city.

In 1974, the project staff carried out reinterviews with over 973 of the original respondents who were living in the same districts as before, plus 63 substitute individuals for household members no longer available. Interviews were also done with 124 original respondents who had moved to other locations in the city or its suburbs, and with 252 people who had moved into dwelling units from which members of the original sample had moved out. Combining the "stayers" from the original sample with the "in-movers" who replaced those who moved out, plus the 63 substitutes for original household members, we got a fairly representative sample of 1,288 members of the community population as of 1974. By looking only at the "stayers" who were reinterviewed, we could make before-and-after comparisons and examine those who changed. The "out-mover" sample provided us with information on who moved out of the districts studied, for what reasons, to what locations, and with what effects on their neighborhood satisfaction and rating of problems and services.

The 1974 interviews were carried out wherever possible by telephone. About half were done in this manner, while the other half were face-to-face interviews, necessitated by absence of a phone, unwillingness to be interviewed by phone, or inability to obtain the number (where new people had moved in or where phone numbers were changed to unlisted). As a check on whether the mode of interview made any difference in results, an experiment was made in one district by using random assignment of respondents who had telephones to either telephone or face-to-face interviews. The results provided reassurance of the quality and lack of substantive effects of telephone compared with face-to-face interviews (and evidence of the greatly reduced cost of phone interviews).[15]

In addition to these four main components of the study, an intensive community case study was carried on in one of the experimental districts. In part this phase was a continuation of the work of one Columbia faculty member and his students. In part, it involved a special survey of 500 persons that concentrated on five ethnic groups and related to their interaction with city agencies. The results of these studies will supplement the broader research, but are not reported in this volume.

Summary of the Research Operations

The administrative analysis component examined the extent to which the decentralization program was actually implemented and the immediate impact on interagency contact and cooperation and on community leadership contacts. The service delivery and cost analysis component measured the resource allocation to all Community Planning Districts for the year 1973 and compared all ten district manager districts with sixteen having district cabinets only and thirty-six having no decentralization arrangements. It measured the cost of operation of the ONG program itself, and it analyzed sixty-five specific projects initiated by the ONG program by describing the extent to which permission of higher authorities was still required, cooperation between agencies was obtained, and changes were actually made in service delivery. A crude measurement of dollar value of benefits was attempted on a project-by-project basis.

The *leadership study* measured the community leaders' contacts with and cooperativeness toward the decentralization program, their perceptions of performance of city agencies before and after and in experimental and control areas, and their attitudes toward city government and the desirability of community advisory or decision-making influence over services. It also measured attitudes of the local officials participating in district cabinets. Further, it produced qualitative case studies of leadership and bureaucratic behavior in districts where the attempt was made to implement the decentralization program.

The *public survey* provided in its base-line survey of 1972 measures in the level of dissatisfaction with the neighborhoods, incidence of problems for district residents, satisfaction with city services, knowledge of the ONG and other decentralized programs (planning boards and school boards), knowledge of where to go with problems of city services, actual contact with city agencies, satisfaction with those contacts, feelings of political potency or alienation, actual political and neighborhood activity, and a large amount of social and demographic background data. The reinterviews in 1974 showed changes in these variables for experimental and "control" districts and for various subgroups in the population. They also provided information on who moved out, where, and with what consequences for their satisfactions and on who moved in to replace them. To the extent that the program of decentralization was implemented to the point of altering practices of the agencies delivering services to the public and avoided doing so in the control areas, the public survey provided a good measure of how much decentralization improved services and the nature of agency contacts for the public. Otherwise, the survey measured "natural" changes over the two-year period, including in- and out-migration.

When put together, these four components and their substudies were designed to give us fairly complete coverage of the intended effects of the decentralization program by combining qualitative and quantitative descriptions and measures. They were designed to tell us how far along the expected processes of change actually proceeded, and at what point they were blocked; how the program evolved as it went along; and how it responded to challenges.

Problems in Maintaining the Experimental Design

The evolution of the Office of Neighborhood Government program took an unplanned turning early in 1973, when it became apparent that Mayor Lindsay, under whose auspices it had begun, was not going to run again. As a means of building political support for continuation of the program, the leadership of the Office of Neighborhood Government began expanding the program into a large number of additional districts, but in a substantially modified form. In each of sixteen "expansion districts," a district cabinet was to be instituted, but without a full-time district manager. Chairing these "expansion cabinets" were to be high-level city officials with full-time jobs as commissioners or assistant commissioners in some city agencies. The Central Office of Neighborhood Government was to provide as much follow-through as possible for projects; task forces were to be set up by the cabinets, and the chairmen were to use their influence on city agencies to obtain support.

As it happened, "expansion cabinets" were set up (without warning to the researchers) in two of the three "control districts" in which public and leader surveys were being carried out on a before-and-after basis for comparison with those in the four "experimental" districts. By the time the researchers became aware of this development, some high-level city officials were already involved as chairmen of these cabinets and the first meetings had been held. The mayor's office clearly chose the two particular "control" districts to be among the sixteen in this program because of the seriousness of their community problems, the fact that a particular potential chairman was interested in helping a particular community, and the requests of local community leaders for help from the city in dealing with their problems.

Efforts to "roll back" the expansion from these districts, involving the Department of Health, Education and Welfare, which was partially funding the ONG as a "research and demonstration" program for services integration, and invoking the scientific importance of keeping the experimental design intact were of no avail. The researchers and the funding agency nevertheless decided to go ahead with the research and to try to take into account the possible contamination by treating the experimental variable of "administrative decentralization" as more of a continuum than a dichotomy. We expected (and it indeed happened) that some of the "expansion cabinets" would be more active than others. One of the "control" districts had a rather active cabinet and chairman from mid-1973 until early 1974, while the others barely functioned. We also hoped that the longer period of operation of the district manager programs in the experimental districts and the slow start-up of programs in the "expansion districts" would leave the public sample relatively uninfluenced by the contaminating programs, even though the response of the community leaders might be more influenced. Finally, we decided to collect additional data to compare coordination between departments in district manager areas, areas with cabinets but no managers, and in some additional areas with neither in order to assess the direct effects of the "contamination." Thus, the possible influence of the violation of experimental design was considered in the analysis.

The Plan of the Book

The following chapters report the results of these studies in detail; each is written by the researchers most directly involved in the particular operation. Chapter 2 describes the evolution of the district manager experiment from its beginning to its (at least temporary) end, and particularly the role of the district manager as it was developed by those who pioneered the job. Chapter 3 gives seven case studies of projects initiated by District Offices of Neighborhood Government to improve services or to solve local problems by coordinating service agencies and mobilizing local resources. Chapter 4 provides a statistical portrait of a sample of sixty-five such projects in four districts and indicates the extent to which it was possible to implement ideas originating at the district level. Chapter 5 reviews the costs of the program and the possible contamination of the experiment by reallocating resources among districts—a common problem when a few areas are singled out for new programs.

Chapters 6 through 9 report the responses of those involved in the experiment. Chapter 6 describes, both statistically and in district-by-district case studies, how community leaders in sections of the big city felt about the program and what they did about it. Chapter 7 reports the results of two surveys of local agency officials that covered both their attitudes and their perceptions of interagency relations. Chapter 8 looks at the state of the public's problems and dissatisfactions at the time the experiment was begun, and Chapter 9 looks at how the public's perceptions of problems, services, and city government generally changed over a two year period, in districts with and without district managers. This chapter also examines public opinion concerning the general idea of administrative and political decentralization.

Finally, Chapter 10 tries to sum up what has been learned, and what has yet to be learned, about decentralization of city government based on our study of the New York City experience in 1972-1974.

Notes

1. Advisory Commission on Intergovernmental Relations, "Neighborhood Subunits of Government," *State Legislative Program* (Washington, D.C.: Government Printing Office, 1970), p. 16; Committee for Economic Development, *Reshaping Government in Metropolitan Areas* (New York: C.E.D., February 1970).

2. Stokely Carmichael and Charles Hamilton, *Black Power* (New York: Vintage, 1967); Alan Altshuler, *Community Control: The Black Demand for Participation in Large American Cities* (New York: Pegasus, 1970); N.I. and S.S. Fainstein, *Urban Political Movements* (Englewood Cliffs, N.J.: Prentice-Hall, 1974).

3. Milton Kotler, *Neighborhood Government* (New York: Bobbs-Merrill, 1969); Howard W. Hallman, *Neighborhood Government in a Metropolitan Setting* (Beverly Hills, Calif.: Sage Publications, 1975). For somewhat contrasting views, see Douglas Yates, *Neighborhood Democracy* (Lexington, Mass.: D.C. Heath, 1973).

4. Alan K. Campbell, ed., *The States and the Urban Crisis* (Englewood Cliffs, N.J.: Spectrum, 1970).

5. David Rogers, *The Management of Big Cities: Interest Groups and Social Change Strategies* (Beverly Hills, Calif.: Sage Publications, 1971); Delbert C. Miller, *Leadership and Power in the Bos-Wash Megalopolis* (New York: Wiley-Interscience, 1975).

6. Robert K. Yin and Douglas Yates, *Street-Level Governments: Assessing Decentralization and Urban Services*, (*An evaluation of policy-related research*), Lexington, Massachusetts: D.C. Heath and Company, 1975.

7. See, for instance, Eric Nordlinger, *Decentralizing the City: A Study of Boston's Little City Halls* (Cambridge, Mass.: MIT Press, 1972); George J. Washnis, *Municipal Decentralization and Neighborhood Resources* (New York: Praeger, 1972).

8. Gerald Rhodes, ed., *The New Government of London: The First Five Years* (White Plains, N.Y.: International Arts and Sciences Press, Inc., 1972); Donald L. Foley, *Governing the London Region: Reorganization and Planning in the 1960s* (Berkeley: University of California Press, 1972); Donna E. Shalala and Astrid Mergit, "The Decentralization Option" and "Decentralization," Ch. 8 and 8, in T.P. Murphy and C.R. Warren, eds., *Organizing Public Services in Metropolitan America* (Lexington, Mass.: D.C. Heath, 1974).

9. Robert C. Wood, *1400 Governments* (Cambridge, Mass.: Harvard University Press, 1961.)

10. S. and N. Fainstein, *Urban Political Movements* (Englewood Cliffs, N.J.: Prentice-Hall, 1974).

11. S. and N. Fainstein, "From the Folks Who Brought You Ocean Hill-Brownsville," *New York Affairs*, vol. 2, no. 2, 1974, pp. 104-15.

12. Mayor John V. Lindsay, *Plan for Neighborhood Government for New York City*, Office of the Mayor, City of New York, June 1970.

13. Mayor John V. Lindsay, *Program for the Decentralization of Municipal Services in New York City Communities*, Office of the Mayor, City of New York, December 1971 (reprinted in the Appendix to this volume).

14. H.W. Riecken and R.F. Boruch, eds., *Social Experimentation: A Method for Planning and Evaluating Social Intervention* (New York: Academic Press, 1974).

15. Theresa F. Rogers, "Interviews by Telephone and in Person: An Experiment to Test Quality of Responses and Field Performance," *Public Opinion Quarterly* 40, Spring 1976.

2

The Evolution of the District Manager Experiment

Stanley J. Heginbotham

Introduction

The primary purpose of this chapter is to provide a brief description of what has been variously called New York City's administrative decentralization program, its experiment in command decentralization and service integration, and its district manager experiment.[a] The task is more complex than it appears to be on the surface because the program changed rather dramatically over time and evolved into a series of rather different experiments in different parts of the city. Therefore, distinguishing between the initial goals and intentions of the experiment and the actual patterns of organization and activity that evolved over time and space is important.

These patterns of evolution have given the experiment a particular fascination, but have also enormously complicated the research tasks involved in evaluating it. When social scientists design base-line survey research to measure the effects of a particular set of stimuli, they are disconcerted when they discover that those stimuli have been changed even before the first questionnaires reach the field. Social evaluation research must come to terms with political and bureaucratic realities, however, and these realities must be understood if one is to understand the dynamics that have shaped the evolution of this experiment.

Eight distinct stages in this evolution can be distinguished, and the main body of this presentation will be organized around a discussion of each stage. An initial period of defining programs goals (stage 1) was followed by an intensive effort to establish the structural characteristics of the program (stage 2). The staff then turned its attention to the mobilization of political and administrative support for the program (stage 3), but a series of problems resulted in a shift of

---

[a]The third option is used here because it emphasizes the structural feature that is most characteristic of and important to the experiment. The other options describe goals. As this chapter will show, however, the goals of the program have undergone significant changes over time. Moreover, the terms *administrative decentralization, command decentralization,* and *service integration* all refer to complex phenomena that have analytically distinct components. A lack of conceptual clarity in dealing with these components has had certain political and tactical advantages for the Office of Neighborhood Government (ONG), but it has also clouded analysis and planning within that organization. The district manager experiment is also occasionally referred to as the ONG program, or in the field, simply as ONG. This usage, however, produces confusion since other ONG activities—Urban Action Task Forces and Neighborhood Action Programs, for example—are often also commonly referred to as Office of Neighborhood Governments or as ONGs.

initiative from central to field officials (stage 4). This stage led to the progressive development of quite distinctive field programs (stage 5). A brief period in which the central office tried to reestablish its control (stage 6) was followed by a major effort to institutionalize the program by expanding it into a much greater number of communities (stage 7). The advent of a new mayor with different perspectives and goals led to a major fight over control of the programs and its eventual transformation into a very different kind of operation (stage 8).

The Eight Stages of the Experiment's Life[b]

General Goal Definition

The Office of Neighborhood Government came into existence in 1970 as a part of the mayor's office. Its first director, Lewis Feldstein, had been a mayoral assistant for several years, but was not a member of the inner circle of mayoral advisors. Even though he was young—having just turned thirty—he had already had experience as a mayoral troubleshooter in one of the most painful and damaging encounters of the mayor's first term: the city school decentralization dispute. Although no one close to the situation seemed to hold Feldstein responsible for the mayor's problems in that confrontation, the negative feelings associated with the experience among the mayor's supporters inevitably reflected, to a degree, on their perceptions of Feldstein.

In taking on the leadership of a new office, therefore, Feldstein was under unusual pressure to produce positive results as quickly as possible. Two significant mayoral programs, the Urban Action Task Force and the Neighborhood Action Program, were placed under the auspices of his office, but clearly Feldstein's mandate was to develop a new program for neighborhood government.

His first effort, presented publicly in the *Plan for Neighborhood Government for New York City* (June 1970), represented a direct step toward political decentralization. It called for the strengthening of a set of existing, appointed Community Planning Boards and held out the prospect of their being transformed into elected district councils. Besides arguing the need for coterminality of service districts, the plan set forth the goal of giving community leaders the ability to "use the executive power of the mayor at the local level to hold

[b]Much of the material in this section is a revised and drastically condensed version of the administrative analysis component's six-part interim report, "Between Community and City Bureaucracy: New York City's District Manager Experiment," by Stanley J. Heginbotham and John M. Boyle, Robin Maas, Howard G. Katz, Geraldine Alpert and Kenneth H. Andrews, Bureau of Applied Social Research, Columbia University, New York, N.Y., December 1974. I greatly appreciate the contribution of my coauthors—Geraldine Alpert, Kenneth Andrews, John Boyle, Howard Katz, and Robin Maas—to that volume and, by extension, to this chapter.

accountable those government officials who are responsible for serving the community."[1]

Hearings on the plan held locally throughout the city demonstrated a widespread sense of public frustration with inadequate responsiveness and coordination of local service delivery by city agencies. The hearings also revealed, however, the absence of anything approaching a consensus on the mechanisms for selecting community boards. In large part because of the clear potential for division and opposition inherent in the issue of selection, the approach presented in the June 1970 plan was shelved.

Deeply in need of a new program format, Feldstein hired two consultants who were clearly held in high regard by administrative and political forces within the Lindsay administration. The consultants suggested that the whole issue of political decentralization be held in abeyance until the outlines of public consensus became discernible, and that the ONG focus instead on bringing about the changes in administrative structure of city agencies that would be necessary preconditions for an effective political decentralization program.

The general argument took the following form: Political decentralization involves the creation of local district legislatures that would have control over the local delivery of services by city agencies; in order for this control to be meaningful, the city agency boundaries have to correspond to the boundaries of the political districts and district-level agency officials have to have sufficient operating autonomy from their agency superiors to allow them to be responsive to the district legislatures; if coherent service delivery is to be achieved at the district level, there must be a single district-level official who can provide coordination both among the district-level agency officials and between those officials and the district legislature.

Program Definition

Out of this general goal, Feldstein and his staff developed a more specific program that was presented to the mayor in June 1971. The long-term goal of political decentralization was deemphasized and remained, throughout the experiment, a hidden agenda that became less and less significant to the ONG staff as time went on. Since it was clear that city agencies would be extremely reluctant to relinquish power over their local personnel to a general purpose district-level administrator, the ONG staff focused on a local coordinator—the district manager—as a beginning step toward the kind of administrative structure that would be consistent with the needs of political decentralization. Since ONG lacked the very considerable political clout that would have been necessary to sell its program on a citywide basis, Feldstein formulated the program as an experimental effort that would be tried out in several parts of the city and then further extended if it proved to be successful. In its initial selection of the eight areas to be included in the experiment, ONG was influenced by staff familiarity with specific communities, the advantage of using districts in which agency boundaries were already roughly coterminous, and the traditional concern for balanced representation of the city's boroughs, social classes, and ethnic communities.

The program design—which went to the mayor in June 1971, emerged in December as his official policy statement, and evolved into the district manager experiment—emphasized six components:[2]

First, a new official, the district manager, was established in each experimental Community Planning District (CPD). The managers were field agents of ONG and were responsible for coordinating service delivery functions in the districts. The men had considerable bureaucratic, professional, and/or political experience, and their initial salaries ranged between $21,000 and $27,000. They were placed on a par with many deputy commissioners (administrators of specialized program offices within the city's departments and agencies).

The salary, prestige of a mayoral appointment, and rank, however, were not matched by the formal powers and personnel resources that would normally accrue to men of this stature. The managers were given no formal line authority over any of the personnel from the operating administrations (or superagencies) that had responsibilities in their districts. Their own staffs consisted of only three to five professionals in the $10,000 to $15,000 salary range.

Second, a district service cabinet was established in each of the experimental CPDs. It was chaired by the district manager, and its members were representatives of each of the city administrations that both directly affected the community and required coordination with programs operated by different offices within the same administration or by other administrations.[c] The mayor's office obtained, before the program began, commitments from the administrations to the idea of assigning appropriate field personnel as members of the cabinets.

Each cabinet was to meet monthly to discuss problems of its district, to share information, and to evolve more effective means of coordinating existing programs that would more effectively meet the needs of the specific community.

Third, the Office of Neighborhood Government was expanded to provide oversight and evaluation of the project. The district managers represented the creation of a new field structure within the city administration. Line authority over those field agents was vested in the hands of the director of ONG. Moreover, the office was to carry on negotiations with the city administrations with regard to their operations in the experimental districts. Finally, the office was to provide and coordinate research and evaluation efforts designed to determine the effectiveness of the experiment.

---

[c]The following administrations and departments were included in the experiment: environmental protection; housing and development; human resources; health services; parks, recreation, and cultural affairs; transportation; and police. The Addiction Services Agency, then in the process of being transferred from the Human Resources Administration to the Health Services Administration was included as a separate entity.

Fourth, administrations that had several departments and agencies delivering services at the local level were to identify—and if necessary create—an official who could speak for the entire organization in the experimental district service cabinets. The powers and responsibilities of these district representatives were, however, unclear from the outset of the experiment. The mayor's official statement on the program specifies at one point that "For each Administration, we have created a local officer *responsible* for all the super-agency's operations in the area" (emphasis added), but in the following paragraph, the same officer is given a much more limited role: "For each central Administration, a single local officer has been designated who is *responsible for the coordination* of all operations in the Community Planning District" (emphasis added).[3]

Fifth, each of the participating city administrations and departments was to redesign its field operations in the experimental areas so that the geographic responsibilities of its representative on the district service cabinet would correspond—in general outline, at least—to the boundaries of the experimental district.

Sixth, the Office of Neighborhood Government began a campaign to get the city administrations to delegate greater decision-making authority to their field personnel. It was assumed that excessive power is retained by centralized supervisors of field personnel and that, in the words of the mayor's program statement, "It is impossible to frame solutions to these individual issues from centralized offices downtown."[4]

Until now, local service chiefs have not had the discretionary authority to adapt their individual operations to meet specific community problems most effectively. . . . Even more detrimental to the functioning of effective government, local agency officers have been unable to work fully with each other at the district level. . . . This program attempts to meet this problem directly by a process of administrative decentralization which will transfer specific powers and responsibilities now vested in central commands to the local agency officers. All local districts will be given greatly expanded responsibilities to vary the deployment of their resources to meet local needs more efficiently and effectively.[5]

Three additional components of interest were in the original experimental package. First, staff members from the Bureau of the Budget and City Planning Commission were to have been assigned to work with the manager and his cabinet. Second, "management information systems" were to have been developed in each district out of the statistics that had been separately collected and maintained by each of the agencies. Third, progress was to have been made on the development of an expense budget for each of the experimental districts. Only limited attention, however, was given to these three elements, and none of them received extensive attention in this study.

Mobilization of Support and Cooperation

Feldstein's original presentation of the district manager program to Mayor Lindsay in June 1971 was only marginally successful. In an often heated session,

Lindsay and other members of his staff voiced serious reservations about the program. Feldstein later recalled to our interviewer his surprise and frustration that the mayor seemed not to understand the administrative goals or implications of the program. Nevertheless, after Feldstein had modified parts of the program and obtained the backing of then-Budget Director Edward Hamilton, the mayor gave ONG permission to go ahead with the program. It was clear to senior administration and political figures in the administration, however, that the program did not seem to be of high priority to the mayor and that it would have to prove itself before the mayor would use his own political capital or risk his own political reputation in its support.

A major factor in ONG's ability to gain the mayor's acquiescence, if not his active support and attention, was Feldstein's ability to generate funding from the federal government. The Department of Health, Education and Welfare was becoming increasingly concerned, during the early 1970s, with the disjointed, disruptive, and conflict-producing impact on state and local government of its numerous specialized mandated programs. Sid Gardner, an erstwhile member of the Lindsay staff, was then the director of DHEW's Office for Community Planning. His approach to the problem of coordinated service delivery was clearly influenced by the Model Cities format and emphasized the development of neighborhood-based general purpose governments in metropolitan centers. Soon after Elliot Richardson became Secretary of DHEW, he created a task force on services Integration, which, with Sid Gardner as chairman, arranged for the funding of a series of twelve research and development grants to support alternative formats for service integration. Feldstein had been in touch with Gardner since mid-1970 about the possibilities of federal funding for an ONG program and, after Gardner left DHEW, he helped in the development of the ONG proposal that won for New York City one of the Services Integration R&D grants. For Lindsay to have rejected Feldstein's proposal, in short, would have been to reject nearly a million dollars of federal funds over a three-year period.

As preparations were made for the inauguration of the district manager experiment, Feldstein explored additional sources of federal funding that might strengthen the political base of the program. The desire of the National Science Foundation (NSF) to develop research "applied to national needs," the interests of the Bureau of Applied Social Research at Columbia University in "quality-of-life" survey research, and the concern of Deputy City Administrator Emanuel Savas that the neighborhood government programs of the administration be effectively studied combined to produce a three-year National Science Foundation grant to Columbia University that called for a $1.4 million effort to evaluate the experiment and its impact on the quality of life in four experimental communities of the city, compared with three "control" communities.

Simultaneously, Feldstein was beginning to explore the possibility of developing a proposal to the Department of Housing and Urban Development. The roots of this enterprise date back to tentative explorations of the city's

Housing and Development Administration as early as 1969 in search of federal housing redevelopment money. Late in 1970, HDA Administrator Albert Walsh received word that the city had reasonable prospects for getting money under section 505 of the 1970 Federal Housing Act. HDA's March 1971 application to HUD was rejected, however, because its thrust was limited to the redevelopment of housing stock and failed to address problems and approaches related to the prevention of general community deterioration. Soon after this rejection was received, Feldstein briefed Walsh on the plans for the ONG decentralization program. Since two of the possible ONG districts were also possible housing rehabilitation areas and the district managers would be able to provide leadership and an institutional base for a coordinated approach to community problems, the new ONG effort seemed like an ideal vehicle on which to launch a revised application to HUD. Feldstein thus became actively involved with HDA, the Community Planning Department and the Bureau of the Budget in the preparation of an ONG request for funds from HUD for a major redevelopment program in two districts. Although the proposal was submitted in October 1971, it underwent a series of modifications in its review by HUD, so that the grant that emerged ten months later was for a three-month effort (costing $310,000) to develop a detailed plan and proposal for a large-scale redevelopment grant covering only one of the two communities.[d]

Quite obviously, then, Feldstein saw the mobilization of federal government resources as a key means of building the political base that would be necessary to keep his program in operation and thus calculated that substantial involvement and investment of three federal agencies—whether direct or, as with NSF, indirect—would constitute a base to assure the survival of the operation over the first several years.

The mobilization of support from within the Lindsay administration was also clearly a central part of Feldstein's agenda. Three of the program's six structural innovations depended on the cooperation of the city's line agencies for implementation, and Feldstein lacked the kind of mayoral backing or independent power base that would have been highly persuasive with the commissioners and administrators whose action was needed.

New York City's administrative structure was, during this period, still adjusting to the dislocations that had resulted from the creation, during the first Lindsay administration, of administrations, or superagencies. Designed to solve what was seen by administrative consultants as a crucial problem of span of control, the superagency concept called for the consolidation of a large number of functionally specialized agencies and departments into a more manageable number of functionally similar administrations. Thus, for example, the depart-

---

[d]Work under this planning grant was completed, but the proposal for the actual redevelopment effort was eventually rejected by HUD in the light of the 1973 freeze on urban housing programs. For a detailed study of the evolution of the HDA district program, see Howard Katz's forthcoming political science dissertation, "Program Implementation in an Urban Bureaucracy," Columbia University, New York, N.Y.

ments for buildings, rent control and code enforcement, and economic development were grouped together into a single Housing Administration. In each case, however, the constituent departments and agencies, and their separate field organizations, remained intact. Attempts of the superagency administrators to establish effective control over the operational components of their domains were, of course, vigorously—and very frequently, successfully—resisted by the bureaucratic, management, union, and client interests associated with the agencies and departments. Among those organizations that ONG was most directly concerned with, the least disruption occurred in the Environmental Protection Administration (EPA) and the Police Department. In the former case, the Department of Sanitation was the dominant component and the only one with a significant field organization. Its commissioner was chosen by, and worked effectively with, the administrator of EPA. No attempt was made to integrate the Police Department into a larger structure, so its organizational integrity remained intact.

The ONG approach to the departments and superagencies called for commitments to participate in the experiment, but encouraged each individual administrative structure to develop the mechanisms whereby it would coordinate with the district managers and participate in their cabinets. Agency resistance came in two forms, depending on the character of the organization's field structure.

For the police and sanitation departments, which had extensive field structures broken down into districts that correspond in size roughly to the Community Planning Districts, the paramount questions related to redistricting. Police precinct captains and district sanitation superintendents were the obvious officials to sit on district cabinets, but major objections were raised to the plan where significant redrawing of agency district boundaries would be required to make them coterminous with those of specific Community Planning Districts. Where ONG was particularly anxious that a district manager experiment be established, however, it was clearly prepared to settle for agency expressions of intent to redistrict within the bounds of administrative feasibility.

In the superagencies with multiple field structures, objections to the structural demands of ONG were of a different order. Since none of the superagencies, as distinct from its component agencies, had its own field structure, acceptance of the precise boundaries of the CPDs as the units of the experiment was easy enough to obtain. The question was one of who would represent the administration on the cabinets. ONG rejected the idea of having a field official from one component represent an entire superagency and argued instead for the appointment of a full-time representative who could coordinate the whole range of superagency activities at the local level and present a consolidated picture for the district manager and the cabinet. The issues then turned on how many such coordinators the agencies could afford to appoint, what qualities and capabilities they would be expected to have, and which districts the superagencies would be willing to work in.

In addition to the question of structural adjustment, ONG clearly felt it needed the support of the agencies in order to get sufficient powers into the hands of the people who would constitute the district service cabinets. Preprogram explorations had indicated that in the Department of Sanitation, for example, decisions that affected a single district were often made by a regional supervisor or in the central office of the chief-of-staff of operations. As a result, a major thrust of the ONG effort was directed at what was called "command decentralization"—that is, more extensive delegation of local operating authority to local operating officials.

Again, the nature of agency response and resistance differed according to whether ONG was working with a single or multiple field structure. In sanitation and police, the questions involved vertical redistribution of power within existing hierarchies. The broader the delegation of power, of course, the more difficult would be the problems of executive control over its use at the local level. Police Commissioner Patrick Murphy was strongly predisposed, however, to strengthen the autonomy of the individual precinct captain and had already delegated extensive powers to the local level and devised new control mechanisms to insure that those powers would be exercised within the confines of central policy guidelines. Commissioner of Sanitation Herbert Elish seemed more reluctant to strengthen the hands of district superintendents and was more constrained by an elaborate set of union regulations that defined many features of district-level operations. Under some pressure from his administrator and with persistent prodding from ONG, however, Elish finally issued, in April of 1972, orders that gave the superintendents in ONG districts formal, if somewhat circumscribed, authority over local routing and scheduling decisions and responses to requests for services from local community groups.

In the health, human resources, and housing and development areas, however, the problems were quite different. The district-level positions that ONG wished to see created were not part of existing power hierarchies. Thus, confusion and ambiguity surrounded the meaning of "command decentralization" in discussions of the powers to be delegated to these officials. Extensive discussions were held between ONG and superagency staff members in which "line authority" and "coordinator" models were considered, but these discussions avoided questions of where the line authority would come from. Lacking coherent and carefully thought out strategies of its own, ONG could do little than accept vague assurances that the district-level representatives would be given "coordinative powers."

Variations in the cooperativeness of superagencies with multiple field structures were shaped by the management goals and strategies of their administrators. Although his statutory and management bases for exercising effective control over the components of the Human Resources Administration were very limited, its administrator, Jule Sugarman, was most receptive to the ONG design. Clearly committed to the notion of locally integrated delivery of social services, Sugarman was already involved in the creation of human resource districts (HRDs) based on Community Planning District lines. He was thus predisposed to appoint the first of his HRD directors in ONG districts, but the ill-defined character of their duties and relationships to other components of HRA led to long delays in the appointment of directors and painfully slow progress in the development of their roles.

In the Housing and Development Administration, the prospect of obtaining federal neighborhood preservation funds prompted reasonably quick appointment of Area Housing Coordinators in the three ONG districts that might qualify under the program. The more complex and intractible problems of defining powers of those officials over the personnel and programs of the superagency's existing hierarchies, however, were neglected by Administrator Walsh, but eventually resolved by his successor, Andrew Kerr, in favor of the existing agency hierarchies.

Gordon Chase, Administrator of Health Services Administration, appeared most resistant to ONG initiatives. His strategy for gaining some measure of control over the health bureaucracies under his nominal command was to focus attention on several programs of key concern and to centralize administrative resources and control over them in the executive staff of HSA. District coordinators made no contribution to this strategy, and Chase did nothing to ease ONG's tasks. Finally, under heavy pressure from Feldstein that he not jeopardize DHEW funding of the experiment, Chase appointed a neighborhood health services manager in one district. The person designated to fill the position was almost immediately appointed a deputy commissioner in the Department of Health, however, and the job was subsequently assigned, as additional duty, to the full-time district health officer in the area.

Thus, by the time the experiment was six months into operation, ONG had achieved only a small fraction of its original goals in negotiations with the city's operating agencies. Although agreement had been obtained for the development of six district cabinets, only very limited redistricting of operational field structures had been carried out. Powerless coordinators of HDA agencies were in place; coordinators were mandated even if their incumbents were not in play, by HRA; and one district health officer had the formal status of a coordinator of local health agency activities. Marginal increases in the formal powers of district sanitation superintendents had also been authorized. These generally disappointing results notwithstanding, however, six separate agencies—sanitation, police parks, recreation, traffic, and addiction services—had agreed to the participation of operating line officials in the district cabinets. Although it was very clear that no powers were thereby given up to the district managers, this highly circumscribed promise of participation provided, more than any other concession from the agencies, the base from which the district manager experiment would evolve.

Shift of Program Dynamic to the Field

In January of 1972, district managers were appointed for the first four experimental areas. Despite the ill-defined responsibilities and virtually nonexistent powers of the managers, the position carried salary and status comparable to those of a deputy commissioner. Feldstein was able to recruit to these positions ambitious and creative people with impressive administrative experience and skills. They, in turn, began almost immediately to recruit staffs, search out local office facilities, and launch a variety of program activities.

The central ONG staff, generally frustrated in its efforts to extract concessions from the city's operational departments and administrations, increasingly turned its attention to the monitoring of its own field operations. Staff members assigned monitoring roles became increasingly involved in the field activities of the managers, however, and within a few months, nearly half of the central ONG staff had been effectively coopted by the managers for their own staffs.

In May, only five months after the beginning of field operations, then-Controller of New York City Abraham Beame released the results of an investigation of the Office of Neighborhood Government that charged its financial manager with a variety of misuses of funds. Feldstein immediately took a leave of absence pending determination of his own legal status and thereby left his deputy, John Mudd, as acting director of the office. Mudd, who had handled many of the details of program development and management under Feldstein, suddenly had to deal also with leaders of the city's administrations and with senior members of the mayor's staff. Problems generated by his own inexperience were compounded by the political cloud that settled over the organization as a result of the mismanagement accusations and by the uncertainty about when, if ever, Feldstein would return to his position as director. At this point in time, the program was clearly a political liability for the mayor, and he made no serious attempt to rescue the office. Feldstein's legal position remained ambiguous for more than a year—he was eventually named by a grand jury in a presentment, but was not indicted—and John Mudd kept the title of acting director throughout that period.

This combination of events—frustration in agency negotiations, administrative dynamism and flexibility in the field, and a deterioration of leadership status and experience in the central office—led to a dramatic shift in program focus toward experimentation in the field. Central staff members were transformed into field staff members and the central office became increasingly preoccupied with fighting political threats to the program, running interference in the central administration for district programs, and keeping up with the demands of various federal funding requirements and prospects. The experiment needed to have demonstrable successes in the field if it were to survive, and the central office had neither the inclination nor the staff resources to exert significant constraints on the ways in which the managers went off in search of programmatic success.

Evolution and Differentiation of Field Roles

As the experimental dynamic shifted to the field, the particular characteristics of the individual districts combined with the background and personality of their managers to generate a distinctive program style, strategy, and focus in each of the districts. A sense of the range and variety of separate district experiments that evolved over the course of the following two years can perhaps best be derived from a brief description of the districts, their managers, and the programs.

The most coherent and, we would argue, the most successful of the experiments evolved very quickly in the Wakefield-Edenwald section of the Bronx. John Sanderson became manager of this remote, predominantly white ethnic, working-class district. Segmented in several distinctive neighborhoods, each of which had its own local organizations but inadequate ties to the larger community, the area's residents felt alienated from the city and its service delivery bureaucracies, suspicious of the Lindsay administration and its neglect of the middle-class constituency, and somewhat fearful of and hostile toward the lower-income, predominantly black residents of the large Edenwald housing project in its midst.

Sanderson combined the class and white ethnic background of his constituency with years of construction and systems design training in the Navy and the Bureau of the Budget that earned him the respect of local agency officials. When his initial management and system analysis interpretation of the district manager role failed to simulate understanding or cooperation among either group, Sanderson violated ONG central's operational guidelines and launched an intensive direct appeal campaign among community organizations, thereby emphasizing his ability to assist in the resolution of problems involving city service delivery. Sanderson clearly had both the political instincts and the management skills to draw expressions of community discontent and needs from local organizations and to translate those expressions into bureaucratically manageable problems. He developed, and was able to maintain, contacts with virtually the full spectrum of ethnic and class interests in each of the district's neighborhoods and gained the personal confidence and professional respect of local agency officials.

Sanderson used his skills and contacts to play a complex and highly successful brokerage role in Wakefield-Edenwald. Central to the notion of brokerage is a nonthreatening posture that is based on an inclusive, mediating, and facilitating pattern of behavior. Rather than attempt to mobilize specific segments of the population behind him, press for specific projects, and create an independent capability for program development and operation, the broker-manager builds and uses resources based on information, contacts, and reputation for trustworthiness and neutrality to help others in the community better achieve their own goals through well-managed joint ventures that they had previously been unable to negotiate for themselves.

Sanderson quickly demonstrated brokerage skills that led him to play significant roles in the Wakefield-Edenwald community. He was active in resolving disputes between contending segments of the community, in defining and evolving solutions to problems that plagued citizen-bureaucrat relationships, and in developing mechanisms whereby functionally related service chiefs could better coordinate their programs in Wakefield-Edenwald.[6]

The brokerage role that Sanderson developed so successfully is not without serious limitations and disadvantages, however. Sanderson was fortunate that the consequences of those problems were minimal in his district. Thus, the achievements of the Wakefield-Edenwald program must be seen not solely as a product of a coherent operational strategy, but also as a product of conditions in the district that made a successful brokerage operation possible.

A broker must accept the basic distribution of power within a community as a given. His role involves working with and strengthening existing organizations. If those are unrepresentative and self-serving, the broker can do little to change the situation. Some marginal shifts in power that strengthen disadvantaged groups can sometimes be engineered by a broker, but the danger of alienating status quo forces is always great. Since the leadership in Wakefield-Edenwald was reasonably representative of the community, the Sanderson strategy of working with existing forces benefited a broad range of the area's residents.

For a new broker to be effective, he must create linkages between significant groups that have common concerns and reconcilable goals but inadequate channels of communication with each other. Wakefield-Edenwald's traditionally separate communities with few umbrella organizations linking them together provided a ready-made setting for a broker-manager. Had the district already contained an effective brokerage institution that created and sustained linkages among communities and between citizens and the public bureaucracies, Sanderson's role would have been much more difficult to establish.

Of course, local political party organizations are potentially most threatened by a broker-manager, both because they often perform brokerage services themselves for the voting citizenry and because their interests are frequently seen as irreconcilable with those of other party organizations: Only one party can win an assembly, councilmanic, or house seat. The seeds of destruction of the Wakefield-Edenwald broker-manager experiment lay dormant for the first two years of its operation in the form of quiet opposition and hostility within the leadership of the district's Democratic Party organization.

Finally, a broker can, in the short term, only have an impact on problems that can effectively be managed by existing institutions within the community. He can marginally increase the amount of, and significantly improve the efficiency in the use of, community and city resources earmarked for expenditure in the district. But if the financial resources, institutional capacity, and organizational sophistication required to deal with an area's major problems are significantly greater than those available to the community, the broker can do little to resolve those problems. In this respect also, Wakefield-Edenwald was an excellent location for the operation of a service delivery-oriented broker since the scope and complexity of the area's problems were manageable within existing resource constraints. Its housing stock was in good repair and most of its major capital infrastructural needs had already been adequately met. The population was, for the most part, capable of meeting its own economic, health, and social needs. Thus, most of the service delivery problems involved relatively minor needs for the improvement of the physical environment of the community and marginal improvements in the quality of health and welfare service delivery.

The pattern of community involvement with the district manager's office in Wakefield-Edenwald represented, then, a fortuitous combination of a skillful broker and a social environment that was highly suited to the services that such a broker was able to provide.

In the Crown Heights area of Brooklyn, Dick Duhan was already involved in a brokerage-type of operation when he was appointed district manager. As director of the Neighborhood Action Program, a Lindsay program administered by the Office of Neighborhood Government and designed to help stabilize transitional neighborhoods, Duhan had developed wide-ranging contacts in the community and had been active in various forms of conflict resolution and program coordination. The merging of that role with a district managership reinforced the resources, status, and access to agency officials that he could devote to further development of a community brokerage role.

The character and needs of Crown Heights were dramatically different from those of Wakefield-Edenwald, however. At the center of class and racial cleavages in Brooklyn, Crown Heights was deeply divided: between middle-class and low-income and between black and Jewish residents. The political cleavages were among the most complex in the city, and many of them were characterized by attitudes that made little allowance for accommodation or compromise.

The problems and needs of the area were, moreover, of a much more complex and intractible nature than those of Wakefield-Edenwald. The northern part of the district was an extension of the Bedford-Stuyvesant ghetto, with low rates of employment, high rates of crime, and increasing problems of housing deterioration and decay. A massive infusion of resources would be needed to stem effectively the progressive deterioration of the area's housing stock. The organizational structure of the district was characterized by radical inequities in the strength and effectiveness with which various segments of the community are represented. The Hassidic community has been one of the most cohesive, well-organized, and—for its size—powerful ethnic collectivities in the city. Middle-class black homeowners were active in effective organizational structures. Poorer blacks and Puerto Ricans—a majority of the total population of the district—were, in contrast, inadequately represented through their participation in contending factions of the Democratic Party and in numerous, but frequently ineffectual, block associations.

In response to these conditions, Duhan soon violated key principles of the brokerage role in an attempt to mobilize greater resources for Crown Heights, thereby greatly increasing, in the process, the difficulties of his own position. That he managed to survive at all in that community is, we would argue, testimony to his energy and his mediating skills.

The specific issue on which Duhan deviated from a brokerage style of operation was ONG's planning grant from HUD. Duhan was actively involved in developing the original ONG proposal, and the very existence of his office and its general acceptance in the community was an important consideration in HUD's decision to award the planning grant for work in Crown Heights. In his role as director of the planning study and major program proposal preparation, with its nominal control over $310,000 and its potential—as perceived by the community—for control over a vastly greater sum of money when the grant was awarded, Duhan met his most severe challenges. Various segments of the community sought to assure themselves positions of influence over the organization that would operate the program. In lengthy sessions with a broadly representative advisory committee, Duhan tried repeatedly to develop program and management formulae that would satisfy the contending segments of his community and HUD. When the program grant was finally turned down, the pressures on Duhan decreased, but he was never able to regenerate the broad-based trust and support that he had built earlier. Nevertheless, he was innovative and resourceful in his efforts to develop relevant programs in a conflict- and problem-ridden district.

The physical needs of Bushwick, the district to the north of Bedford-Stuyvesant in Brooklyn, were much more severe even than those of Crown Heights. The long rows of wood frame houses had deteriorated badly in the preceding twenty years under the pressure of heavy overcrowding by low-income tenants. The community's Italian immigrants had largely deserted the southern half of the district and had been replaced by black and Puerto Rican residents. The area was highly susceptible to devastating fires, and the social, health, and housing needs of the community's low-income population were among the greatest in the city. Few organizations existed to effectively represent these interests and needs, however. Population turnover was rapid, and Puerto Rican or black institutions were few in number and generally ineffectual. Numerous Italian organizations remained intact in the northern part of the district, but their concerns did not extend to the district as a whole.

Sid Jones, the Bushwick district manager, was clearly the most cautious of the initial appointees. He showed the most persistent commitment to developing service cabinet relationships and programs and was hesitant to violate ONG guidelines that recommended limited contact with and mobilization of community organizations. Obviously, part of his reluctance to replicate the kind of program that seemed to be achieving significant successes in Wakefield-Edenwald stemmed from his conviction that focusing his office's attention on minor environmental problems in Bushwick would prevent him from working on the major human and capital investment projects that his district so desperately needed.

In a series of frustrating staff efforts over the course of nearly two years, Jones came face to face with the limitations of the cabinet as a program development institution. The limited concerns, incentives, and programmatic flexibility of agency representatives simply did not provide the basis on which significant planned change was to be generated in Bushwick. Jones, like the other managers, was able to improve coordination of routine service delivery tasks but these accomplishments frequently seemed like hollow victories in the context of Bushwick's needs. The limited range and representativeness of organizations also reduced the applicability of the Wakefield-Edenwald model to Bushwick.

In mid-1973, Jones began shifting toward a strategy that built more aggressively on community support and local political power as a basis for drawing greater public resources to Bushwick. Clearly, however, a great deal of work would have to go into developing the organizations on which such an effort could be based. By establishing an advisory council and working in support of block associations, Jones became more directly involved in community organizations and the politics of planning and capital budgeting.

The alternative to a brokerage strategy for the district manager is what might be called an entrepreneurial strategy—that is, one in which the manager sets out to build an independent power base through the mobilization of selected segments of the community, the espousal of specific programmatic goals, the development of alliances with political forces, and the accumulation of financial and staff resources for program implementation.

The most effective use of an entrepreneurial strategy was made by Janet Langsam in the Rockaways. The district manager program was begun in this remote Queens community nearly six months after its establishment in the first four districts.[e] It had already become clear that community participation was going to be a more important component than had been anticipated by ONG planners, so they decided to experiment with the selection of a district manager with community, rather than bureaucratic, experience. Langsam had been the chairman of a community planning board in northern Queens and had well-established contacts in the county Democratic Party organization and the City Planning Commission.

Although the Rockaways had a higher mean family income than Wakefield-Edenwald, its problems were of a radically different character. As an area that had doubled in population during the past twenty-five years while population levels had been relatively stable in most of the rest of the city, the Rockaways

---

[e]At the same time, the program was also extended to the South Bronx. In that community, however, the experiment was grafted onto a much larger and more generously funded Model Cities program that had already been in effect for a number of years. The BASR research effort made no attempt to follow or access the South Bronx experiment.

had still not experienced the infrastructural development necessary to support its increased population. Its problems were compounded by the presence of both middle-income Jewish families and a significant number of lower-income black families. The orientations of these two groups toward the Rockaways and its pattern of future development differed radically.

Langsam was determined to do something about the infrastructural needs of the community and saw community groups as central actors in her efforts. Clearly, her goals were mobilizing the Community Planning Board to take a more active planning role and supplementing and supporting community activity with whatever independent political and administrative influences she could exercise. Her effective use of personal contacts soon made obvious that she was a political force to be reckoned with.

By pressing for the development of specific planning projects, Langsam quickly began to alienate segments of the community that saw her actions and goals as inimical to their interests. Through her initiative, organizing skills, and influence, however, she was able to bring limited planning and service delivery benefits to the Rockaways and to produce, in conjunction with the Community Planning Board, a prototype district planning document.

The Langsam entrepreneurial strategy produced active and aggressive leadership in a community with serious long-term problems requiring complex decision making and determined movement through the nearly impenetrable tangle of political and administrative obstacles that characterizes the planning and capital budgeting processes in New York City. She exhibited concern for maintaining a balanced community, but her exercise of power and influence apparently threatened and alienated many leaders throughout the community. Although her style generated great initial skepticism among the members of her service delivery cabinet, Langsam's ability to represent their interests in bureaucratic and political power centers won her the respect of many of them.

Donald Middleton, the district manager in Washington Heights, pursued an entrepreneurial strategy with considerably less success than Langsam. Although the district was remarkably diverse in its ethnic make-up, economic status, and the characteristics of its neighborhoods, it had two active institutions whose leaders saw themselves to be representatives of the district as a whole. Its Community Planning Board was among the most active in the city and had established a number of subcommittees concerned with service delivery issues. Working closely with the board was the second districtwide institution: Jordan Linfield's Neighborhood Action Program, which operated in Washington Heights under the auspices of the Office of Neighborhood Government.

In their search for a Washington Heights district manager with administrative experience, Feldstein and his staff committed what is, in retrospect, almost universally regarded as a major tactical blunder. They bypassed Linfield—but left him in full control of the Neighborhood Action Program—and appointed an ambitious young man who had grown up in the district and was believed to have thoughts of using his old home turf as a personal political base. The plan seemed feasible because the formal role definitions of the NAP director, Community Planning Board, and district manager were quite distinct and potentially complementary. Linfield would work with community organizations, the board would develop a community planning capability, and the district manager would coordinate local service delivery. Initial assent to Middleton's appointment was given by Linfield and the board on the understanding that he would be an administrative technician who would work almost exclusively to improve operating relationships among the city agencies in the district.

In reality, however, Linfield, the board leadership, and Middleton were all clearly interested in playing linkage roles between the community and service delivery bureaucracies. Thus, Middleton quickly came to be seen by NAP and Community Planning Board leaders as a competitor for, rather than as supplement to, their community leadership and representation roles. Middleton, in turn, perceived these institutions as representing narrow interests and the political ambitions of their leaders and made clear that he would not be responsive to their claims to speak for the community on service delivery needs, goals, and priorities. The political influence of his opponents far outweighed the support he could mobilize as a new mayoral appointee in the Office of Neighborhood Government, however, and Middleton was soon forced to accept a written agreement with the board and NAP that severely limited his role.

As a program management specialist who had begun to make a name for himself through the development of a new program in the Addiction Services Agency (ASA), Middleton was clearly intent on applying executive management techniques and political entrepreneurship to the mobilization and rejuvenation of an unresponsive bureaucracy. Deprived of the political base that he was unable to build, Middleton had little leverage over his district service cabinet members, and unused to exercising influence without formal authority, he was slow to develop the personal loyalties of service chiefs that Sanderson seemed to stimulate so naturally. Middleton concentrated his initial program efforts on the extension of an idea he had developed in ASA to improve the handling of addicts arrested on misdemeanor charges. Slowly, he also began to build a minimal political base to protect his position within the district, and his conflict with Linfield and the board stabilized into an uncomfortable standoff.

Attempts to Consolidate Central Authority

By late 1972, the initial directions of the individual district experiments had been clearly established. The central office staff, however, had become seriously depleted, and the consequent lack of central authority and direction had important long-term implications for ONG's survival. Sid Gardner helped the central staff define the problems and evolve a new management strategy when he returned in a consultant capacity to undertake a brief review of the experiment. One disturbing pattern was the very distinct drift in district program emphasis and successes toward environmental community service problems: safety, recreation, traffic, garbage collection, and street cleaning. Few serious program efforts—and even fewer program successes—had dealt with the social, health, and educational problems that were of primary concern to the program reviewers in the Department of Health, Education and Welfare. The divergence between DHEW goals and ONG performance was accentuated by the emergence within DHEW of more explicit criteria for the evaluation of human service integration efforts. It was apparent that failure to make credible efforts to develop more effective programs involving human service agencies would jeopardize ONG's refunding prospects for a third year.

A second trend was the increasing autonomy and district-orientation of the managers, who were clearly conscious of the distinctive characteristics, needs, and constraints associated with their districts. Their activities became increasingly focused on meeting specific local needs and taking advantage of specific local opportunities as they arose. The central office staff seemed aware that many useful things were being done in the field, but they were unable either to direct activities along particular lines or to define and document patterns of successes in ways that would justify continuation of the program.

Finally, the internal research capability that had been mandated in the DHEW grant had deteriorated badly. Bureaucratic entanglements with the city university system had brought sponsored research by a team from Queens College to a standstill, and the central staff lacked both research personnel and defined research goals. Thus, the ONG commitment to DHEW for evaluation of their own experiment was not being met.

In an effort to reverse these trends, a concerted effort was made to expand and strengthen the capacity of the central office in three areas. One section tried to revive negotiations with the operating departments and administrations, particularly those in fields of social, health, and housing. Its efforts, however, produced only marginal advances in patterns of agency cooperation with ONG. A Department of Health reorganization effort was well underway before ONG became aware of the strong convergence of interests between its own goals and those of officials involved in efforts to restructure the health bureaucracy.[7] ONG intervened much more vigorously in HRA planning processes for that administration's field reorganization and managed to focus initial attention on the needs of the human resource districts in which there were also district managers. The HRA reorganization left most of the field operations of its individual agencies unchanged, however, and the district-based community social services programs that developed in Crown Heights and Washington Heights were able to have only limited impact.

A second section in ONG's central office began systematic monitoring of the district experiments and developed program designs that could be replicated across districts. This effort was more successful in meeting its goals. It forced the managers to categorize their many varied activities into specified projects and to report regularly on progress being made toward the achievement of specific goals. Although these reporting procedures were seen as distractions from their primary tasks by some managers, they imposed some minimal coherence on the disparate activities of the various experiments and produced tangible and documented evidence of ONG's achievements.

A third section in ONG focused on the generation of the office's own research and evaluation of the experiment. This effort was slow to get established and its staff's attention was frequently diverted to other tasks, but it eventually developed and presented with some effect the case for the district manager and the district service cabinet as mechanisms of service integration.

The basic dynamic of the program, and the primary sources of its political support, however, remained in the districts. John Mudd remained outside the centers of power within the Lindsay administration and was unable to establish himself as an influential spokesman in behalf of ONG interests. Leadership in the city's departments and administrations changed over time, but the Office of Neighborhood Government continued to be generally perceived as one of the many minor irritants with which operating agencies had to contend. Support from DHEW had clearly waned and negotiations with HUD had consumed inordinate amounts of staff time and energy. Only the NSF-BASR interest remained firm, but even there, the danger of unfavorable interim research reports gave a double-edged quality to that involvement.

Institutionalization through Expansion

By March of 1973, the political context in which ONG operated had changed dramatically. John Lindsay announced that he would not again run for mayor, and it soon seemed probable that Abraham Beame—not an open supporter of the district manager concept—would be mayor within nine months. Attention thus turned toward the problems of securing the political base of the program. The primary strategy that was chosen involved extending the community constituency of ONG by expanding the experiment to additional districts. Since funds were unavailable for the hiring of new district managers, the expansion was made only into districts that already had Neighborhood Action Programs or skeleton Urban Action Task Forces. By using small full-time staffs and coopting commissioners from various agencies to chair monthly cabinet meetings, minimal district service cabinet programs were established in eighteen new districts. These expansion cabinets lacked the most significant element in the initial experiments—the full-time district managers—but it was hoped that even this minimal program would generate significant community support in many parts of the city.

A second strategy was to assure the continuation of DHEW funding for a third full year so that the program would have federal support to carry it at least six months into the term of a new mayor. In the face of considerable doubts in DHEW as to the viability of the district manager and cabinet concept as a vehicle for client-based service integration, ONG mobilized sufficient political support to win refunding at two-thirds of the previous level of annual support.

The Fight for Political Control

A hallmark of the Beame administration, after its inauguration on January 1, 1974, was its reliance on established bureaucratic institutions. One manifestation of this allegiance to the routinization of government was a proclaimed intention to reestablish the functionally specialized bureaus, agencies, and departments as the pillars of city administration. The strong civil service tradition of this mayor and his senior advisors relied on the agencies themselves to coordinate with each other and was basically hostile to the notion that special coordinators were needed to provide geographic coherence to local service delivery. The inter-agency coordination role of the district managers was, in short, of doubtful legitimacy in the new regime.

A second feature of the new administration was the strength of its roots in the established Democratic Party organization throughout the city. This aggregation of local district institutions had traditionally provided an important link between citizens and local bureaucracy. Although its bases had been seriously eroded over the past fifty years by the drastic reduction of patronage positions that resulted from civil service reform, the party's local clubs still attempted to alleviate citizen grievances related to public service delivery.

Both within the administrative and the political traditions of the new mayoral team, then, there had long been a predisposition to see the district manager experiment primarily as a constituency servicing program rather than as an administrative reform program. Even during the Lindsay years, many of that mayor's political opponents saw the experiment as just one more in a series of his efforts to build a citywide servicing organization that would institutionalize an alternative to the Democratic clubs as a basis of political support. In this perception, the jobs of the district managers and their staffs represented significant patronage opportunities.

The first battle over these positions in the new administration came in the district where the experiment had had its most visible successes: Wakefield-Eden-wald. There, the district Democratic Party leadership moved quickly within the new administration to secure the removal of Sanderson's successor, Robert House, and his staff assistants. House reacted by attempting to mobilize community support in opposition to the firings, and though the effort failed, the political battle that ensued probably discouraged the administration from moving quickly into similar confrontations with the other Lindsay-appointed district managers.

The Beam administration's approach to the program as a whole seems to have been characterized by a reluctance to dismantle what could be a useful servicing institution, but an inability to hit upon a formula for distributing patronage opportunities in ways that would both satisfy its multiple constituencies and its own concerns for operational control. Appropriately concerned with eliminating the multiple and overlapping programs of the Office of Neighborhood Government, the new director of the office, John Carty, attempted to design a program that could be implemented uniformly throughout the city. The use of city councilmanic districts as bases for ONG districts was long considered and finally rejected. Extended debate ensued on the mode of appointment of district managers. With increasing concern for fiscal austerity in the administration, attention subsequently turned to the possibility of locating district representatives in the central office and linking them to their communities by special telephone exchanges.

The citywide program that was eventually established to replace the district manager experiment called for districts over twice the size of the experimental areas and staffing patterns representing less than half the personnel and expertise that was available under the earlier programs. This fourfold diminution of resources for a given area had a serious impact on the ability of the program to cope with local problems. Even more detrimental to the program, however, was the deterioration in ability of local coordinators to work effectively with agency field personnel. The large districts represented a dramatic increase in the numbers of agency personnel with whom a district manager needed to coordinate, and the lack of agency coterminality increased the coordinative burden on all participants in the system, because any one official was likely to have to deal with several officials from each of the other agencies with which he worked.

Conclusion

As the foregoing summary of the evolution of the district manager experiment suggests, considerable diversity existed in the goals and the operating patterns of the program. Its most distinctive and significant defining characteristic, however, was the tendency of district managers to combine the administrative role of fostering interagency cooperation with the quasi-political role of linking communities to the local representatives of the city's bureaucracies. Where managers had the professional experience and skills to work effectively with agency officials and the political instincts to work with community groups, these two roles were mutually reinforcing and stabilizing. Broad-based community backing strengthened the managers in their efforts to increase bureaucratic responsiveness, and the managers' professional competence and influence with agency officials drew community participation and legitimized and reinforced the nonpartisan character of their leadership.

This achievement represents considerably less than the elaborate administrative reorganization and eventual political decentralization originally envisioned when the program was formulated. The experiment never established an effective model for a citywide program because it failed to find a manageable formula for the rationalization of agency boundaries and field bureaucracies. The needs for improved interagency cooperation were almost certainly overstated, and the formula for "command decentralization" that evolved from experience with the sanitation and police departments was inappropriate to the needs of other city agencies.

The freedom of the individual managers to experiment—and the generally intelligent and skillful manner in which they pursued their various goals—demonstrated, however, the very positive effects that sensitive and energetic people can have in the performance of urban brokerage roles. In a large city with its complex economic, social, and political linkages, the coherence of its component localities tends to atrophy. It was this deterioration that the ONG staff perceived in their early explorations with community leaders throughout the city. As members of the mayor's staff, it was appropriate that they be particularly sensitive to the lack of local coherence in mayoral agencies. As John Boyle's chapter shows, however, the informal mechanisms of interagency communication seem to have been more adequate than most observers suspected. An extensive and important variety of integrative roles linking these agencies to other institutions—especially public and private schools and local community organizations—were, however, simply not being performed throughout much of the city. The managers demonstrated that the city administration can play an important part in reestablishing the coherence of local communities through the mechanism of district-political-administrative brokers.

Notes

1. Mayor John V. Lindsay, *Plan for Neighborhood Government for New York City*, Office of the Mayor, City of New York, June 1970, p. 12.

2. For the official formulation of the program, see Mayor John V. Lindsay, *Program for the Decentralized Administration of Municipal Services in New York City Communities*, Office of the Mayor, City of New York, December 1971 (reprinted in the Appendix to this volume).

3. Ibid., p. 266, this volume.

4. Ibid., p. 265.

5. Ibid., pp. 265-266.

6. For more detailed discussions of the first year of district programs, see

Parts I, III, and IV of Stanley J. Heginbotham and John M. Boyle, Robin Maas, Howard G. Katz, Geraldine Alpert and Kenneth H. Andrews, *Between Community and City Bureaucracy: New York's District Manager Experiment*, Bureau of Applied Social Research, Columbia University, New York, N.Y., December 1974. The appendix to Part IV contains brief descriptions of 121 program activities in the five districts.

7. See Geraldine Alpert, *Professional Values and Bureaucratic Behavior: The New York City Department of Health Revisited*, Bureau of Applied Social Research, Columbia University, New York, N.Y., 1974, for an analysis of the reorganization. A chapter in Dr. Alpert's political science dissertation discusses the HSA response to the district manager experiment. See Alpert, "The Limits of Structural Reform: Professional Values and Administrative Reorganization in the NYC Health Care Bureaucracy," Unpublished Ph.D. dissertation, Columbia University, New York, N.Y., 1975.

3

Service Integration at the District Level: Seven Examples

Ronald Brumback

What did the district Offices of Neighborhood Government actually do in the New York City district manager demonstration program? Behind the abstractions of "service integration," "interagency cooperation," and "agency-community relations" were the day-to-day problems of getting vacant lots cleaned up, finding community work for people on relief, and trying to keep a community's housing stock from deteriorating. Therefore, we offer seven case histories of "projects" initiated by local Office of Neighborhood Government. The case histories include some projects that became operational, some that failed to get going, and one large one that was still under development when the field research ended. In the chapter that follows this one, we will proceed to a statistical description of sixty-five projects that were studied in this way. The seven examples in this chapter, which detail the complexities of such seemingly simple problems as cleaning up vacant lots, will provide the reader with a better understanding of what the demonstration program was about, and why it produced both applause and frustration from those involved.

Abbreviations

ASA   —Addiction Services Agency of New York City
CB   —Community Board (earlier called Community Planning Board, CPB)
CPC   —City Planning Commission
CPD   —Community Planning District (sixty-two in New York City, each with a Community Board appointed by the borough president)
DCD   —Department of Community Development (part of HRA)
DHEW—U.S. Department of Health, Education and Welfare
DM   —District manager (head of a district ONG)
EPA   —Environmental Protection Administration of New York City (includes Department of Sanitation)
HRA   —Human Resources Administration of New York City
HSA   —Health Services Administration of New York City
HUD   —U.S. Department of Housing and Urban Development
NAP   —Neighborhood Action Program (an ONG-directed program that preceded the district manager program in setting up offices in several CPDs as intermediaries between residents and the city bureaucracies)
OCS   —Office of Community Services (part of HRA)

ONG —Office of Neighborhood Government (can refer either to the central office, an agency in the office of the mayor, or to the district offices set up in several CPDs, which included BONG, the Bushwick ONG; CHONG, the Crown Heights ONG; WEONG, the Wakefield-Edenwald ONG; and WHONG, the Washington Heights ONG)

PRCA —Parks, Recreation, and Cultural Affairs Administration of New York City

WREP —Work Relief Employment Program (an HRA-administered program that used welfare recipients as supplementary manpower for city work and included sanitation department Self-Help workers)

YSA —Youth Services Agency (part of HRA)

How to Clean a Vacant Lot

District: Bushwick.

Project: Vacant lot cleaning.

Status as of December 31, 1973: Operational.

Purpose: To develop a procedure whereby the district's numerous vacant lots, most of which are privately owned, could be cleaned and kept clean.

Reason for Project: Bushwick has more than 350 vacant lots (i.e., more than 350 tax lots that are organized into 200 to 300 separate parcels) all of which are the source of such problems as refuse accumulation, rat breeding, fires, loitering, and criminal activity. Most of the lots are privately owned. The procedure for cleaning private lots is very cumbersome. Resources for cleaning vacant lots are available on an irregular basis. Once cleaned, lots tend to return to their previous condition fairly quickly.

Client Group: All service consumers in the district, particularly those near the greatest concentration of vacant lots in the southern two-thirds of the district below Myrtle and Knickerbocker Avenues.

Location of Benefit: Entire district, particularly the southern two-thirds of the district below Myrtle and Knickerbocker Avenues.

Agencies: Department of Sanitation Self-Help, Department of Sanitation (Districts 37 and 41, borough lot-cleaning crew), Human Resources Administration (WREP program), Department of Highways, Department of Health, Finance Administration (Department of Tax Collection), Department of Real Estate, Wildcat Corporation.

ONG Role: Identifying the severity of the problem; ascertaining the agency procedures involved. Developing modified interagency procedures; lobbying with the sanitation and health departments for more resources; providing EX-107 funds for additional equipment; coordinating the various lot-cleaning subagencies and other agencies involved; designating some of the decentralized highways budget for fencing cleaned vacant lots; developing lot use plans.

Program Category: Refuse removal, environmental beautification, health.

Nature of Change in Service Production: Prior to BONG's arrival in Bushwick, vacant lots were cleaned as time permitted by the North Brooklyn borough lot-cleaning crew in response to specific complaints. Legally, the sanitation department can clean only city-owned lots (prior to December 1973, there were only six such lots in Bushwick) and private lots certified as health hazards. Because the interagency procedure for cleaning private lots is very cumbersome and there is no organized public or private pressure to conduct lot cleaning, only a small proportion of Bushwick's vacant lots were cleaned prior to BONG's arrival. Inspired primarily by a desire to encourage block associations (most of which BONG had organized) and to help them with their clean-up efforts, BONG tried to increase the amount of sanitation department lot-cleaning activity in the district.

Initially, BONG developed an informal procedure whereby the sanitation department Self-Help workers and Sanitation District 37 crew cleaned private lots without securing health department certification. (The District 37 superintendent took this action following a mayoral statement at a district service cabinet meeting to the effect that the sanitation superintendent should clean as many lots as time and productivity goals permitted without regard to legal ownership.) In addition, the borough lot-cleaning crew agreed to commit its crews one day per week to Bushwick, thus ensuring some regularly scheduled cleaning. However, since all these changes depended on the good will of the people then in command, BONG attempted to institutionalize the changes to assure regular cleaning of lots.

The *usual procedure* for dealing with private vacant lots is as follows: someone reports a dirty vacant lot to the sanitation central office; someone from the borough sanitation office verifies the condition of the lot and determines its precise location by both street address and tax block number; this information is then transmitted to central sanitation and from there across to the health department's central office; an order then goes out to the borough office of the health department's inspection force that verifies the condition of the lot, determines who owns the lot, and notifies the health commissioner's office; the health commissioner then notifies the lot owner in writing that he has two weeks to clean his lot, after which it will be cleaned by the city at his expense (rarely collected, however); the lot is reinspected after two weeks, and if the lot is still dirty, a letter is sent by the health commissioner to sanitation central ordering sanitation to clean the lot; at sanitation central an order is prepared and transferred to the central lot-cleaning staff who in turn notify the borough lot-cleaning section that eventually cleans the lot—assuming the order has not been lost somewhere in the shuffle of paper work.

The *procedure developed by BONG* in conjunction with the sanitation and health departments is as follows: when a dirty vacant lot is discovered, the local Department of Sanitation Self-Help superintendent inspects the lot to verify its condition; a member of his crew (all of whom are WREP employees) determines the location of the lot from the lot and block book; then Self-Help notifies the sanitation department's borough lot-cleaning office, which determines the owner of the lot and reports back to the district Self-Help superintendent; the Self-Help superintendent then notifies a health department sanitarian who was outstationed in Bushwick to handle vacant lots and other matters; the sanitarian inspects the lot; if it is dirty, the district health officer (not the commissioner, as in the normal procedure) sends a letter to the lot owner informing him that he has two weeks to clean the lot, after which the city will clean the lot and bill him; the sanitarian reinspects the lot after two weeks; if the lot has not been cleaned, the district health officer fills out a lot-cleaning order on a form designed by BONG and the Self-Help superintendent to closely resemble a Department of Sanitation work order; this form is sent to the sanitation borough office where copies are distributed to the borough lot-cleaning crew, the appropriate district superintendent, and the Self-Help superintendent; the lot is cleaned by Self-Help, if it can be done with hand tools, and by the borough lot-cleaning crew, if heavy equipment is required. Although the process for handling private vacant lots is still rather involved, conducting it primarily at the local level—where it can be monitored—made the process far more effective. Other proposed aspects of this project included use of EX-107 money to purchase equipment needed by the sanitation department for lot cleaning, use of a Wildcat pest control crew to clean some lots, and use of part of one of the capital budget lump-sum lines in the decentralized highways budgeting experiment to fence some of the cleaned lots to reduce the rate at which the lots become relittered.

Results and Sources of Benefits: Despite the fact that certain aspects of the project were still being negotiated at the time of the change of city administrations, most of Bushwick's more than 350 vacant lots were cleaned at least once. Although a request to fence 29 lots was submitted as part of the decentralized highways budgeting project, no lots were fenced. Since in the past only a handful of lots had been cleaned each year and virtually no fencing was ever done, the project produced a marked increase in cleanliness and a reduction of fire and health hazards. Although the project required additional resources, it also resulted in more efficient use of the sanitation department Self-Help crew (comprised of welfare recipients who were essentially free resources to the agency). If the fencing had been done, the project should also have resulted in a per lot reduction in the cost of maintaining an acceptable state of cleanliness. In addition, by carrying out most of the coordination at the local level, there was greater assurance that local priorities would be met and that a dirty lot once discovered would be cleaned. The reduction in paper shuffling within and among agencies should have increased the efficiency of the process. Another project, vacant lot development, provided for development of some of the lots into useful community resources. Two side effects of the project were the use by Department of Sanitation Self-Help of the Bushwick Self-Help program as a model for its expansion into other districts and the establishment of a central interagency committee to try to develop a similar mechanism for lot cleaning and development throughout the city.

Resources: The cost of cleaning an average lot was approximately $300 to $350, although this cost obviously varied depending on how dirty the lot was, which crew did the cleaning, lot size, and so forth. For example, required incremental city expenditure was greater for sanitation department employees than for Department of Sanitation Self-Help (which used WREP workers who would otherwise have been collecting welfare checks without providing a service in return) or Wildcats (whose expenses were only partly paid by the city). Although not done, the cost of fencing the requested lots in the district was within the $11,273 lump-sum line allocation to the district for such purposes as part of the decentralized highways budgeting project. In total, the actual incremental cost of the project was probably in the neighborhood of $40,000 to $80,000. As a result of the systematic lot cleaning and development projects, the annual cost of maintaining an acceptable state of cleanliness was probably far less than this; this cost would have been even lower if fencing had been installed.

Implementation Problems: The sanitation department's reluctance to have the district health officer fill out a Department of Sanitation work order; the health department's use of an out-of-date real estate directory to determine the names and addresses of current owners; the health department's initial reluctance to outstation a sanitarian; lack of adequate equipment for local lot cleaning; HSA's reluctance to enter into a contract for pest control with the Wildcat Corporation; the highway department's failure to live up to its commitment to provide the requested fencing as part of the decentralized highways budgeting project; failure of the Brooklyn Borough Improvement Board to approve the EX-107 capital budget package, which included funds for additional lot-cleaning equipment (this delay was due to political maneuvering over the future of the ONG program).

Effect of Noncoterminality: Bushwick is served primarily by two sanitation districts. One of the district superintendents was more willing to cooperate in an informal lot-cleaning arrangement than was the other. However, implementation of the new procedure eliminated this problem.

Probability of Accomplishment without Program: Very low, probably zero. Since Bushwick is not the kind of community that pressures the service delivery system to improve services, it is unlikely that many of the vacant lots would have been cleaned in the absence of a community spokesman such as ONG. In addition, streamlining the interagency procedure for dealing with private lots probably would have been infeasible without BONG to devise the new procedures, to act as intermediary among the affected agencies, and to prod the agencies continually for action.

Comment: This project required a large amount of BONG staff time and effort. The district Self-Help superintendent was extremely valuable in working with the sanitation department.

Preserving a Neighborhood

District: Washington Heights.

Project: Neighborhood preservation. (Variations of this project were also conducted in two other experimental districts—Bushwick and Crown Heights.)

Status as of December 31, 1973: Project development.

Purpose: To rehabilitate 1,000 housing units in Washington Heights and to encourage the Clearinghouse Banks to seriously consider recommitting $100 million in mortgage money to the district in order to stem deterioration of the housing stock.

Reason for Project: To persuade the Housing and Development Administration (HDA) to undertake the neighborhood preservation program that it initially opposed; to ensure inclusion of three of the ONG experimental districts—Bushwick, Crown Heights, and Washington Heights—in the program; to facilitate development and implementation of the program.

Client Group: Directly, tenants and owners of the rehabilitated housing stock; indirectly, all service consumers in the vicinity of the rehabilitated housing on the assumption that the project will stem the neighborhood's evolution to a slum.

Location of Benefit: Small sections of Jumel, East Inwood, and Fort George—three of seven subneighborhoods in Washington Heights.

Agencies: Housing and Development Administration (Office of Neighborhood Preservation, Code Enforcement), Fire Department, Human Resources Administration (the Washington Heights offices of the Department of Community Development and the Office of Community Services), Department of Health, City Planning Commission, Neighborhood Action Program, Manhattan Community Planning Board 12.

ONG Role: Helping to persuade HDA to undertake the neighborhood preservation program; persuading HDA to commit $10 million of municipal loan funds to Washington Heights; lobbying with HDA for greater authority for the area housing director and for decentralization of staff, particularly code enforcement inspectors; trying to persuade the Clearinghouse Banks to recommit up to $100 million in mortgage funds to the district; assisting in developing and coordinating interagency inspection teams; helping to obtain Fire Department approval for HDA to copy fire violation reports for the purpose of establishing a complete violation file on the target buildings; providing a mechanism for HDA/HRA cooperation; attempting to procure HEW funding of complementary social services in the affected areas.

Program Category: Housing (rehabilitation of private stock) primarily; also social services.

Nature of Change in Service Production: According to an internal memorandum of HDA prepared in 1973, "Neighborhood Preservation/Rehabilitation Program," the neighborhood preservation program constituted ". . . the first attempt to concentrate and coordinate the application of . . . various HDA housing maintenance and rehabilitation programs on a neighborhood or community basis." More specifically, the neighborhood preservation program was intended to concentrate selected HDA programs in "transitional" neighborhoods to try to preserve the existing housing stock still within the price range of lower-middle-income families. The program in Washington Heights was to include $10 million in municipal loan funds plus various other loan, enforcement, repair, and rehabilitation programs—all coordinated by the local area housing office. In addition, in Washington Heights, as in Crown Heights, the demonstration of a sincere concerted effort by the city to cope with the problems of transitional neighborhoods was expected to prompt the Clearinghouse Banks to revive an earlier commitment of $100 million in private mortgage funds to the district.

To assist the area housing staff in pinpointing problem buildings, WHONG developed a pilot project whereby teams of DCD social workers who had been trained by HDA catalogued the violations in fifteen buildings scheduled for inclusion in the program. This prior screening of the buildings permitted more efficient use of the limited number of HDA inspectors who followed to actually enforce the housing code in the selected buildings. In addition, as the DCD team discovered unmet health or social service needs, they notified the Department of

Health and OCS as appropriate. WHONG assisted the area housing office in obtaining Fire Department code violation records in order to compile a comprehensive violations file for the district. In an effort to deal with some of the social problems that accompany housing stock deterioration, ONG unsuccessfully sought DHEW funding for increased complementary social services in and around the target areas.

Results and Sources of Benefit: Although no units had been rehabilitated as of December 31, 1973, the target areas had been selected and activities—increased code enforcement, loan applications, housing court action, and so forth—preliminary to actual rehabilitation had begun. The program, if fully implemented as planned, had the potential for approximately 1,000 units to be rehabilitated with the $10 million in municipal loans earmarked for the district, a number of other housing units to be repaired by the owner as a result of various HDA actions and programs, and a substantial number of units to be saved from deterioration and abandonment through the $100 million Clearinghouse Bank Commitment. While the foregoing constitutes more of an evaluation of the neighborhood preservation program than of ONG involvement, it can be argued that any success achieved by the program would be enhanced by ONG involvement.

Development of the area housing office that coordinates HDA action locally was a direct consequence of the ONG decentralization program. Involvement of other agencies to facilitate HDA efforts would have been unlikely without the ONG service integration mechanism. In addition, WHONG's knowledge of the district was valuable to the program in that it facilitated consideration of special local factors affecting the durability of housing improvement. In summary, while the neighborhood preservation program could have been conducted without ONG, there is little doubt that in the end ONG involvement will have increased the effectiveness of the program.

Resources: The one obvious increase in city resources to the district was the $10 million municipal loan commitment. Beyond that, it is difficult to determine whether other resources used in the program constituted net additions for the district. While it is likely that the concentrated effort in a few target areas coupled with normal HDA activity elsewhere in the district did result in some increased use of HDA resources in Washington Heights, the magnitude was probably small relative to the municipal loan funds and certainly small relative to the $100 million private sector commitment by the Clearinghouse Banks. At any rate, ONG's impact on the program was not to increase substantially the level of resource use, except insofar as the program probably would not have been undertaken without ONG advocacy.

Implementation Problems: HDA reluctance to undertake the program; HDA reluctance to implement the program once it had tentatively agreed to undertake it; HDA delay in assigning staff for the program; HDA resistance to granting the area housing director more authority; Clearinghouse Banks' reluctance to recommit themselves to investment in the district following earlier city failures to follow through on promises; Fire Department reluctance to open up its files to HDA.

Effects of Noncoterminality: None.

Probability of Accomplishment without Program: Without ONG prodding, HDA probably would not have undertaken the neighborhood preservation program. Once initiated, the program could have been conducted by HDA alone though perhaps not as efficiently. However, as discussed above (Results and Sources of Benefit), several aspects of the Washington Heights program (e.g., DCD inspection, access to Fire Department violation files, knowledge of specific neighborhood considerations) would not have occurred without ONG involvement.

Allocating Summer Youth Jobs

District: Wakefield-Edenwald.

Project: Summer youth programming.

Status as of December 31, 1973: Operational—recurs each summer.

Purpose: To calm community (primarily black versus Italian) tensions with regard to the distribution of summer recreation resources in the district; to develop a local procedure for allocating recreational resources in the district in order to spread resources more evenly over the entire district.

Reason for Project: Italian and black displeasure with what each group perceived to be a disproportionate allocation of summer recreation resources to the other; centralized allocation of summer resources to community groups based on political considerations and friendship. lack of coordination among recreation and youth agencies; lack of a source of information for the community on the availability of summer recreational programs.

Client Group: Youth in the district, particularly those associated with a few black and Italian community organizations; indirectly, all service consumers in the district on the assumption that the alleged negative relationship between recreational activities and antisocial behavior does exist.

Location of Benefit: Most of the district, either directly or indirectly.

Agencies: Department of Recreation; Youth Services Agency, including Neighborhood Youth Corps; PRCA (central office); Office of the Mayor (allocates some summer recreation resources).

ONG Role: Detecting the intensity of the community concern over the allocation of summer recreational resources; bringing agency and community representatives together in a meeting chaired by WEONG to discuss the issue; mediating between the blacks and Italians and between the community and various levels of the agencies involved; having a key role in drawing up the plan for resource distribution; allocating some of the resources and jobs; serving as a convenient information source on program schedules; securing an additional $10,000 from PRCA for an Italian sports program to balance a YSA allocation to blacks.

Program Category: Recreation (summer youth recreation).

Nature of Change in Service Production: WEONG held several meetings attended by community and agency representatives and did a lot of behind-the-scenes maneuvering to try to reduce racial tensions between the blacks and Italians over the summer resource allocation issue. The basic problem was that the Italians were upset over the fact that YSA resources were concentrated in black areas. In addition, YSA had just announced a new program that would provide the district with another $36,000 for a year-round program to benefit blacks primarily. (The Italians interpreted the program as a payoff to gangs. In the end, only about $9,000 of this money was ever spent, the rest having been frozen as a result of a scandal involving the YSA commissioner. As a result, the blacks probably received no more resources than the whites.)

The final resolution of the issue included establishment of a community council to oversee the distribution of resources, procurement of an additional $10,000 from PRCA for an Italian sports program (which meant that instead of drastically redistributing existing resources, new resources were used to achieve a more equal distribution among groups), establishment of the employment service project (see separate project description), and development of specific procedures for distributing each agency's resources. As an example of the changes in agency allocation procedures, the Department of Recreation divided the district into quadrants and rotated its resources among designated locations in each quadrant. Prior to the project, the recreation department's mobile vans were distributed without regard for the resulting spatial distribution pattern.

Results and Sources of Benefit: The project reduced racial tensions in the district through a combination of additional summer recreational resources (as opposed to redistributing resources routinely assigned to the district), community participation in allocating resources, and revised agency allocation procedures. The additional resources included $10,000 from PRCA, seventy additional Neighborhood Youth Corps jobs, and, probably, a larger allocation of buses from the mayor's summer recreation program. Programs such as the Department of Recreation's mobile van program were probably distributed more evenly throughout the district, and Neighborhood Youth Corps jobs were allocated in a more open manner. Reducing racial tensions was a top WEONG priority at the time the project was initiated because of a number of racial incidents occurring at the time, the most widely-publicized of which was "Kill Whitey Day" when some black and Puerto Rican groups allegedly threatened to kill any white student who attended school on a specified day. The day passed without serious incident, at least partially due to ONG efforts at coordinating the various law enforcement, transportation, school, and social service agencies involved.

Resources: Additional resources for the project included a $10,000 PRCA grant (actually funded by the U.S. Department of the Interior), some additional buses from the mayor's summer recreation program, and an increase of 70 Neighborhood Youth Corps jobs, which brought the district total to 250 such jobs. For the summer of 1973 season, the district was awarded 200 state-funded summer jobs due to WEONG's employment and summer recreation projects.

Implementation Problems: YSA's reluctance to alter its highly centralized resource allocation procedures, and divisive racial tensions in the district.

Effects of Noncoterminality: None.

Probability of Accomplishment without Program: Very low, probably zero. There was no person or program other than ONG to bring the community and agencies together, to persuade the agencies to alter their procedures, or to monitor the service delivery change to see that the project ran smoothly.

Finding a Parking Place for a Museum

District: Crown Heights.

Project: Children's museum parking.

Status as of December 31, 1973: Terminated.

Purpose: To develop parking arrangements for museum patrons' cars and buses consistent with both museum and community needs and desires. (The Bureau of the Budget had approved construction of the museum but turned down the underground parking planned for the project without providing alternative parking facilities. Bus parking was not included in the original plan.)

Reason for Project: Without some parking arrangement, museum patrons' cars would have created an enormous parking problem in the neighborhood already plagued by insufficient parking spaces.

Client Group: Museum users and residents around the museum, which is located in the northwest corner of Brower Park.

Location of Benefit: The area adjacent to the northwest corner of Brower Park at the corner of St. Mark's Place.

Agencies: Department of Cultural Affairs (Brooklyn Childrens' Museum), schools (P.S. 289 and School District 17), Department of Parks, Police Department (Precinct 077), Department of Traffic (Brooklyn), Department of Highways.

ONG Role: Raising the issue while there was still time to rectify the problem prior to the museum's opening; developing alternative solutions; coordinating agencies and community groups; mediating the disputes among the community and agencies.

Program Category: Cultural affairs (facilities development); transportation (parking).

Nature of Change in Service Production: CHONG assisted in developing a plan for bus parking that called for having the buses drop their passengers at the children's museum and then proceed to the Brooklyn museum parking area. Several alternative proposals for solving the automobile parking problem were considered either individually or as part of a package solution: (1) angle parking on adjacent streets (St. Mark's Place and Park Place); (2) parking on a demapped street in Brower Park; (3) parking on a dirt mound at the northeast corner of Brower Park at Park Place and Brooklyn Avenue; (4) parking in an adjacent school yard with provisions to accommodate the school children in the park when redeveloped; (5) parking at some distance from the museum with a circuit bus connection. One of the last plans suggested by ONG involved a three phase combination of solutions 1, 3, and 4. The redevelopment of Brower Park, which is an integral part of the parking plan, was scheduled for fiscal year 1975-76.

Results and Sources of Benefit: Since the project was terminated prior to implementation of any of the alternative solutions, the only benefits generated were a clarification of the problem and a clear statement of alternate solutions.

A substantial source of irritation for the community and museum users could have been eliminated if the project participants had been willing to reach a compromise based on the CHONG solutions.

Resources: Since none of the proposed changes were implemented, the only resource absorbed by the project was the time spent by ONG, agency, and community representatives in trying to devise a solution. An estimate of probable resource use is not feasible without knowing which proposal would have been adopted if the participants had been more cooperative.

Implementation Problems: The community initially balked at any on-street parking scheme and demanded increased police protection as a payoff. The street was too narrow to accommodate angle parking without widening the street. The community also refused to approve the destruction of any trees for development of an angle parking plan. The highways department initially refused to participate in any plan requiring them to work around the trees. Similar inflexibility prevented the other project participants from consenting to any plan that required their agencies to modify their routine ways of providing services.

Effects of Noncoterminalty: None.

Probability of Accomplishment without Program: Very low. Without ONG, the problem might not have been raised until the museum opened because there was no other person or program to raise the issue before it became a real problem or to coordinate the various agencies and the community at the local level.

Diverting Arrested Addicts into Treatment

District: Crown Heights.

Project: Drug arrest diversion.

Status as of December 31, 1973: Terminated.

Purpose: To increase the number of policemen on patrol by streamlining drug-related arrest procedures; to increase the likelihood of addicts being removed from the streets by the police; to reduce the probability that arrested drug abusers would resume criminal behavior upon release from the criminal justice system (pilot program).

Reason for Project: Police are deterred from arresting street addicts because of the large amount of time involved in "going downtown" to file complaints and, subsequently, to appear in court. When an arrest is made, the arresting officer is removed from patrol duty for a substantial amount of time. In addition, it is sometimes argued that placing non-violent offenders among a criminal population merely breeds hardened criminals and overburdens an already crowded detention system. One source estimates that as many as 40 percent of the arrests in New York City are drug-related.

Client/Target Group: Target Group: suspected criminal offenders arrested on nonviolent drug-related misdemeanor charges. Client group: all service consumers in the district on the assumption that the project would actually lead to lower levels of criminal activity.

Location of Benefit: That part of the district covered by the cooperating police precincts (071 and 077).

Agencies: Police Department (Precincts 071 and 077), Addiction Services Agency (Brooklyn), participating drug treatment centers.

ONG Role: CHONG had only a minimal role in developing the project; it was initially suggested by the WHONG district manager. WHONG and ONG central suggested testing the project at the district level, worked with ASA and the police in debugging the idea, and attempted to persuade ASA to cooperate.

Program Category: Crime control, health (drug abuse).

Nature of Change in Service Production: In the absence of the proposed procedure, the arresting officer must take the suspect "downtown" to a central booking point and must subsequently make several court appearances. Under the proposed change in procedure, some arrested addicts were to be given a court appearance ticket and diverted into a drug treatment program. Cases were to be judged individually depending on the nature of the criminal charge, the accused person's record of prior convictions, and other pertinent criteria. The project was to be staffed by two specially trained policemen and two ASA addiction specialists; in addition, two policemen from each of the Neighborhood Police Teams were to receive special training to serve as back-ups and to provide community drug education and prevention services. When not actually working with arrested addicts, the addiction specialists were to try to persuade other street addicts to enter treatment programs before they were arrested.

Results and Sources of Benefit: None; the project was terminated. Had the project been implemented and proved successful, it should have resulted in more patrol hours per policemen and fewer street addicts and, hence, fewer drug-related crimes. However, there is reason to question whether the workload would have been great enough to use the ASA workers efficiently, although the probable inefficient use of ASA workers might still have been more efficient than tying up police manpower.

Turning a Highway into a Park

District: Wakefield-Edenwald.

Project: Bronx River Shoelace Park.

Status as of December 31, 1973: Operational—park is completed and open to the public.

Purpose: To increase the recreational facilities in the area by turning an abandoned stretch of highway into a park.

Reason for Project: Community leaders indicated an interest in more park facilities; an abandoned stretch of roadway provided an opportunity for creation of a new park; the local Department of Parks foreman was willing to assume a major role in designing the park.

Client Group: Potentially, all service consumers in the district; primarily, residents (particularly youth) who live near the park.

Location of Benefit: The park is located along the western edge of the district between 212th and 223rd Streets. Potential benefit is presumably greater for residents near the park.

Agencies: Department of Parks, Department of Recreation, PRCA (central office), City Planning Commission, Department of Highways, Department of Sewers, Bureau of Gas and Electricity, Police Department, Department of Sanitation.

ONG Role: Providing the forum for a community concern to be aired and for local agency development of a plan to deal with it; securing approvals from the participating agencies for the various aspects of the rather unorthodox procedure of having the proposed facility designed locally and constructed with the maintenance resources of a number of agencies; having a major role in actually designing the facility; coordinating the agencies during the planning and construction of the park.

Program Category: Recreation (facility development).

Nature of Change in Service Production: The park is approximately 1.2 miles long and varies between 75 and 150 yards in width. WEONG, and the local parks department foreman designed the park with some assistance from the City Planning Commission. Other agency participation included: sewers department, which cleaned the catch basins in the park; sanitation department, which swept the area in preparation for paving and subsequently initiated a regular schedule of refuse collection for the park; highways department, which repaved a thirty-foot stretch of roadway; parks department, which helped design the park (done by the local foreman), erected basketball standards, and marked off areas for a number of recreational activities; recreation department, which assigned a staff person in charge of programming to the park; the Bureau of Gas and Electricity, which installed lighting in the summer of 1974. Except for the lighting, this project was completed in less than a year; normally such a facility would have been dragged through the capital budget process for several years. Had it not been for ONG, the park would not have been built so quickly, if at all.

Results and Sources of Benefit: The park opened in the summer of 1973, and casual observation suggests that it is used fairly intensively. Development of the park turned an otherwise wasted strip of city-owned land into a productive community resource. Local development of the project permitted the park to be constructed several years earlier than would be the case if it had gone through the capital budget process.

Resources: Cost of the project cannot be easily determined since WEONG made no attempt to account for agency resources. Resources used include: approximately 2-1/2 to 3 man-months of WEONG staff time; resurfacing of a 1.2 mile long, thirty-foot wide strip of roadway, which required a highways department paving crew, asphalt spreader, and roller for eight days; a sewers department crew for three days; 1-1/2 months time for the parks department foreman; two weeks time for each of two City Planning Commission draftsmen; a recreation department director and assistant for the park; basketball standards, paint, and maintenance personnel from the Department of Parks; lighting from the Bureau of Gas and Electricity. All things considered, the total cost of constructing the park was probably between $150,000 and $350,000. Annual operating costs are low and, with the exception of two summer recreation department employees, are covered by stretching agency resources in the district a bit further.

Implementation Problems: The project experienced no major difficulties, although each agency had to be sold on the idea. Recreation was reluctant to assign a recreation director. City Planning delayed completion of the drawings.

Effects of Noncoterminality: None.

Probability of Accomplishment without Program: Very low. Although there is no reason why this project could not have been put through the capital budget process, this probably would not have happened because the community probably would not have generated sufficient pressure to persuade the Department of Parks to undertake it in the absence of ONG. If attempted according to routine procedure, construction of the park would have been delayed for several years by having to go through the regular capital budget process.

Finding Community Jobs for Relief Recipients

District: Washington Heights.

Project: Development of WREP employment opportunities.

Status as of December 31, 1973: Operational.

Purpose: To develop useful jobs in public and private nonprofit organizations for as many Work Relief Employment Program (WREP) workers as possible (pilot project).

Reason for Project: The frequently wasteful use of WREP workers by agencies that do not want to be bothered with them; the availability of WREP workers as a "free" addition to available resources; the capability to match WREP workers to identified needs of agencies and nonprofit private organizations at the local level; the possibility of placing WREP workers in private nonprofit organizations where the job could become permanent, thus permitting the workers to end their dependence on public assistance.

Client Group: WREP workers employed in the CPD; service consumers in the district who received an enhanced level and/or quality of services as a result of increased manpower.

Location of Benefit: Potentially, the entire district, depending on where and how the agencies employ the WREP workers.

Agencies: Human Resources Administration (Department of Community Development, Work Relief Employment Program; city agencies in employing WREP workers in the district (Department of Parks, Police Department, Housing and Development Administration [area office], Human Resources Administration [area office], ONG, Neighborhood Action Program); various local nonprofit organizations employing WREP workers (day-care centers, senior citizen centers, outreach programs for the elderly, senior citizen transportation programs, and so forth).

ONG Role: Helped to persuade HRA to make Washington Heights a pilot project area; worked with local DCD to set up program; set up meetings between DCD and the cooperating agencies; assisted DCD in trying to persuade the Bureau of the Budget to bend the rules a bit regarding assignment of "public employees" to private organizations; generally performed the tasks of an intermediary among interested parties.

Program Category: Social services (public assistance); various program areas in which the WREP workers are employed.

Nature of Change in Service Production: The Work Relief Employment Program places employable public assistance recipients in city agencies to "work off" their welfare payment. Usually WREP workers are assigned to agencies centrally to be distributed within the agency as that agency desires. Agencies frequently view WREP workers as a burden to be minimized. The WHONG pilot project had WREP workers assigned to the district DCD office, which worked with public and private nonprofit organizations in the district to develop useful positions. WREP workers are, in effect, free resources for the agency because their salary is paid by the public assistance program.

Results and Sources of Benefit: Approximately 175 WREP workers were employed in Washington Heights. Of these, approximately 60 were employed by city agencies and the remaining 115 worked for various private, nonprofit organizations. Of those working for public agencies, about 40 were used to beef up chronically understaffed parks department maintenance crews. This project has several advantages over the usual procedure for assigning WREP employees: (1) use of local WREP workers in their district of residence to the extent possible; (2) DCD's involvement in assisting city and private agencies in developing useful jobs, supervising the workers, and mediating between agencies and workers; (3) presence of the ONG program to encourage local interagency coordination between DCD and the cooperating agencies; (4) the opportunity to match more closely people and jobs on the basis of interest and ability; (5) the possibility of placing workers in jobs that occasionally became permanent. This project generated a clear gain in productivity of WREP employees and in the effectiveness of the WREP program in reducing client dependency.

Resources: No additional resources were involved from the city's point of view. Although employers had additional manpower at their disposal, salaries were substituted for public assistance checks thereby generating no net increase in expenditure by the city. The project did, however, represent an increase in public resources to the district.

Implementation Problems: Some initial reluctance by HRA to approve the pilot project; delays in HRA's outstationing of the DCD staff; the necessity to bend the rules whereby city resources going to private organizations must be covered by a contract requiring Board of Estimate approval (an issue that was never resolved, but did not hamper operation of the project).

Effects of Noncoterminality: None.

Probability of Accomplishment without Program Very low. There was no person or program other than ONG with responsibility for bringing the various agencies together.

4

An Analysis of the Service Integration Projects of the District Offices

Joel D. Koblentz
and
Ronald Brumback

Introduction

Now that we have described some typical projects initiated by the district Offices of Neighborhood Government, we will proceed to analyze the whole sample of sixty-five projects that were intensively studied through interviews with ONG personnel and examination of ONG documents. First, preliminary interviews were conducted with ONG program managers to determine the scope and structure of the program and the probable types of changes in service delivery to be expected from the program. Second, an analytical framework and interview schedule were created to permit a uniform treatment of all of the major ONG activities (projects). Third, hundreds of hours of interviews were conducted with ONG personnel at all levels and with service agency personnel. These interviews, supplemented by examination of ONG and interagency memos and reports, made it possible to assess what each project probably accomplished (and what it might have accomplished in the case of those who were not fully or at all implemented) by contrasting what ONG appeared to accomplish or advocate with the way agencies operated routinely. This information was analyzed within the framework mentioned above. The presumption underlying this method of evaluation is that by gaining a thorough knowledge of routine agency practice and of the changes that ONG actually achieved, and by attempting to be objective by using a rigorous, uniform analytical framework, creating a reasonably accurate assessment of what actually occurred is possible.

Types of ONG Activities

An assumption underlying the ONG program was that opportunities existed for service improvement that the established organization of the service delivery system was unable to achieve. Here we present a brief catalogue of the types of ONG activities with examples of each. Most attention is given to the service integration activities, because these distinguish the ONG program from other neighborhood city hall-type operations. In addition, we describe community-

Valuable assistance was provided by Leslie Allen, Philip Hanser, David Kennett, Margaret Konefsky, Jeannette Michelson, and Bronwyn Richards. Pnina Grinberg rendered valuable data-processing assistance. The Mayor's Office, the Controller's Office, ONG, and other City agencies—City Planning, Fire, Health, Housing, Human Resource agencies, Parks, Police, Sanitation, Transportation—were extraordinarily cooperative, patient and open.

oriented programs that aimed to improve agency-community relationships and single-agency activities in which ONG worked to improve services of particular agencies within the district.

Service Integration Activities

A major expectation of the designers of the ONG program was that the appropriate degree and types of service integration between previously nonco-operating agencies can improve service delivery at minimal cost. Observation of the ONG program suggests ten situations in which local service integration might have a salutory effect.

1. Common Client or Target Groups. City agencies share client or target groups, and yet interagency cooperation in such cases is at best sporadic if not completely lacking. For example, an apartment building in Crown Heights was renovated by its landlord with the assistance of several housing programs under the direction of HDA. HRA then placed a heavy concentration of welfare cases in the building. Being in an area of high gang activity, the tenants were harassed by youth gangs who had established themselves in one of the building's apartments from which the tenants fled. When CHONG learned of the situation, HRA had a homemaker working out of one of the apartments, the Youth Services Agency was trying to work with some of the gang members, the police had been called to the building to investigate rapes and muggings, HDA was upset because the landlord had warned he would probably be unable to pay for the rehabilitation work, the local schools were plagued with the building's resident gang, tenants in neighboring buildings were complaining about the building's effect on the neighborhood, and HRA caseworkers were dealing with individual cases. Despite this confluence of interests, the agencies involved were each trying to cope with their own small piece of the problem without knowing what action other agencies were taking. ONG succeeded in bringing several of the agencies together to develop a strategy for dealing with the building's problems. Although this strategy provided no instant cure for a situation that could have been averted from the outset by interagency cooperation, some progress was made.

As the service delivery system is currently organized, clients with multiple problems are not routinely referred from one agency to the next to ensure comprehensive treatment of their problems. The neighborhood social services information system (NSSIS) in Crown Heights attempted to remedy this problem by establishing a common intake and referral mechanism involving the schools, social service and youth agencies, health and drug agencies, hospitals, housing department and, in a slightly different capacity, the police. The project as initially proposed was vetoed by the CHONG service cabinet because it feared violating client confidentiality. The watered-down version of the project that was finally initiated generated very few referrals. The project failed, not because all appropriate referrals were made routinely, but because agency people had very little incentive to make referrals.

2. Common Complaint Intake Systems. Environmental services, like human services, have no common complaint intake system at the district level, nor do they have follow-up mechanisms for existing single-agency complaints. Consequently, service consumers fail to lodge complaints, or they make them to the wrong agencies and see their complaints go unanswered because of the absence of a monitoring system. If a complaint involves more than one agency, its resolution is unlikely due to the lack of interagency communication at the operating level. To try to alleviate this problem, ONG developed a common complaint-intake-system—the environmental information system (EIS).

Under this system, environmental service problems were reported to ONG by service consumers and city agencies for transmittal to the appropriate agency. A common reporting form was distributed to city agencies and in some districts to community groups in order to try to identify service problems as soon as they developed. Forms received by ONG were checked to determine whether the necessary information had been reported and to determine what agencies to notify. Requests were prioritized: relatively minor routine service problems were usually transmitted in a batch once a week while more serious or more complex problems were relayed immediately by phone. This filtering of complaints through ONG ensured that adequate information reached the appropriate agency. By monitoring the request, ONG was able to press a laggard agency for quicker response. The environmental information system was also a valuable management tool for monitoring the quality of service and spotting trends of serious service problems or lagging agency performance.

3. Regulation of Common or Related Targets. Lack of coordination among the regulatory components of city agencies at best reduces their effectiveness and sometimes leads them to operate at cross purposes. For example, when Fire Department inspectors force a landlord to shut down a faulty boiler because it is unsafe, tenants may be deprived of heat and hot water for an extended period of time if the landlord chooses to delay the necessary repairs. If, in responding to a complaint, a housing inspector orders the landlord to restore heat and hot water, he may do so by restarting the faulty boiler, thereby creating a fire hazard. Because fire and housing inspectors act independently, landlords are able to violate one regulation in order to obey another of more immediate concern. In Crown Heights, an agreement between the Fire Department and HDA to exchange enforcement reports on boilers permitted each agency to monitor landlord compliance so that the regulatory activities of both agencies were more effective.

4. Regulatory Functions that Directly Affect Operating Agencies. The city's regulatory functions are intended to affect, inter alia, the need for and effectiveness of the services provided by operating agencies. Cooperation at the service district level would be beneficial in some instances, but rarely occurs. A case in point is the establishment of parking regulations. For example, a commercial street in Wakefield-Edenwald did not receive effective street cleaning because the area did not technically meet the criteria for a certain type of parking regulation. As a result, street sweepers that traveled the street enroute to other areas were not able to sweep next to the curb because of parked cars. WEONG coordinated the traffic and sanitation departments to eliminate this blatant inefficiency.

A slightly racier example occurred in Crown Heights. Police and community complaints about prostitutes operating in cars around one of the district's parks prompted the traffic department to install signs forbidding parking around the park from 7:00 p.m. to 5:00 a.m. Crown Heights now has the only such parking regulations in the city, and the prostitutes have gone elsewhere.

5. Service Failures or Inadequacies that Cross Operating Agency Boundaries. Without some form of service integration at the operating level, problems that require the attention of more than one agency frequently remain untreated. For example, the process whereby litter-strewn, privately owned vacant lots are certified as a health hazard by health department inspectors and cleaned by sanitation department crews if the owner refused to clean the lot was the focus of a major Bushwick project. Although a clearly defined interagency procedure exists for certifying a lot as a health hazard and initiating cleaning action by the sanitation department, it frequently breaks down because lot cleaning is not one of the sanitation department's top priorities in most districts and because the interagency procedure has many steps, each of which affords an opportunity for losing the paperwork. The previous chapter's first case study describing the old and new procedures demonstrates not only the interdependence of operating and regulatory functions, but also the complexity of negotiating a procedural change.

It appears highly unlikely that anyone in the service delivery system other than ONG would have attempted this procedural change, despite the fact that the ineffectiveness of the former procedure permitted serious health and safety hazards to persist in districts like Bushwick.

6. Service Improvement Opportunities that Cross Operating Agency Boundaries. Service delivery issues that cross agency functional boundaries sometimes result only in reduced effectiveness of an otherwise reasonable process rather than outright failure of the system. A significant instance of this occurred in the city's utilization of Work Relief Employment Program (WREP) workers. (WREP is the city program under which able-bodied public assistance recipients "work off" their welfare checks in city jobs that do not complete with existing union or civil service jobs). The case is described in detail in the previous chapter. This project undoubtedly resulted in a substantial increase in the productivity of the WREP workers and at the same time increased service levels in the district as a result of the expanded agency staffs.

7. Interagency Sharing of Information. Because agencies frequently deal with common clients or targets, information obtained by one agency can frequently be used by another. For example, to facilitate the identification of areas within the district most likely to benefit from the neighborhood preservation project, WHONG negotiated access for HDA to Fire Department code enforcement records. The surprising things about this transaction to one unfamiliar with New York's service delivery system are, first, that two agencies with overlapping responsibilities are not already sharing information, and second, that months of negotiations were necessary for one agency to gain access to information contained in another agency's files. That agencies not only fail to share information but also fiercely protect information gained through their own efforts is ample evidence of the need for an active effort to induce greater interagency cooperation.

8. Related Capital Improvements. When one agency repairs streets and another tears them up, when one agency affects population distribution in an area and another provides services to that population, when one agency seeks a site for a school and another for a housing project, it stands to reason that the capital improvement projects of these agencies are sufficiently interdependent to require interagency coordination. Although major capital budget projects are monitored centrally by the City Planning Commission, foul-ups inevitably arise because the central monitoring mechanism lacks anyone with the contextual knowledge of a district to spot conflicting agency plans. In addition, expenditures from agency lump-sum lines are not monitored. Agencies also tend to be provincial in their concerns—that is, they sometimes conduct their activities to meet their own agency's objectives without concern for the effects on other agencies. For example, in Crown Heights, cabinet members and community spokesmen complained about a several-block section of Pacific Street that was in uncommonly bad disrepair. The street had been torn up to lay a new water main. The contractor had done a temporary paving job pending a subsequent planned reopening of the cut to search for leaks. The temporary patch crumbled and thus forced traffic onto the edges of the street, which also began to deteriorate as a result of heavier use. Although the highways department was initially blamed for the problem, they denied any responsibility and pointed to the Bureau of Water Supply as the culprit. Although the bureau insisted the contractor would soon repair the cut permanently, there was reason to believe that the contractor would try to slip out without making the permanent repairs.

In addition, CHONG argued that repairing the cut alone would still leave the street in worse condition than when the contractor started because of the subsequent deterioration of the remaining street surface. Since the contractor was legally required to restore the street to its precut condition, CHONG argued that he should be required to do a complete resurfacing job on the worst blocks. After months of badgering water supply and/or highways to act, CHONG finally succeeded in bringing representatives of both agencies together to examine the street and fix the blame. In their face-to-face meeting, the agency representatives agreed with CHONG's assessment of the cause and severity of the street's condition and determined that, indeed, the contractor should be required to make most of the repairs CHONG sought. As a result, the users of the street were spared the misery of riding on a deteriorated street, and the city was spared the expense estimated at more than $200,000 of resurfacing the street that would have certainly been necessary if the contractor had either failed to make the permanent repairs or had only resurfaced his cut. The astonishing thing about this project is the fact that one city agency seemed to care very little about the impact of its operations on the services provided by another agency and that both seemed reluctant to reach a mutual agreement that the outside contractor should be held to the terms of his contract.

9. Capital Improvements Directly Affecting Operating Agencies. The construction and maintenance of capital facilities by city agencies affects the operating effectiveness of other agencies that appear at first glance to be functionally independent. For example, the initial construction plans for a children's museum in Crown Heights provided for an underground parking lot. The Bureau of the Budget determined that the planned parking lot was too expensive and deleted it from the plans without making an alternative provision for patron parking. CHONG learned of the problem from the museum director while helping to solve a drainage problem at the construction site. At least seven agencies—traffic, highways, police, sanitation, parks, education, and cultural affairs—were involved in the attempt to solve the problem. (See the description in the previous chapter.) Despite months of negotiation and preparation of five alternative plans by ONG and the affected agencies, no agreement was reached because the restrictions placed on the solution by each agency to meet its own inflexible operating criteria eliminated any possibility of agreeing on a single course of action. This type of problem is likely to be identified first at the local level, and alternative solutions can probably best be developed by a local professional staff with a multi-agency perspective such as ONG. However, this instance illustrates the additional need for an ONG-type program to have strong mayoral support to resolve deadlocks.

10. Local Planning and Budgeting. The interdependence of city agencies at the operating level suggests the utility of locally integrated input into planning and budgeting. A strong a priori case can, therefore, be made that neighborhood-based plans and budgets should comprise the first step in the citywide planning and budgeting process. This case is strengthened by the fact that a great deal more information on unique neighborhood conditions is available at the service district level than at the central level. Evidence of the worth of locally conducted neighborhood budgeting was provided by the Crown Heights capital budget package project, which created a district level capital budget for eight agencies operating in the district. This project had a number of beneficial effects on service delivery in Crown Heights.

1. It provided local service chiefs an opportunity to advise their agency's central budget department on their assessment of local resource needs. As evidence of the appropriateness of the requests, both the police precinct captain and the parks department foreman had some of their requests acted on immediately rather than delayed until the proposed capital budget allocation became effective the following fiscal year.

2. It required the service chiefs to review the entire range of their operations locally. As a result, the parks department foreman identified not only items to be requested from central, but also items that he could take care of immediately. Evidently, he had no incentive to undertake a thorough assessment of his operations prior to this project.

3. It identified areas in which interagency cooperation would be helpful and/or necessary. For example, during a discussion of the capital budget package at a CHONG cabinet meeting, the police precinct captain listed among his budget requests funds for removal of a troublesome post in the middle of the driveway leading into the precinct house parking lot. Although the post had caused several accidents, previous attempts to have it removed had been unsuccessful. The Department of Water Resources cabinet representative offered to remove the pole immediately, thereby sparing the police the delay and bureaucratic hassle involved in obtaining approval for removal of the pole.

4. It identified central agency oversights. ONG had prevailed upon the Department of Sanitation to create a single sanitation district roughly coterminous with the Crown Heights CPD, which has previously been split among five districts. In preparing his agency's portion of the Crown Heights capital budget package, the sanitation superintendent discovered that the central sanitation budget staff had failed to allocate equipment for the new district. The agency then allocated equipment to the new district on the basis of the Crown Heights capital budget package. (This work eventually came to no avail because following the change in city administrations, plans for the new coterminous service district were shelved even though preparations had been completed. This action should not obscure the fact, however, that the district-level budgeting process had uncovered a serious oversight.)

5. It identified conflicting site use plans. During the preparation of the capital budget proposal for the local school district, CHONG spotted a potential

site selection conflict involving the Board of Education and a local community group working with CHONG and HDA to develop a low-income housing project for the elderly. The conflict arose primarily because the need for additional classroom space had shifted within the district during the gestation period for its construction. As a result, the central Board of Education decided to have the capital budget line-item designation changed. It had not, however, announced the site it intended to use, which, in fact, was the same one that the housing group was planning to develop. Having identified the conflict during preparation of the capital budget package, CHONG then served as mediator in resolving the conflict. The most significant outcome of this process was the creation of a site selection committee comprised of representatives from HDA, the local school districts, ONG, and the Brooklyn Department of City Planning to review all site use plans for the district.

Although a neighborhood-based capital budget that considers the allocation of equipment (e.g., small sanitation, crime, and fire-fighting equipment) and contracts under agency lump-sum lines (e.g., contracts let to private contractors for water main construction, major street resurfacing, emergency housing repairs) as well as line items (e.g., construction of schools, housing projects, major park facilities) might be developed in any one of several ways, the CHONG project certainly demonstrated the capacity of this approach to improve the resource allocation process.

The district capital budget package was one element of a broader unrealized ONG objective: creation of an operational district plan. The annual district plan would identify the changes in both expense and capital budget items necessary to adapt agency capability to changing service needs and identified community priorities. The plan would facilitate more effective utilization of the existing level of resources rather than become a forum for major new demands for resources. The Crown Heights capital budget package indicated the feasibility and appropriateness of such an undertaking. Efforts in this direction by several ONG districts were tabled as a result of the uncertainty over the existence and future shape of the program following the change in city administrations.

Summary. These examples suggest several conclusions. First, many opportunities for improving service delivery through local service integration are missed by the service delivery system as currently organized. Second, service integration opportunities are not only missed, but in some instances agencies actually resist them. Third, an ONG-type mechanism can induce beneficial service integration. Fourth, although capable of initiating service integration activities, ONG as constituted in the experimental program was powerless to compel their implementation, regardless of merit; stronger mayoral support to compel agency cooperation is essential to the success of a program of this type.

Community-Oriented Services

The ONG offices also engaged in a number of community-oriented activities. These were primarily to improve understanding and utilization of city services and to reduce the friction between agencies and community groups that result from poor communications. The activities included a variety of direct services to service consumers, integrating community efforts at service delivery, and conflict mediation.

Direct services. The ONG offices provided a variety of services directly to community residents including the following.

1. Providing assistance in resolving routine and nonroutine service complaints: Bewildered service consumers frequently straggled into ONG offices after trying to no avail to find the appropriate nerve center in the bureaucracy to respond to their problems. For example, a Crown Heights resident was experiencing severe basement flooding because his next door neighbor insisted on sprinkling his lawn all night long. After being rebuffed at a variety of city service complaint numbers, he sought help from ONG. Hours of work trying to find his way through the bureaucracy enabled a CHONG staff member to reach the person in the water resources department who could solve the problem. Although it was no simple matter to have an inspector dispatched to the far reaches of central Brooklyn in the dead of night, the man's problem was solved several days after he contacted ONG.

2. Aiding potential community sponsors in filing applications for city programs: Community groups filing applications for city programs such as playlot development or senior citizens centers are frequently bewildered by the application forms and file them incorrectly as a result. Several of the ONG offices provided assistance to community groups in filing these applications. Such assistance can easily involve weeks of staff time for a major funding program such as that for senior citizen centers. In some instances, ONG offices identified potential applicants in areas of their districts lacking such facilities and provided them with a variety of types of assistance.

3. Enabling people to apply locally rather than downtown to participate in city programs: Traveling "downtown" to apply for participation in programs like the senior citizen's half-fare transit program can be a real burden for some service consumers. For others, it is merely an inconvenience. To alleviate this problem, some of the ONG offices received authorization to permit applicants to file applications with them to be forwarded to the appropriate central office. In one experimental district not studied, this service resulted in thousands of applications for various programs being filed in the district.

4. Enhancing community organization: ONG was also responsible for a

substantial amount of community organization, particularly in Bushwick and Crown Heights. In Bushwick, tenant and block associations that BONG had organized and nurtured became a significant positive factor in their case for Bushwick's inclusion in the neighborhood preservation program. In some districts, requests to ONG for assistance in organizing a block or tenant organization were ordinarily referred to HRA's Department of Community Development office, while in others ONG itself provided assistance. The choice generally depended upon the effectiveness of the local HRA office.

Integrating Community Efforts at Improving Service Delivery. Some districts have a number of private and quasi-public groups that focus their attention on particular functional programs areas. For example, in Crown Heights, where deteriorating housing threatens neighborhood stability and where a concentration of medical facilities generates considerable consumer interest in health issues, there are a number of health and housing groups. These groups range from quasi-public groups, such as Community Planning Board committees, Community Corporation committees, institutional advisory boards, and so forth to ad hoc citizen groups. To improve the effectiveness of these groups, CHONG staff members attended the meetings of these groups, provided them with general and technical information on how to deal with city agencies, kept them informed as to what each group was doing, tried to bring groups with similar interests together to avoid wasteful duplication of effort, assisted them in the preparation of program proposals, and sometimes acted as a liaison between the groups and city agencies. The ONG staff role in each of these undertakings was a combination of information source, project manager, and mediator.

Conflict Mediation. Conflict mediation at the neighborhood level was a major ONG function in some districts. Although occasionally arising among community groups, the conflicts more frequently involved citizens and city agencies or city-licensed agencies. For example, in both Bushwick and Crown Heights, a multicenter drug program with a bad reputation tried to expand its operations. Although these districts with their significant drug problems did not object to the establishment of drug centers per se, they did object strongly to poorly run centers. In both districts, ONG investigated the charges against the program, determined them to be sound, and provided the community groups with technical assistance to force the drug centers to upgrade their programs if they wished to expand in the district. In each of these instances of conflict mediation, the ONG staff, which is knowledgeable about the workings of the service delivery system, facilitated resolution of conflicts at a much lower cost in terms of both hard feelings and agency time than would otherwise have been the case.

Single-Agency Activities

Even local service needs and problems that do not cross agency boundaries sometimes remain untreated. ONG's single-agency activities ranged from merely trying to attract additional discretionary resources to attempting to rectify operating inefficiencies that a centralized agency staff could not be expected to detect. At one end of the spectrum, several district managers were able to convince the traffic department to conduct districtwide surveys to identify missing and inappropriate traffic control signs and devices; this action resulted in the replacement, or new installation, of approximately 450 such devices. Although the need for all devices installed met the traffic department's technical criteria, the benefits of the new devices were clearly an instance of a district manager's obtaining special treatment for his district.

Some single-agency activities aimed to improve the efficiency of resources already allocated to the district. For example, in one district ONG succeeded in obtaining minor changes in bus routes serving the district to eliminate a triple fare for district residents traveling to a nearby shopping area. Although this change may sound trivial, it actually represents quite an accomplishment. Because of the incredible maze of red tape and municipal union constraints, bus routes are very rarely changed to conform to changing ridership patterns.

Other single-agency activities in which ONG engaged in one or another district include assisting the police in determining crime patterns in a major park, assisting the parks department foremen in prioritizing and preparing a list of spruce-up projects for submission to parks department central, prodding the transit authority to improve sanitary and safety conditions in a subway station, and so forth. Although many of these activities appear to be inconsequential given New York's many problems, such little service problems can create a substantial amount of ill will if permitted to fester, but cost little to remedy.

Modification of Service Delivery
System Structure

Opportunities to improve services by modifying the structure, procedures, and relationships within the service delivery system are rarely seized upon because no one in the system has the appropriate perspective and knowledge to relate inferior services to organizational and management deficiencies and to develop the appropriate remedy. ONG activities directed at these opportunities included developing neighborhood budgeting capability, trying to persuade agencies to accept a greater degree of administrative decentralization, fostering agency co-location, arguing for greater coterminality of service district boundaries, and developing both intra- and interagency procedural changes. The advantages of having changes of this type initiated by the district manager are that he responds to identified problems, he is knowledgeable about both agency and neighborhood conditions that should affect the design of such changes, and he is present in the district to monitor implementation of the change.

Service Delivery System Deficiencies

Since most of the types of activities discussed in the previous sections are not regularly conducted under the current system without ONG, probing into the reasons why these opportunities for improving services are routinely neglected is necessary. This section summarizes the deficiencies in the service delivery to which the ONGs reacted in attempting to implement their projects. These deficiencies constitute one of the major arguments for creation of an ONG-type program.

Table 4-1 shows why the sixty-five ONG projects in the four districts studied probably would not have been implemented without ONG. (A project can have a number of reasons for initiation.) Half of the projects (51 percent)

30-69%

Table 4-1
Deficiencies in the Service Delivery System that Induced Projects

Deficiency	Percent of Projects
No procedure to identify local issues and priorities regarding routine service delivery	48
No procedure to identify local issues and priorities regarding changes in agency emphasis	20
Summary: No procedure to identify local issues and priorities	65
Lack of agency presence in the district	5
Lack of resources	65
No intra-agency procedure to deal with the problem	8
No interagency procedure to deal with the problem	45
Summary: No procedure to deal with the problem	51
Cumbersome or unreliable intra-agency operating procedure	34
Cumbersome or unreliable interagency operating procedure	15
Summary: Cumbersome or unreliable operating procedure	43
Summary: Cumbersome unreliable, or no operating procedure	82
No one likely to initiate or develop the service delivery change	97
No one to coordinate or manage the implementation of the service delivery change	80
No one to coordinate or manage the ongoing operation of the service delivery change	32
Inadequate mechanism for advising public of available programs	8
No local mechanism for channeling complaints and problems to appropriate agency	11

Note: N = 65 projects.

were initiated at least partially because no agency procedures existed to deal with the problem. For example, no interagency coordinating mechanism exists to facilitate efficient and equitable distribution of the perennially scarce resources for summer youth programs. As a result, needless duplication of programs exists in one section of a district while another section of the same district goes without programs for the entire summer. Projects aimed at mitigating this problem were conducted in three of the four districts studied.

Almost as serious a problem as nonexistent procedures was the problem of cumbersome or unreliable procedures for providing services (43 percent). For example, the water resources department contractors who open a street to install or repair a water main are required by the terms of their contract to return the street to its precut condition. Unfortunately, unsatisfactory repair jobs occur frequently and result in substandard street quality for prolonged periods until the highways department either patches or repaves the street at city expense. One instance of this sort discovered by CHONG saved the city an estimated $200,000 in street repairs, but only after prolonged negotiations with the water supply bureau and highways department to fix responsibility and settle on a course of action.

Absence of a reliable mechanism for determining local issues and priorities was a factor in 65 percent of the projects. For example, the parks department has traditionally allocated its capital budget lump-sum lines for parks spruce-up and repairs without consulting even the local foremen to determine usage patterns, need for change in facilities due to changing population characteristics, and so forth. ONG pressure in several districts persuaded the parks department to permit the local foreman to submit a prioritized list of such activities. The list reflected community priorities, suggestions from service cabinet members, and the foreman's evaluation of service needs. ONG transmitted community priorities to the foreman, conducted its own evaluation of the district's park needs, and assisted the foreman in preparing the prioritized list of budget requests.

Lack of resources was a major reason for 65 percent of the projects. For example, the existence of a large number of littered vacant lots that created a health and safety hazard in some sections of the district was a particularly acute problem in Bushwick. Although BONG's vacant-lot-cleaning project eliminated a number of bottlenecks in the lot-cleaning process, implementation was partially frustrated by lack of manpower and an inappropriate mix of equipment.

These service delivery system deficiencies are typical of the problems that commonly persist for years in the absence of an ONG-type mechanism.

Role of ONG in Projects

By considering what ONG had to do to achieve service delivery changes, one can better understand the need for a local service integration mechanism. Table 4-2

Table 4-2
ONG Roles in 65 Projects

ONG Role	Percent of Projects
Project development phase	
Issue definition	97
Providing supporting information for proposed service delivery change	29
Seeking approval beyond operating level	86
Assistance in development of the service delivery change	91
Coordination during project development phase	83
Implementation phase	
Assistance in implementation of the service delivery change	62
Coordination during implementation phase	69
Operating phase	
Assistance in construction or ongoing service delivery operation	17
Coordination during construction or ongoing operation phase	35
Assistance for agencies with non-ONG projects	9
Line authority over agency resources	2
Direct service provision	2
Roles in relation to community	
Complaint conduit	20
Information collection and handling	22
Information source for community	17
Technical assistance for community	9
Community consultation	40
Community organization	5
Conflict mediation	6
Roles in obtaining resources	
Procuring noncity resources	12
Researcher's assessment of probability of service delivery change without ONG	
Low	92
Medium	8
High	0

summarizes the major ONG roles in the service delivery change projects. (Each project can exemplify several ONG roles.)

The most striking feature in Table 4-2 is the large proportion of projects in which ONG played a significant role in coordinating and assisting in the conduct of the project (rows 4 through 9). Although the percentages decline as the projects progress from the development phase through the implementation and ongoing operation phases, ONG still performed an important coordinating role in over one-third of the projects in the later phases. This agency dependence on ONG, coupled with the fact that ONG played a key role in defining the problem in an overwhelming proportion (97 percent) of the projects, suggests that few, if any, of these projects would have been undertaken without ONG. The primary reasons appear to be that agencies rarely cooperate with each other to achieve more complex objectives than those for which their individual agencies are routinely responsible and that since their field operations generally work near capacity, district service chiefs have little time for staff work required to initiate local service integration.

By demonstrating the modest agency decentralization that existed during the experiment, the table indicates ONG had to seek approval from agency decisionmakers above the district level in 85 percent of the projects. What this figure does not show, however, is the reluctance with which many agencies granted ONG requests, as indicated by the months of inaction that frequently followed ONG requests.

ONG's community consultation role, occurring in 40 percent of the projects, is probably not fully reported in Table 4-2. ONG informally consulted with community representatives on a large proportion of the projects at various stages of planning, development, and implementation. In addition, in some districts, a more formal consultation process was utilized with a community board which met periodically to review the projects.

The ONG capital budget funds were used in 22 percent of the projects, most frequently in Bushwick, where they were an integral part of 43 percent of the projects. Unfortunately, neither Bushwick nor Crown Heights received their allocations for FY 1974 because the Brooklyn Borough Improvement Board, comprised of the borough president and city councilmen representing the borough, decided to hold the allocations captive while they and the mayor scrapped over control of the ONG program.

ONG provided supporting information for the proposed service delivery changes in 29 percent of the projects. These projects included such activities as preparing a well-documented case for Bushwick's inclusion in the neighborhood preservation program based on a block-by-block survey of the district to identify those areas in which the program would be most beneficial in stemming neighborhood deterioration.

In 22 percent of the projects, ONG played a crucial middleman role as a collector of information to be passed on to agencies. For example, the environmental information system that operated in three districts received information from agencies and the community on faulty hydrants, unsealed abandoned buildings, parks vandalism, and so forth, analyzed it to determine the nature and urgency of the problem, and transferred it to the appropriate agency for action.

The deficiencies in the service delivery system previously enumerated, coupled with the major role played by ONG in developing and implementing the projects, suggests that a local service integrator such as the ONG district manager is probably essential if the types of activities outlined in the second section of this chapter are to be routinely performed.

Implementation Problems

The ONG experiment experienced a number of difficulties that limited its ability to improve service delivery. As a result, only 38 percent of the attempted projects became fully operational, although 77 percent were at least partially implemented. Twenty (20) percent of the projects were completely dormant or terminated as were parts of another 17 percent, as of December 31, 1973 (and have remained so since). The proportion of fully operational projects ranged from 25 to 30 percent in three districts, but reached 73 percent in Wakefield-Edenwald (Table 4-3).

Project Implementation Problems

The immediately apparent reason for the low project completion rate is that agencies frequently did not cooperate to the proposed extent. Table 4-4 summarizes some of the reasons for agency noncooperation. Sixty-eight (68) percent of the projects were victims of a major cause of delay or termination. Of these, 40 percent had more than one cause of agency noncooperation. On the brighter side, 32 percent of the projects experienced no major problems, while 26 percent were plagued by only one major problem. These figures, however, fail

Table 4-3
Status of ONG Projects, December 31, 1973

Status	District				
	Bushwick (Percent)	Crown Heights (Percent)	Wakefield-Edenwald (Percent)	Washington Heights (Percent)	Total
Fully operational or completed	29	30	73	25	38%
Partially operational or completed	50	50	20	31	39%
Pending	7	0	0	0	3%
Completely dormant or terminated	14	20	7	44	20%
	100%	100%	100%	100%	100%
Number of projects	14	20	15	16	65

Table 4-4

Reasons for Agency Noncooperation which Contributed to Delay or Termination of Projects

Reason	Percent of Projects[a]
Project violated agency technical, ethical, or legal standards	20
Agency placed low priority on project	38
ONG placed low priority on project	5
Union or civil service restrictions	17
Community objection	5
Uncertainty following change in city administration	15
Resources not readily available	11
Change implemented incorrectly	2
General bureaucratic delay	12
Other	6
Summary: Projects in which agency cooperation was not completely satisfactory[b]	68
Summary: Projects with no major cause of delay[b]	32
Summary: Projects with only one major cause of delay[b]	26
Summary: Projects with more than one major cause of delay[b]	40

Note: N = 65 projects.

[a]Percentages include projects for which the reason applies to at least part of the project.

[b]Summaries are derived from original data base and therefore cannot generally be calculated from other data in this table.

to portray the extent of difficulty in implementing even the simplest service delivery changes. Projects experiencing no major agency resistance still required as much as a year of planning and cajoling before being implemented. If the list of projects seems short, it is partially because each small victory generally required at least a major skirmish.

Table 4-4 indicates that only two problems—the agency placed low priority on the project (38 percent), and the project violated agency technical, ethical, or legal standards (20 percent)—accounted for agency noncooperation in at least 20 percent of the projects. A sprinkling of other factors accounted for the rest: union or civil sevice restrictions (17 percent), uncertainty following the change in city administration (15 percent), general bureaucratic delay (12 percent), and resources not readily available (11 percent).

Although understated in the table, most service delivery changes that had not been implemented by late 1973 fell victim to the "uncertainty following change in city administration" in January 1974. Since the new administration initially displayed only minimal interest in the program, and subsequently changed the nature of the program substantially, virtually none of the projects pending in late 1973 were ever implemented.

The two most prevalent major problems—"project violated agency standards" and "agency placed low priority on project"—are somewhat misleading. While standing alone these problems seem to imply that the projects were in some sense a bad idea, this was generally not the case. Inflexible application of agency rules was sometimes used to thwart well-conceived projects. For example, the Manhattan and Bronx Surface Transit Operating Authority, which operates the city bus lines in Manhattan and the Bronx, placed a very low priority on a change in bus routes proposed by WEONG. The proposed route would have converted the trip from the Wakefield section of the district to the Fordham Road shopping area from a three-to one-fare trip. When the change was finally implemented as the result of an ONG project, ridership on the altered routes actually increased.

A technically feasible project that violated agency criteria was Bushwick's pest control project. The Wildcat Corporation, a nonprofit organization engaged in helping former addicts enter the work force, was eager to obtain a contract with the city for extermination work in the city's slums. Not only would Wildcat perform a service not otherwise provided in the district, but it would also provide the service more cheaply because the addict rehabilitation program was federally supported, and the former addicts were paid low wages while in the program. Although the conditions Wildcat sought to eliminate were in clear violation of the health code, the project violated health department criteria because they generally do not fund pest control work outside Model Cities areas, for which substantial direct federal support is available. That severe health and safety hazards could be removed at a fraction of normal cost while contributing to the rehabilitation of ex-addicts was of little consequence in the decision.

Union and civil service restrictions prevented effective implementation of several proposed service delivery changes. For example, one reason a Bushwick proposal to have housing inspectors collect chips of paint from the walls of ghetto dwellings during their regular inspections could not be undertaken was that the task did not appear in the housing inspectors' job description. The collection of paint chips, used as partial evidence of the existence of a lead paint poisoning hazard, was the exclusive domain of Department of Health sanitarians. Although the instances when restrictive regulations and work rules delayed or prevented a project's implementation can be documented, it is impossible to know the extent to which the knowledge that they would obstruct service delivery changes discouraged ONG from even proposing some projects.

The extent of agency participation and cooperation varied by agency and by district depending on: the severity of internal agency organizational problems; the general willingness of the agency to cooperate; the competence, interest, and rank of the cabinet member; agency capability in the district; personal friendships; and situations that foster local cooperation such as co-location. ONG experience suggests that superior performance in one of these areas can compensate for shortcomings in another. For example, although HRA was an ineffective participant in some districts, its accomplishments in Washington Heights contributed significantly to a couple of WHONG's most outstanding projects. The more productive HRA role in Washington Heights is attributable to highly qualified district directors; personal friendships between the district manager and one of the HRA district directors; the co-location of ONG, HRA, and HDA for several months after the WHONG office was established in the district; and the fact that the HRA agencies in Washington Heights were adequately staffed because the district was considered a good place to work by HRA employees.

Underlying Implementation Problems

The underlying reasons for the program's failure to accomplish more include the short time period over which it was tested, weak mayoral support, and district rivalries.

The brief period during which the program was actively operational was, perhaps, its most crippling handicap. Under the best conditions, it takes time for even a minor governmental reorganization such as this to become productive. Unfortunately, the ONG program had an active life in the field of only a year and a half. Even though planning began in mid-1971, most field offices were not fully operational until at least early in the summer of 1972. For the next year and a half until the end of 1973, the program was fully operational, although its ability to achieve results began to wane by the end of summer 1973 as the mayoral election approached and employees began to leave for other jobs. Although the program continued for a full year after Mayor Beame's inauguration, its record of accomplishment ended in December 1973.

Weak mayoral support plagued the program from the outset and explains why each undertaking was such a struggle. Although Mayor Lindsay voiced strong support for the experimental program as a vehicle to improve the management of the service delivery system, his office clearly did not impress his commissioners with the fact that they should cooperate with ONG. Accordingly, it became clear that despite token changes made by some agencies, most agencies viewed ONG as little more than a passing fad to be tolerated, and while district service chiefs generally accepted the program, central agency officials showed little enthusiasm. The result was that approvals took months instead of days, district service chiefs were told to cooperate but given little or no additional authority to facilitate cooperation, and several agencies with internal organizational problems used this lack of authority as an excuse for noncooperation.

Already-established rivals initially hampered ONG activities in several districts. In Washington Heights a Neighborhood Action Program (NAP) office had preceded the district manager by several years; in Bushwick the primary rival was the powerful Community Corporation. Although in both cases the rivals had responsibilities distinct from those of ONG, the rivalries still sapped the program's strength. In Crown Heights, on the other hand, the district manager was also the NAP director for the district and the power of the Community Corporation was less pervasive. This experience suggests the importance of firmly establishing a single district-level office to solve service problems.

Summary

A brief summary of the findings and major conclusions follows.

Capabilities of the District Manager Program

1. The district manager's nonpartisan, single-community, multi-agency, consumer-oriented perspective enabled him to fill a substantial gap in the service delivery system. Many service problems that commonly remain untreated can be identified and effectively solved from such a perspective.

2. To exploit commonly missed opportunities to improve service delivery, the program initiated:

Activities to integrate services at the district level;
Activities to improve the performance of individual agencies;
Activities to improve consumer utilization of service and to improve communication among agencies and community groups;
Activities to modify the formal and informal structure and procedures within the service delivery system.

3. Observation of the program suggests twelve situations in which local integration can have salutary effects:

Shared client groups;
Shared client and target groups;
Common client intake and referral systems;
Common complaint intake systems;
Regulation of related or common targets;
Regulatory functions that directly affect operating agencies;
Service failures or inadequacies that cross agency boundaries;
Service improvement opportunities that cross agency boundaries;
Interagency sharing of information;
Related capital improvements;

Capital improvements directly affecting operating agencies;
Local planning and budgeting.

4. The deficiency in the service delivery system that ONG sought to remedy most frequently was cumbersome, unreliable, or nonexistent agency procedures to cope with service problems; this type of deficiency induced about four-fifths of the projects.

5. Integrating both human and environmental services through one common integrator—the district manager—often produced satisfactory solutions to service problems.

6. Multi-agency procedural changes tested in one district could be easily implemented in other districts with the assistance of the district manager.

7. While the ONG program produced only nominal improvements in physical productivity, it emphasized other, less tangible characteristics of services:

Quality;
Accessibility, convenience, and other determinants of the rate of consumer
    utilization;
Spatial distribution;
Range.

In the absence of a district-level service integrator, the district service chiefs lacked the requisite information or incentive to pay sufficient attention to these attributes.

Impediments to Success

1. Two-thirds of the ONG projects experienced long delays or were terminated because agencies did not cooperate sufficiently.

2. Weak mayoral support for the program permitted the agencies to disregard ONG's requests for cooperation.

3. The agencies did not delegate sufficient authority to their district service chiefs.

4. Agencies with serious internal management problems were generally ineffective participants in the experiment.

5. Competition with rival district-level organizations sapped ONG's strength in some districts.

6. Restrictive union and civil service regulations hampered nearly a fifth of ONG's projects and probably prevented others from being seriously considered.

The ONG experiment identified a substantial number of opportunities to improve service delivery that could not be consistently and effectively exploited in the absence of a district-level service integration mechanism primarily because of gaps in the distribution of responsibility among agencies and the inherent multi-agency nature of many service problems. The substantial role ONG played in attempting to develop and implement projects further underscored the need for a local service integration staff and demonstrated the ability of such a staff to facilitate the resolution of a number of complex problems requiring specific local information and a multi-agency perspective. ONG also demonstrated its utility as a nonpartisan neighborhood outpost of city government.

Although judging the program a success on the basis of its actual accomplishments during its one-and-one-half-year active life is difficult, the program would have probably been very successful were it not faced with the obstacles to effective implementation that resulted from lack of mayoral support and the resulting noncooperative spirit of some central agency administrators.

5

Costs of the Program and Resource Allocation Effects

Joel D. Koblentz
and
Ronald Brumback

Cost of the ONG Program

The costs of the ONG experiment in the four districts studied fall into four categories depending on their origin: costs of maintaining the district and central ONG structure; costs of agency participation in the experiment; agency costs incurred as a result of ONG projects; and agency costs associated with activities other than service delivery projects. This section deals briefly with the first and second categories—ONG administrative costs and agency participation costs. The other two categories are costs of specific activities, which are netted against their accompanying benefits. Since only four of the eight districts in which ONG conducted the experiment were studied, the ONG administrative costs and agency participation costs were prorated.

ONG Administrative Costs

Table 5-1 summarizes the costs of the ONG administrative structure by location for three periods: the start-up period, the active operational period, and the combined start-up and active operational period. Because of the program's initial difficulties, its active life is defined as the eighteen-month period from July 1972 through December 1973. The first year of the program (July 1971 through June 1972) was spent securing DHEW funding, attempting to secure political and bureaucratic support, resolving a minor scandal over lax control of funds for several other ONG programs, and establishing field offices.

As indicated in Table 5-1, the total cost of the program for the four districts during the first two-and-one half years was approximately $1,712,000 of which $1,270,000 represented costs during the eighteen-month active life of the program and $442,000 arose during the start-up period. Although central expenditure dominated the start-up period, 62 percent ($788,000) of the cost of the active life of the program was for district-level expenses.

Table 5-2 shows that the city paid 70 percent ($1,206,824) of the total cost of the program for the four districts, while the federal government funded the other 30 percent ($505,690). The federal share included the DHEW grant originally obtained by the city to pay for the experiment and a planning grant from HUD to develop strategies to combat neighborhood deterioration in Crown Heights. (Both grants were considerably larger than the amounts indicated in

93

Table 5-1
Total Cost of ONG Administrative Structure in Four Districts, by Location

Location	7/71-6/72 (12-Month Start-Up Period)	7/72-12/73 (18-Month Active Period)	7/71-12/73 (30-Month Total)
Bushwick	$37,000	$183,000	$220,000
Crown Heights	50,000	311,000	361,000
Wakefield-Edenwald	32,000	148,000	180,000
Washington Heights	34,000	146,000	180,000
Total costs for districts	153,000	788,000	941,000
Central (prorated share of 4 districts)	289,000	482,000	771,000
ONG total administrative cost (4 districts)	$442,000	$1,270,000	$1,712,000

Note: Cost figures in this table include personal services, other than personal services, fringe benefits calculated at 9 and 3/4 percent of personal services, and rent (actual or imputed).

Despite the apparent precision, cost estimates include as much as a 10 percent margin of error. Central administration costs are prorated.

Table 5-2, which reflects only the cost attributable to the operation of the experimental program in the four districts under study.) Since total resource use rather than expenditure is the appropriate cost figure to compare with benefits, the cost of several items that ONG did not actually purchase is included in "imputed and unallocated costs." The cost of these items—rent on central and district office space in city-owned buildings and central telephone expense— amounts to 7 percent ($121,621) of the total program cost.

Agency Participation Costs

Agency participation costs totalled $117,000 divided between start-up costs of $42,000 and participation costs of $75,000 for the active operational period. The start-up costs cover time spent by agencies negotiating the form and extent of their cooperation with the experimental program. The participation costs borne by agencies during the active operational period resulted from the time spent by district service chiefs serving in the service cabinet; they included none of the resources required for ONG-generated activities. The cost of agency participation is by far the most rough-and-ready cost estimate. Although the

Table 5-2

Total Cost of ONG Administrative Structure in Four Districts, by Funding Source

Source	7/71-6/72 (12-Month Start-UP Period)	7/72-12/73 (18-Month Active Period)		7/71-12/73 (30-Month Total)	
ONG capital budget line	*	$72,000	6	$72,000	4
NAP capital budget line	$190,000	625,000	49	815,000	47
Mayoralty line	39,000	28,000	2	61,000	4
Other agencies	38,000	100,000	8	138,000	8
DHEW grant	137,000	327,000	25	464,000	28
HUD grant	*	41,000	3	41,500	2
Imputed and unallocated costs	44,000	78,000	6	122,000	7
Total Cost (4 districts)	$442,000	$1,271,000	100	$1,713,000	100

Note: Cost figures in this table include personal services, other than personal services, fringe benefits calculated at 9 and 3/4 percent of personal services, and rent (actual or imputed). Central administration costs prorated.

Despite the apparent precision, cost estimates include as much as a 10 percent margin of error.

"Capital budget lines" do not imply expenditures on construction or durable equipment, but reflect the city's practice of charging certain administrative expenses to the capital budget and thus financing them by borrowing.

*Source not used during this period.

$75,000 for the eighteen-month period is the estimated agency participation cost, there was no comparable increase in expenditure; instead, working with ONG constituted an additional duty for existing agency personnel.

Projected Cost of Citywide Program

The annual cost of operating an ongoing ONG-type program citywide would be approximately $8,146,000, or about one dollar per inhabitant. This estimate includes: the cost of maintaining ONG field offices, $6,567,000; the cost of central ONG administration, $804,000; and the cost of agency participation, $775,000. The annual cost per field office of $106,000 is based on an average of the expenses of three of the four district offices studied, excluding the Crown Heights office because its disproportionately large size would probably not be duplicated in a citywide program. To account for probable economies of scale in central administration, the annual costs for central administration are projected to be only two and one-half times the costs attributable to the four districts studied. Agency participation costs are a proportional extrapolation to sixty-two districts of the $12,500 per district cost estimated for the experimental program.

Depending on the design and method of funding a citywide program, at least two additional adjustments might be required. First, fringe benefits were calculated at 9 and 3/4 percent of the expenditure on personal services because the program was staffed by mayoral appointees and provisional employees who do not receive pension fund benefits. Had the regular rate of 28 and 3/4 percent for civil servants been used, the fringe benefit cost in Tables 5-1 and 5-2 for the active period of the program would have been $183,000 higher. Second, the cost of office furniture was excluded from calculations of the current program costs because estimates were not available and the annual cost of office furniture for the program was relatively small. Such items should be included in cost projections for a citywide program. Considerable savings in cash outlay, if not of real resource use, could be achieved by staffing the program with provisional employees, utilizing city-owned or privately donated office space, and scavenging furniture from existing city inventories.

Source of Project Resources. As Table 5-3 indicates, service delivery change projects drew resources from several sources. The most frequent sources were the ONG capital budget line and extensive ONG staff time (82 percent of projects), resources assigned from a central or regional pool (74 percent), and resources regularly assigned to the district (65 percent). In addition, as many as 74 percent of the projects probably utilized resources shifted from service districts not serving the CPDs studied.

Table 5-3 must be read with caution for several reasons. First, the percentages reflect the frequency with which a source was tapped rather than the magnitude of resources obtained. Second, all sources of resources for projects are indicated regardless of whether they were a regular or incremental expenditure in the ONG districts. Third, the sources are not mutually exclusive; for example, resources transferred from a central pool might also have been normally assigned to the district.

The large proportion of projects for which resources were shifted from other districts (74 percent) suggests that the program depended on a substantial infusion of resources. These incremental resources were, however, nominal compared to total city expenditure in the districts. Furthermore, results of the resource allocation analysis reported later in this chapter indicate that these districts were not favored with greater city resources for routine operations than would be expected considering the population of the districts and the agencies' workload in the districts except for highways department street repaving and, perhaps, parks department maintenance.

Table 5-3
Sources of Public Resources Used in Projects

Source	Percent of Projects
Resources new to the service delivery system	9
Resources regularly assigned to the district	65
Resources shifted within the service district serving the CPD	22
Resources assigned from a central or regional pool	74
Resources shifted from a service district not serving the CPD[a]	74
ONG resources for planning and development (extensive staff time)	80
ONG resources for implementation (capital budget funds or extensive staff time)	42
Summary: ONG capital budget funds or extensive ONG staff time	82
Resources provided by the private sector	11

Note: Percentages include projects for which sources were either proposed or actually used.
[a]Although precise information on the origin of resources used in ONG projects was not available, a high proportion of projects probably used resources transferred from other districts. Estimates were made project by project on the basis of informed judgment.

There are two sides to the question of whether a program such as this should be heavily dependent on shifting resources within the city. On the one hand, shifting would be more difficult in a citywide program in which each district manager is vying for his district's share of the spoils. On the other hand, if, as has generally happened with the current experimental program, the resources are used as efficiently or more so from a citywide perspective, the shifting of resources is not harmful and is sometimes beneficial. In fact, such shifting should enable the service delivery system to move closer to marginal equality of the productivity of resources used for alternative purposes by drawing resources from activities with low priorities. It may also force agencies that now distribute discretionary resources arbitrarily to improve their efficiency and consistency by clarifying their allocative criteria.

Benefits: Definition and Source. The definitions of *benefit* and *efficiency* used here are broader than those normally employed in quantitative cost-benefit studies. Since the ONG program emphasized the more intangible aspects of service delivery, this study assessed its impact on both the tangible and less tangible dimensions of service delivery including quantity of service provided for a given expenditure (physical productivity); qualitative characteristics of services; spatial distribution of services; accessibility, convenience, and other determinants of consumer utilization of services; and the appropriate range of services for the district.

Although the ideal measure of benefit—the value placed on services by consumers—cannot be obtained, factors that might influence consumer valuation of services were identified. Any improvement in these factors not accompanied by a reduction in quantity of services should result in increased consumer valuation. If the improvement occurs without increased quantity of resources, the change increases the efficiency (benefit/cost) of the service delivery system, at least from a local perspective. If additional resources are shifted from elsewhere in the service delivery system, however, the effect on efficiency from a citywide perspective is ambiguous. An increase in efficiency from a district perspective may result in increased, decreased, or unchanged efficiency from a citywide perspective depending on whether the value of the resources in their new use is greater than, less than, or equal to their value in their former use. A method for reducing this ambiguity is discussed below.

The major sources of project benefits from the perspective of city agencies and service consumers in the ONG districts are summarized in Table 5-4. Of the sixty-five projects proposed by the ONG offices, only 18 percent were likely to increase physical productivity if implemented. In contrast, a much larger percentage of projects either did, or would if implemented, give rise to other sources of benefits: improved qualitative characteristics (89 percent), broadened range of services (54 percent), changed spatial distribution (43 percent), and increased rate of consumer utilization of services (38 percent). In addition, the second most prevalent source of benefits from the district perspective (71 percent) was increased production capability due to increased resources, which

Table 5-4
Sources of Benefits from the Perspective of City Agencies and Service Consumers in the District

Source	Percent of Projects
Production capability due to increased resources	71
Physical productivity	18
Rate of consumer utilization of services	38
Range of services	54
Spatial distribution of services	43
Qualitative characteristics of services	89
Direct change in private sector profitability	5

Note: Realized benefits are combined with the benefits expected if the projects had been implemented.

means that 71 percent of the projects proposed (and 52 percent of those implemented) should have resulted in an increased level of service in the district as a result of augmented resources.

Because the less tangible sources of benefits are not self-explanatory, several examples from ONG experience follow. Construction of a park provides a new recreational facility and thereby increases the range of services. Coordinating the distribution of summer recreation resources can improve the spatial distribution of services by ensuring more even coverage of the district. Repairing playground equipment probably increases consumer utilization of park services. Replacing a litter-strewn vacant lot with a playlot transforms the characteristics of the lot from undesirable to desirable. Establishment of a district-level complaint intake and service monitoring system can improve the qualitative characteristics of municipal services in two ways: first, it makes reporting problems easier for both citizens and agencies and increases the probability that complaints will be acted on; second, by expediting the agency response and increasing the likelihood of resolution of the problem, the system reduces the number and severity of problems at any point in time.

Although measuring the value of these less tangible aspects of service delivery is virtually impossible, the lack of attention generally given them by city agencies is undoubtedly a significant source of dissatisfaction with municipal services.

Impact on Level of Resource Allocation
to Routine Services

To determine whether the experimental districts received preferential resource allocation, the resource levels for eight services in the eight CPDs with appointed district managers were compared with resource levels in the other fifty-four CPDs for FY 1973. The services selected for evaluation were police, fire, sanitation, public assistance, group day care, park maintenance, pothole patching, and street repaving. Although other services were included in the experiment, these services were chosen at the outset of the study for a combination of the following reasons: (1) high a priori probability that the service would be affected by the experiment, (2) substantial expected agency participation in the experiment, (3) expenditure on the service constituted a substantial proportion of total city expenditure identifiable at the neighborhood level, and (4) high degree of administrative discretion in resource allocation.

This section presents a brief description of how the community level data base was created, how the indices of neighborhood characteristics were developed, and how the hypothesis that ONG affected resource allocation to the experimental districts was tested. The analysis suggests that the experimental CPDs did not receive preferential treatment for routine services except for street repaving and, perhaps, park maintenance.

Two Simple Models

Two plausible simple models of agency resource allocation were used to test for differences in service levels between the eight CPDs with a district manager and the other fifty-four CPDs. The first model assumes that agencies allocate resources according to workload measures; for example, robberies for police or eligible population for public assistance. The second assumes that agencies distribute resources according to neighborhood population and housing characteristics. Both models also include population to control for the scale of the CPDs.

If ONG had a significant effect on the quantity of resources allocated to the experimental districts, the effect should be detectable as a deviation from the resource allocation pattern estimated by the workload measures or indices of neighborhood characteristics. This was tested by regressing resource levels (e.g., number of policemen, spaces for children in group day care centers) first on workload plus a dummy variable for the presence of a district manager, and second on neighborhood characteristics plus the dummy variable. A significant positive coefficient on the presence of district manager indicates that the ONG districts received a larger amount of resources than would be expected on the basis of either workload or neighborhood characteristics alone. Similarly, a significantly negative coefficient indicates that ONG districts were allocated less than expected. If, as most frequently occurred, the coefficient is not significant, the pattern of agency resource allocation was probably not affected by ONG. Unfortunately, the conclusions from the regression analysis alone are ambiguous. It is not possible to distinguish whether the observed resource allocation patterns existed prior to establishment of the experiment, whether the allocation pattern was a consequence of ONG efforts, or whether both resource allocation and selection of the CPDs for the experiment were manifestations of a basic policy to favor certain CPDs.

Community-Level Data Base

Sufficient information on agency operations, budgets, and expenditures to test these models is available from the agencies, the budget bureau, and the controller's office; however, the data is organized by the unique, noncoterminous sets of agency service districts and cost centers; for example, police precincts, fire companies, child day care resource areas, park sectors, and so forth. To permit evaluation of this CPD-oriented program, agency data was reorganized by CPDs. The resulting data base constitutes a community level break-out of agency data for most of the major agencies administered by the mayor. This information could be used for planning, budgeting, and monitoring services at the point of delivery—the neighborhood.

The agency information was integrated with 1970 *Census of Population and Housing* (fourth count) data aggregated to CPDs. Additional socioeconomic data that was also integrated included such items as the number of reported narcotic addicts, number and type of vacant buildings, number of buildings with tax arrears and the amount of the arrearage, and so forth.

The experience of creating this archive for FY 1973 suggests that the city could generate a comparable set of statistics by CPD annually for a nominal expenditure. However, availability of information by CPD or other community-level geographical unit is entirely dependent on the extent to which agencies already generate data for their own internal management. For example, the uniformed services maintain detailed data files on their operations, selected items of which are included in the community data base. In contrast, the parks department maintains only the most rudimentary records for internal management.

Indices of Neighborhood Characteristics

The indices of neighborhood characteristics used in some of the regressions were derived from the 1970 *Census of Population and Housing* by principal components analysis.[a] These indices, rather than the original variables, were used in the regressions in order to retain the largest possible amount of information from the variables while minimizing the statistical problems of multicollinearity among the original variables and insufficient degrees of freedom if all meaningful descriptors of neighborhoods were included. The original data set consisted of eighteen classes of census variables selected to characterize the communities by ethnicity, life cycle, family composition, income, education, occupation, labor force participation, unemployment, mode of travel to work, size and age of residential structures, crowdedness of dwelling units, homeownership and residential mobility. From this data a set of eight indices were derived.

Regression Results

Of the eight pairs of regressions of service levels on workload measures (Table 5-5) and on neighborhood characteristics (Table 5-6), four indicate no difference in resource allocation related to presence of a district manager: number of policemen, public assistance cases, children in group day care, and potholes

---

[a]The indices are principal component scores obtained by multiplying the factor score coefficients for each census variable in a component by the standardized census data for each CPD. For a complete explanation of principal components techniques, see R.J. Rummel, *Applied Factor Analysis*, (Evanston, Ill.: Northwestern University Press, 1970); and H.H. Harman, *Modern Factor Analysis*, rev. ed. (Chicago: University of Chicago Press, 1967).

Table 5-5
Regression of Level of Selected Services on Workload Measures and Presence of District Manager

Service	Constant	Population (1000s)	Acres	Density (1000 Population/Acre)	Assessed Value ($1,000,000)	Percent Families Below Poverty Level	Percent Population Age 0-17	Robberies	Index of False Alarms and Fires (1000s)	Tons of Refuse per Truck Shift	Number of Parks	Park Acres	District Manager	R^2
Policemen	50.9	0.9[b] (5.81)			.04[a] (3.61)			0.02[b] (11.86)					-49.9 (0.96)	.42
Firemen	56.4	0.04 (0.07)	0.01[b] (12.58)		0.01 (1.00)				1.7[b] (30.09)				31.66[a] (2.53)	.46
Sanitationmen	8.4	1.0[b] (117.75)	0.0[b] (3.90)							79.6[a] (3.41)			-8.8 (0.56)	.70
Public Assistance Cases	-1027.8	38.5[b] (53.62)				393.9[b] (50.63)							-330.8 (0.17)	.86
Children in Group Daycare	-524.9	4.0[b] (19.07)				26.4[b] (13.31)	6.4 (0.94)						86.0 (0.43)	.65
Park Maintenance Personnel Expense	102,917.2	-588.9 (0.33)		1,796,347.5[b] (4.38)							8866.5[b] (4.16)	340.7 (1.44)	140,883.8[b] (4.38)	.22
Potholes Patched	22,203.6	-38.6 (0.51)	7.9[b] (27.58)		-1.6 (0.22)								2655.0 (0.11)	.34
Man-Days of Street Resurfacing	863.6	-11.9[a] (2.85)	1.3[b] (41.57)		-.04 (0.87)								2191.9[b] (4.22)	.46

Note: F values are in parentheses.

Data were organized by the sixty-two Community Planning Districts ($N = 62$ CPDs).

[a]Denotes significance at 5 percent level.

[b]Denotes significance at 1 percent level.

Source: Agency data are from representative periods during FY 1973. Population, family income, and age data are based on the 1970 *Census of Population and Housing*. Acreage data were provided by the Regional Plan Association.

Table 5-6

Regression of Level of Selected Services on Presence of District Manager and Eight Community Variables

Service	District Manager	R^2 (All 10 Predictors)
Policemen	−28.6 (0.33)	.57
Firemen	25.3 (1.59)	.53
Sanitationmen	−17.1[a] (2.75)	.78
Public assistance cases	−279.4 (0.14)	.89
Children in group day care	−25.2 (0.05)	.78
Park maintenance personnel expense	245,845.[b] (5.00)	.33
Potholes patched	−486.0 (0.00)	.37
Man-days of street resurfacing	1758.8 (2.17)	.34

Note: F values are in parentheses.

N = 62 CPDs.

Population of district and eight community characteristic variables derived from census data by factor analysis are entered into the regression along with a dummy variable for "presence of district manager." The coefficients for "district manager" are thus the "effects" of having a district manager net of population size and community characteristics.

[a]Denotes significance at 5 percent level.

[b]Denotes significance at 1 percent level.

patched. Two are consistent with preferential treatment of experimental districts: number of man-days spent resurfacing streets and expenditure for park maintenance personnel. And two exhibit mixed results: number of firemen and sanitationmen.

These results are generally consistent with expectations based on the analysis of ONG activities. Although resources were sought for specific projects, the only services of those tested for which ONG tried to influence resource allocation for routine service delivery were parks and street resurfacing. Extensive activities were initiated in all ONG districts to improve the condition of parks and to obtain the districts' pro rata share of asphalt resurfacing of streets from the highways department. Although the results are ambiguous, the analysis indicates that these efforts succeeded in attracting a larger share of resources for these two services than would be expected on the basis of either workload or neighborhood characteristics.

The insignificant or marginally significant coefficients for the other services suggests that there was no substantial infusion of resources into the districts selected for the experiment. The possibility remains, however, that the level of resources was raised from 1971 to 1973 to bring these districts into conformance with the prevailing citywide pattern of allocation.

Summary

Costs of the Program

Annual operating cost of a typical district manager office for a district of 150,000 was about $100,000, to which should be added about $12,500 in agency participation costs. Central office costs per district were about $80,000 a year, but per district, these would be expected to fall drastically if the program moved from a few experimental districts to a citywide operation. We therefore estimate that the total cost of a citywide program would be about $8,000,000 in New York City, a little over $1 per inhabitant.

Effects on Allocating of Resources among Districts

Although resources were transferred into the experimental districts for specific projects, city agencies did not favor these districts with more resources for routine services, with two exceptions, than would be expected considering the population, housing, and agency workload in the district. The two exceptions were street repaving and, perhaps, park maintenance.

District Budget Feasibility

To facilitate interagency planning and budgeting at the level of the sixty-two Community Planning Districts, substantial budget and operations data for most city agencies could be prepared for a nominal expenditure by using the methods developed in the research program to analyze resource allocations.

Appendix 5A
An Attempt at Judgemental
Evaluation of Project
Benefits

Introduction

The service delivery component of the research was interested in measuring the benefits as well as the costs of the ONG program so that the two could be compared. However, a direct quantitative assessment of the impact of the program on service delivery is difficult for several reasons. First, the well-known problem of measuring the output of almost any public service was compounded by the fact that ONG activities ranged over virtually the whole range of public services. Second, the small increment of resources—an office in each CPD costing approximately $100,000 per year to operate—relative to the total agency resources allocated to each district—about $200 million—suggests that even if the program had been an impressive success in a cost-benefit sense, its impact would be small even compared with the measurement error for such budget and output data. Third, the changes in service delivery sought by the district managers were frequently of a qualitative nature. Many of these changes included attempts to expedite the solution of service problems, to see that all aspects of a service problem were treated, and other types of changes in the quality rather than the quantity of services. Although such changes may significantly affect consumer valuation of services, it is not feasible to measure their impact. Fourth, the large number (between one hundred and three hundred activities depending on how they are defined) and variety of ONG activities, each requiring a unique evaluation model, made direct quantitative measurement prohibitively expensive.

However, we did attempt, for each of the sixty-five projects that were intensively examined, to estimate whether any benefits were produced and to assign a rough order of magnitude to the dollar value of these benefits by making certain assumptions about the value of the services involved in terms of their costs and about the extent of improvement resulting from the ONG's activities in that specific project (or potentially results on the case of projects not carried to completion). This process is obviously a highly judgmental one, and we do not argue strongly for the results. However, we believe the estimates are worth presenting as the judgments, on a project-by-project basis, of a well-informed analyst. It should be clear that they do not represent "hard data" on benefits, even though we do proceed to compare them with the costs, which are much more objectively measured. We present this exercise in "judgmental evaluation" only as such.

Criteria for Increased Efficiency from
a Citywide Perspective

Since the ONG program generated no additional resources to support ongoing operation of the service delivery system, its ability to improve service delivery from a citywide perspective depended on its impact on the efficiency of the service delivery system. Put another way, in order for the program to have generated positive net benefits, the resources used to support program activities must have been used more efficiently than prior to the program. Since direct measurement of the benefits of free government services in dollar terms is impossible, direct comparison of benefits and costs, which are for the most part measurable in dollar terms, is likewise impossible. In addition, since the true cost of using resources in one activity is the value of their best alternative use, the evaluation problem is compounded when the alternative use of the resources cannot be specified.

Here we have attempted an indirect comparative technique of evaluating benefits. This approach requires specifying criteria by which resources can be reasonably assumed to have been used at least as efficiently or more efficiently than in their alternative use.

The criteria for assessing net benefits from the service delivery change projects fall into two groups: those criteria that had to be met for resources to have been used *at least* as efficiently as in their alternative use, and those that had to be met for resources to have been used *more* efficiently than in their alternative use. Satisfying the criteria that resources are used at least as efficiently as in their alternative use implies non-negative net benefits. Satisfying the criteria that resources are used more efficiently than in their alternative use implies positive net benefits. Either of the following criteria suggest that resources were used at least as efficiently in ONG projects as in their alternative use: (1) resources were used for the same purpose as in their alternative use but were directed toward locally identified priorities; or (2) resources were shifted functionally or spatially within a district by mutual agreement of the district manager and local agency service chiefs.

If resources were directed toward locally identified priorities and one or more of the following criteria were met, a project was expected to have produced *positive* net benefits: (1) the efforts of more than one agency were coordinated to provide greater assurance that the total problem was dealt with; (2) the resources of one or more agencies were concentrated in an area small enough to benefit from the neighborhood effects of service improvement; (3) a more efficient intra- or interagency procedure was used in the project; or (4) the project dealt with a severe problem deserving high priority from a citywide perspective.

Measurement of Net Benefits

To compare program costs and benefits, the dollar value of net benefits generated by projects was estimated. First, the cost of agency resources for the project was estimated. Second, the evaluation criteria described above were used to determine the probable effect of the project on efficiency from a citywide perspective. Third, net benefits were roughly estimated in order of magnitude categories for each project.

The rationale for this technique follows. Since the actual value of free government services is not known, a working assumption must be made that permits a reasonable estimate of net benefits. A plausible assumption is that if what agencies currently do is justifiable (and we have no way of judging that it is not), then doing it better represents an improvement in efficiency from a citywide perspective. Although one might doubt that the service consumers of New York City received a dollar's worth of services for their tax dollar, the issue raised generally has to do with the relative efficiency (cost per unit of output, however measured) of agency operations rather than with the particular services provided. Since a substantial amount of information is available on which to base a decision, it seems reasonable to accept the premise that, for the most part, what city agencies do is considered worth doing. It, therefore, follows that improving the efficiency (value produced/cost) of agency operations produces positive net benefits. Although it is not possible to measure the percentage gain in efficiency without a measure of gross benefit, it is possible to estimate whether the change was high, medium, or low, on a project-by-project basis. By using this qualitative assessment of efficiency gain and a reasonable estimate of cost, net benefits can be estimated in broad ranges of dollar values.

Realized and Potential Benefits

Since the study sought to evaluate the concept of the district manager experiment more than to report on the accomplishments of New York City's experiment, it was necessary to strip away the effects of the institutional barriers that hampered the program to expose the program's true potential. For this purpose, both realized and potential net benefits are presented. Those that were unrealized would probably have accrued had the projects been fully implemented, which were blocked by bureaucratic and political problems some at least of which were peculiar to the situation of a "lame duck" administration with a hostile city council.

Magnitude of Net Benefits

By using the estimates of net benefits, projects were assigned to categories corresponding to the order of magnitude of their probable net benefits: $0; ± $1 to $10,000; ± $10,001 to $100,000; greater than ± $100,000. Tables 5A-1 and 5A-2 summarizes the results. Six (6) percent of the projects generated realized net benefits estimated to be in the over $100,000 range, 40 percent in the $10,000 to $100,000 range, and 14 percent in the less than $10,000 range. In terms of potential net benefits, 15 percent of the projects were estimated to be in the over $100,000 range and 57 percent were in the $10,000 to $100,000. The differences between realized and potential net benefits result primarily from

Table 5A-1

Realized Net Benefits from a Citywide Perspective (Frequency of projects)

	District				
Benefit	Bushwick (*N* = 14)	Crown Heights (*N* = 20)	Wakefield- Edenwald (*N* = 15)	Washington Heights (*N* = 16)	All Districts (*N* = 65)
Greater than +$100,000	0	1	0	2	3
+$10,001 to +$100,000	10	5	8	4	27
+$1 to +$10,000	0	3	5	1	9
$0	1	4	1	3	9
−$1 to −$10,000	3	6	1	6	16
−$10,001 to $100,000	0	1	0	0	1
Less than −$100,000	0	0	0	0	0

Table 5A-2

Potential Net Benefits from a Citywide Perspective (Frequency of projects)

	District				
Benefit	Bushwick (*N* = 14)	Crown Heights (*N* = 20)	Wakefield- Edenwald (*N* = 15)	Washington Heights (*N* = 16)	All Districts (*N* = 65)
Greater than +$100,000	2	4	0	4	10
+$10,001 to +$100,000	10	11	9	7	37
+$1 to +$10,000	0	3	4	2	9
$0	2	2	2	3	9
−$1 to −$10,000	0	0	0	0	0
−$10,001 to −$100,000	0	0	0	0	0
Less than −$100,000	0	0	0	0	0

worthwhile projects that were indefinitely delayed or terminated or did not mature before the change of city administrations. Twenty-five (25) percent of the projects bore nothing but expenses, and another 15 percent were rated as producing no net benefit or as being unratable.

The next step in creating the dollar measurement of net benefits from projects was to calculate an aggregate value of net benefits generated by each district's projects. A conservative value for each range described above was multiplied by the number of projects in that range. The values for each category were: $0 for the $0 range; $5,000 for the $1 to $10,000 range; $25,000 for the $10,001 to $100,000 range; and $100,000 for the greater than $100,000 range. These estimates significantly understate the net benefits of a number of projects, but understatement was preferred given the imprecise estimates.

Table 5A-3 provides a district-by-district summary of the project net benefits. Only $895,000 or 51 percent, of the projects' potential net benefits were realized. This result contrasts with the fact that approximately 75 percent of the projects were at least partially implemented. It appears, therefore, that the implementation problems described in Chapter 4 cost consumers significant improvements in municipal services.

*Interdistrict Variations in Potential
Net Benefits*

While the magnitude of realized net benefits was similar in all four districts, there were substantial differences in the magnitude of potential net benefits and in the percentage of benefits realized. Wakefield-Edenwald had by far the lowest potential net benefits from a citywide perspective: $245,000 compared to an

Table 5A-3
Realized and Potential Net Benefits from Projects from a Citywide Perspective

District	Realized Net Benefits	Potential Net Benefits	Percentage of Potential Benefits Realized
Bushwick	$240,000	$450,000	53
Crown Heights	210,000	590,000	36
Wakefield-Edenwald	220,000	245,000	90
Washington Heights	275,000	585,000	47
All districts	$945,000	$1,870,000	51

Note: Potential net benefits are defined as realized plus unrealized net benefits.

average for the other three districts of approximately $540,000. This difference is due primarily to two factors. First, all of WEONG's projects yielding net benefits in excess of $100,000 from a district perspective involved substantial inflows of resources for which there was no reason to claim that the resources were used substantially more efficiently than in their alternative use. Second, several of WEONG's projects used only WEONG staff time as inputs. While projects of this sort did not usually generate large net benefits, they generally constituted an effective use of staff time.

An important question arising from this comparison of net benefits among districts is what Wakefield-Edenwald's relatively low level of potential project net benefits portends for a citywide program. Wakefield-Edenwald is the only predominantly white, working-class neighborhood studied. Citywide, however, there are a substantial number of such districts. If it is assumed that Wakefield-Edenwald's service problems are representative of those of similar communities in New York City and that WEONG tackled a representative set of problems for such a district, generalizing from this sample of one leads to the conclusion that the potential project net benefits for a program of the ONG-type in neighborhoods like Wakefield-Edenwald are likely to be substantially lower than in districts with more severe problems. In other words, although establishing offices in such neighborhoods may still be worthwhile, the benefits from projects alone will be less in those neighborhoods. On the other hand, under a citywide program, in which shifting resources among districts would be more difficult, some of the higher valued projects conducted in the other three districts may be harder to achieve. If so, then perhaps most districts will engage more in activities requiring few, if any, additional resources. These include strictly integrative activities, provision of direct services to the community, service monitoring, and so forth.

The proportion of potential project net benefits that were realized ranges from a high of 90 percent for Wakefield-Edenwald to a low of 27 percent in Crown Heights, with Bushwick (53 percent) and Washington Heights (47 percent) in between. Several factors contributed to this interdistrict variation: the extent to which the projects required a procedural change or a change in the mix of agency resources; the persistence with which ONG fought for a project; the general cooperativeness of the participating agency's central administration; and the competence, interest, and rank of the district's cabinet representative from the participating agencies. These differences in turn were due to the type and severity of service problems in the district; personal friendships among service cabinet members and between cabinet members and the district manager; the district manager's own interests and philosophy about the program; the district manager's prior experience and agency contacts; and factors such as agency co-location that foster interagency cooperation.

Net Benefits from District and
Citywide Perspectives

Whether benefits are viewed from a district or citywide perspective greatly affects the perception of net benefit. As Table 5A-4 indicates, only 47 percent of the realized project net benefits viewed from a district perspective could also be considered net benefits for the city as a whole. The lower level of citywide benefits occurred because resources transferred into the district were not necessarily used more productively. Significantly, however, none of the projects resulted in a reduction in efficiency from a citywide perspective. Resources transferred into the ONG districts were, therefore, used at least as efficiently, and frequently more so, compared with their alternative uses.

A similar, although less pronounced pattern, was observed when potential, rather than realized, net benefits were considered; in this case, 56 percent of the net benefits from a district perspective were also net benefits from a citywide perspective, thereby indicating that the projects that have yet to bear fruit or were terminated were on balance less provincial than those already implemented. Either way, however, the experimental program had a propensity for engaging in provincial projects.

The evidence suggests the importance of designing the program so as to discourage the robbing-Peter-to-pay-Paul-type of project that does not also require a basic service delivery change—resource concentration that internalizes externalities, procedural change, service integration, and so forth—to ensure more efficient use of resources.

Comparison of Net Benefits and Administrative Cost

Comparison of the net benefits from projects calculated above with the administrative costs of the program indicates that the projects alone did not generate sufficient realized net benefits to cover the cost of administering the program (Table 5A-5). Potential net benefits, however, were great enough to justify the administrative cost of the program (Table 5A-6). (The question marks in both tables indicate that the program generated a substantial, but unknown, value of net benefits from other activities.)

Both the realized and potential net benefits from service delivery change projects were sufficient to cover the aggregate district level costs for the eighteen-month active period. The similarity ends here, however: Realized net benefits fell short of total costs by $884,171, while the potential net benefits exceeded total costs by $40,829. Since this excess is only about 2 percent of

Table 5A-4
Net Benefits from Projects from District and Citywide Perspectives

District	Realized Net Benefits				Potential Net Benefits			
	District Perspective	Citywide Perspective	Difference	Citywide as Percent of District	District Perspective	Citywide Perspective	Difference	Citywide as Percent of District
Bushwick	$560,000	$240,000	$320,000	43	$950,000	$450,000	$500,000	47
Crown Heights	450,000	210,000	240,000	47	905,000	590,000	315,000	65
Wakefield-Edenwald	415,000	220,000	195,000	53	540,000	245,000	295,000	45
Washington Heights	575,000	275,000	300,000	48	950,000	585,000	365,000	61
All districts	$2,000,000	$945,000	$1,055,000	47	$3,345,000	$1,870,000	$1,475,000	56

Note: Potential net benefits are defined as realized plus unrealized net benefits.

Table 5A-5

Realized Net Benefits from ONG Projects and Other Activities from a Citywide Perspective

District	Realized Net Benefits from Projects	Realized Net Benefits from Other Activities	Cost of ONG District Administrative Structure for 18-Month Active Period	Residual Net Benefit
Bushwick	$240,000	?	$183,000	$57,000 + ?
Crown Heights	210,000	?	311,000	(101,000) + ?
Wakefield-Edenwald	220,000	?	148,000	72,000 + ?
Washington Heights	275,000	?	146,000	129,000 + ?
All districts	$945,000	?	$788,000	$157,000 + ?
Less: ONG central administrative costs				$482,000
Residual after ONG administrative costs				($325,000) + ?
Less: Operating agency participation costs				75,000
Residual after total cost of active period				($400,000) + ?
Less: ONG start-up costs:				
District start-up costs			$153,000	
Central start-up costs			289,000	$442,000
Residual after ONG start-up costs				($842,000) + ?
Less: Agency start-up costs				40,000
Residual after all costs				($882,000) + ?

Note: Parentheses indicate negative amounts.

Despite the apparent precision of these calculations, the cost estimates are only accurate within 10 percent and the benefit calculations are even rougher approximations.

Question marks indicate that the net benefits from nonproject activities are not included. This probably represents a substantial omission.

total costs for the four districts, it is within the expected margin of error for these calculations. Although the estimates erred on the side of overestimating costs and underestimating benefits, it is not possible to say that the project benefits alone clearly covered the cost of the administrative structure.

Since the program was plagued with a variety of problems during its first year, the better test of its worth is the comparison of net benefits and costs for the active period alone. Although even on this basis costs exceeded realized project net benefits by $400,000, potential project net benefits surpassed costs

Table 5A-6

Potential Net Benefits from ONG Projects and Other Activities from a Citywide Perspective

District	Potential Net Benefits from Projects	Potential Net Benefits from Other Activities	Cost of ONG District Administrative Structure for 18-Month Active Period	Residual Net Benefit
Bushwick	$450,000	?	$183,000	$267,000 + ?
Crown Heights	590,000	?	311,000	279,000 + ?
Wakefield-Edenwald	245,000	?	148,000	97,473 + ?
Washington Heights	585,000	?	146,000	439,000 + ?
All districts	$1,870,000	?	$788,000	$1,082,000 + ?
Less: ONG central administrative costs				$482,000
Residual after ONG administrative costs				$600,000 + ?
Less: Operating agency participation costs				75,000
Residual after total cost of active period				$525,000 + ?
Less: ONG start-up costs:				
District start-up costs			$153,000	
Central start-up costs			289,000	$442,000
Residual after ONG start-up costs				$83,000 + ?
Less: Agency start-up costs				42,000
Residual after all costs				$41,000 + ?

Note: Potential net benefits are defined as realized plus unrealized net benefits.

Despite the apparent precision of these calculations, the cost estimates are only accurate within 10 percent and the benefit calculations are approximations.

Question marks indicate that the net benefits from nonproject activities are not included. This probably represents a substantial omission.

for the active period by a substantial margin of $524,000, thus indicating that if the program had received support and cooperation, it would have been a valuable modification of the service delivery system.

Crown Heights was the only district whose net benefits from service delivery change projects were insufficient to cover its administrative costs. This imbalance was due to several factors. First, CHONG lost at least eight months during FY 1973 while it helped administer a $350,000 HUD planning grant to develop ways of stemming the deterioration of "transitional neighborhoods."

The much larger grant to implement the planned program never materialized, and CHONG was left with little to show, despite the fact that the planning grant had robbed it of about half of the ONG experiment's active life. That project also inflated CHONG's staff and, thereby, its expenses. Second, CHONG's larger staff was also due in part to its attempt to integrate its community work responsibilities under the Neighborhood Action Program (NAP) with its service integration activities under the experimental program. This increased CHONG's expenses without generating a corresponding increase in the number and quality of service delivery change projects. Third, CHONG had the largest number of community-and agency-oriented activities that were aimed at improving service delivery, but did not meet the criteria to be called projects. Consequently, the benefits from these activities, although substantial, are excluded from Tables 5A-5 and 5A-6. Fourth, a number of CHONG's projects rated as potentially producing positive net benefits were either terminated due to agency resistance or were still active but had not borne fruit by December 31, 1973. Table 5A-5 reveals that, despite its disproportionately large expense, CHONG's potential net benefits left a substantial residual net benefit after covering the district-level administrative costs for the eighteen-month active period.

Conclusion

Realized net benefits generated by projects did not cover the total ONG and agency administrative costs for the four districts studied from the program's inception until December 31, 1973, when the active period of the program ended. Even the potential net benefits only barely covered the total costs over that period. The more meaningful comparison for analysis of the program's true potential, however, is that of potential project net benefits and administrative costs for the active period, since this comparison eliminates the experimental program's inordinately high start-up costs and the effects of the bureaucratic and political impediments that plagued the program. Comparing the ONG and agency administrative costs for the active period ($1,345,000 for the four districts) with the potential net benefits ($1,870,000) from projects alone suggests that the program has the capability of improving the efficiency of the service delivery system.

There are several reasons why the true potential of the program is substantially greater than stated. First, the estimate of project net benefits is understated. The estimates are deliberately conservative, particularly for the more significant projects (net benefits in excess of $100,000) for which $100,000 was a low estimate; several of these projects either could or did produce net benefits several times that amount. Also, a number of procedural changes are durable and will, therefore, provide a continuing stream of benefits. Furthermore, a substantial number of the projects could be replicated in other parts of the city with payoffs comparable to those in the ONG districts.

Second, benefits from a large number of ONG activities are not included in Tables 5A-5 and 5A-6, which only include the benefits from those activities that met the criteria for projects. Other agency- and community-oriented activities aimed at improving service delivery generate substantial benefits in one of three ways: they increase consumer satisfaction with city services by reducing consumer irritation and expense in resolving service problems; they reduce agency cost of handling problems by having ONG filter complaints to ensure that the correct information is transmitted to the appropriate place in the bureaucracy; or they facilitate more efficient functioning of the service delivery system by altering its structure and procedures in response to identified service problems.

Third, had the program received stronger mayoral support and, as a result, greater agency cooperation from the outset, less effort would have been required for each activity. Not only would this have increased the proportion of potential benefits that were realized, but it also would have enabled ONG to engage in more projects and other activities. ONG did not exhaust the supply of opportunities for improving service delivery; rather the difficulty in achieving change stretched ONG's resources to the limit.

In summary, the combined effect of an unfavorable operating environment, a conservative evaluation of projects, and unmeasured benefits resulted in a substantial understatement of the value of the program. On balance, however, a properly designed and implemented program of the ONG type should be capable of producing a substantial surplus of benefits over costs.

The concept of a neighborhood-level service integration mechanism is sound. It requires a favorable environment in order to function properly; but once that environment is attained, the payoffs can be substantial.

6

Community Leadership and the Office of Neighborhood Government

Susan S. Fainstein, Norman I. Fainstein, Charles L. Bennett, Neil Bomberg, Fran LaSpina Clark, Peter Roggemann, and Mary Jane Wilson

Introduction

One of the principal aims of the Office of Neighborhood Government program was to reduce the distance between city government and its citizens. The linkage was established primarily through the role of the district manager, who acted as intermediary between the organized community and the service cabinet.[a] The close, frequently informal communication that took place through the manager between local organization leaders and cabinet members permitted ONG to circumvent the elaborate chain of command that normally determined bureaucratic procedures. Effective operation by the manager in this dual role required both that he work closely with the cabinet, as anticipated in the original ONG formulation, and that he develop ties with community groups and mobilize new groups where existing organizations did not fulfill his purposes. Thus, while ONG was initially conceived as a program of administrative decentralization with no formal component of citizen participation, the district managers in the three localities we studied intensively (Bushwick, Crown Heights, and Wakefield-Edenwald) all devoted considerable time and energy to developing ties with community organizations.

The managers described how they and their staffs spent their first months in office appearing at every local meeting they could locate, seeking to familiarize people with their offices, and requesting that the people bring their problems to the offices. They aimed at developing routine, ongoing contacts with the principal organizations in their areas, thereby remaining in touch with local issues and providing assistance to a variety of projects. While the managers did deal with individual citizen complaints and demands for services, their primary emphasis was on acting as the interface between organized client groups and bureaucracies. Reliance on organizations made ONG susceptible to the criticism that it ignored the interests of the weaker, unorganized elements in the communities; given the extent of its resources and its need to establish roots in the communities, however, such dependence was inevitable.

---

[a]Needleman and Needleman, in discussing the role of planners under various schemes of decentralization, describe the community planner as serving a similar linkage function by providing "bureaucratic enfranchisement" to community groups. See Martin L. Needleman and Carolyn Emerson Needleman, *Guerillas in the Bureaucracy: The Community Planning Experiment in the United States* (New York: John Wiley, 1974), pp. 47, 72 and *passim.* Warren describes horizontal and vertical patterns of relationships in communities. Within his paradigm the district manager connects the horizontal and vertical patterns. See Roland Warren, *The Community in America*, 2nd ed. (Chicago: Rand McNally, 1972), pp. 240-44.

The importance of just the informational function performed by community organizations in city neighborhoods, which rarely are covered by the mass media, cannot be exaggerated. Moreover, the district manager required support from these organizations if he was to have any influence over the bureaucrats. With relatively little mandated authority, ONG had to develop power resources on the local level if its requests to the service providers were to produce any response. By acting as a spokesman for neighborhood groups and assisting those groups in keeping a watch over city bureaucrats, the district manager enhanced his effectiveness vis-a-vis the line agencies. In turn, his increased effectiveness there raised his legitimacy in the community.

The result of this method of operation was that the actual community contacts of ONG tended to be limited to a small number of leaders. Thus, attempts to tap community sentiment toward the new offices elicited very low recognition among the general public but very high response among the leadership stratum. Only 26 out of 146 respondents in our 1974 survey of community leaders in four ONG districts indicated that they had had no contacts with ONG in the previous two years.

The research reported in this chapter relies on an analysis of the leadership group, which was studied in a number of ways. In order to determine leadership attitudes toward ONG and its effectiveness, and more generally toward decentralization, community control, and the quality of city government, we developed four primary sources of empirical data. First, a closed-ended field survey (Wave 1) of a total sample of 362 community leaders was carried out during 1972 in four (Bushwick, Crown Heights, Wakefield-Edenwald, and Washington Heights) of the five original experimental Community Planning Districts (CPDs) and in three control districts. (The survey was pretested in the other ONG district, the Rockaways.) A follow-up survey of 201 leaders was done in 1974 (Wave 2); this survey included a panel of 151 respondents from the first wave.

Second, intensive, semistructured interviews were conducted during 1973 with a sample of 114 community leaders (chosen by procedures different from those used in the survey) who were active in three of the experimental CPDs. Third, voluntary organizations, protest groups, quasi-government agencies, and political clubs and parties were observed directly during 1973 and 1974 in the same three districts. The discussion that follows depends mainly on the first two sources of data, which we designate, respectively, the *survey* of community leaders and the *interviews* with community leaders. Field observation data will be used illustratively and, finally, the cabinet interviews will be examined for the effects of community interaction on the attitudes of normally insulated agency officials.

Leadership Attitudes toward ONG

The extent to which the managers succeeded in developing the community leadership stratum into a supportive constituency was indicated by the widespread endorsement ONG received in Bushwick, Crown Heights, and Wakefield in the 1974 Wave 2 survey (Table 6-1). In Washington Heights, where the ONG never successfully established its legitimacy due to rivalries with other city offices, ratings of the district ONG were much lower (Table 6-2).

In the four districts taken together, 61 percent of those answering the question rated ONG's performance as good or very good. In contrast, just 43 percent gave that high a rating to the community school board, which was the most important other decentralized administrative mechanism in the locality.

The great majority of leaders in all four districts reported having some contact with their local ONG, and in the three most favorable districts, nearly 70 percent reported either quite a bit or a great deal of contact (Table 6-3).

Interviews with leaders in the three most favorable districts showed that they considered ONG to be an effective community agency and that evaluation of its effectiveness became more positive with greater familiarity with the office. A number of leaders commented that ONG was most appreciated by the most knowledgeable section of the community while it was unrecognized in the district at large. When we divided our 1974 survey sample in the four districts

Table 6-1
Leadership Rating of ONG in Bushwick, Crown Heights, and Wakefield in 1974

Rating	Percent $(N = 92)$[a]
Very good or good	71
Fair	22
Poor or very poor	7
	100

Note: The survey item was phrased as follows: "Overall, what kind of a job has the ONG been doing in this area?"

[a]An additional fifteen respondents either indicated "don't know" or failed to respond to this question.

Table 6-2
Leadership Rating of ONG in Washington Heights in 1974

Rating	Percent $(N = 30)$[a]
Very good or good	33
Fair	37
Poor or very poor	30
	100

Note: This table is based on the same survey item as in Table 6-1.

[a]Nine respondents either indicated "don't know" or did not respond.

Table 6-3
Leaders' Reported Contact with ONG, 1974

Degree of Contact	Bushwick, Crown Heights, Wakefield (Percent) (N = 107)	Washington Heights (Percent) (N = 39)
A great deal	40	13
Quite a bit	28	31
A little	15	36
None	3	10
No response or other	14	10

Note: The survey question was worded as follows: "Over the last two years, how much contact have you or your organization had with the local ONG?"

according to race and ethnicity, we found virtually no difference between minority and white leaders in the various districts in their evaluations.

Based on the data in the intensive interviews in three districts, we attempted to determine whether the type of position held by a leader affected his or her attitude toward ONG (Table 6-4). Of particular interest was the question whether holders of political office or members of quasi-governmental organizations such as the Community (Planning) Board or poverty board found ONG a competitor for status or resources. We divided the one-hundred leaders from the interview sample who stated definite opinions on ONG into two groups, governmental and nongovernmental, according to their principal organizational affiliation. We classified as governmental those leaders who either occupied an elected official position such as councilman, assemblyman, or district leader or who sat on quasi-governmental bodies such as the community school board, planning board, or poverty board. Nongovernmental leaders were those who were associated with block or tenant organizations, service delivery agencies, or other community groups without authoritative status.

Our analysis indicated virtually identical ratings of ONG for both governmental and nongovernmental leaders. ONG was seen as a threat in some isolated instances, especially by leaders connected with the Community Corporation (the official antipoverty organization) in Crown Heights. Many leaders, however, found that ONG's existence increased the power of their own office. Community Board (CB) members looked to ONG for staff assistance since the CBs had no staffs of their own. Elected officials used ONG to assist in responding to constituency complaints, which they clearly felt it could handle better than their own offices. In the words of one councilman, "Yes there is a duplication [of effort], but there is more than enough work to go around." Another remarked, "It frees me to do my other work to be able to refer service complaints to them.

Table 6-4

Attitude toward ONG: Governmental vs. Nongovernmental Leaders in Bushwick, Crown Heights, and Wakefield, 1973

Rating	Governmental (Percent) ($N = 46$)	Nongovernmental (Percent) ($N = 54$)
Positive	59	63
Mixed	21	20
Negative	20	17

I do work with them closely, however, in developing long-range plans for the district." Another councilman, while opposing further decentralization and arguing that the community school boards were "a disaster," stated that the district manager was "one of the best things to come to this community in a long time." He added that while he saw a potential for a conflict of roles between himself and the district manager, so far that problem had been avoided. A state assemblyman said, "We collectively work toward the same end results and so they're not a threat. . . . I see the district manager as an administrator, not a political figure."

The minority view among elected officials was that ONG did constitute a rival for constituency support. One councilman contended:

I consider it a patronage set-up. City councilmen and the Community Boards should be handling the same things ONG is supposed to be doing.

Under the Beame administration, there were several proposals reflecting this minority viewpoint for the continuation of ONG as essentially an adjunct to the councilmanic offices, with ONG district boundaries to coincide with councilmanic ones. Strong opposition to these proposals from the ONG staff and others who felt that councilmanic districts made no sense as administrative boundaries resulted in an impasse that threatened to jettison altogether the concept of the neighborhood office as a permanent presence in local districts. Nonetheless, among the councilmen we interviewed who had actual experience with a neighborhood office, there was little objection to its continuation along Community Planning District lines.

The popularity of ONG as an institution is further evident in the responses to an item in our 1974 survey that inquired whether ONG should be continued in the respondent's district (Table 6-5). The survey item—"Should the ONG in this area be continued?"—was phrased to allow the respondent to check as many as appropriate of the following:

Table 6-5

Attitude toward Continuation of ONG in Bushwick, Crown Heights, Wakefield, Washington Heights, 1974

Attitude	N	%[a]
More authority over city agencies	61	68
More local control	54	
Continue as is	12	8
Reduced authority	2	1
Discontinue	6	4
No response or other	28	19
Total respondents	146	100

[a]Since respondents could check more than one response, percentages are calculated on the basis of the mutually exclusive alternatives.

No, it should not be continued
Yes, set up as it is now
Yes, but with *more* local control over its activities
Yes, but with *more* authority over city agencies in this area
Yes, but with *reduced* authority
Other

The great majority of respondents, including those in Washington Heights where the actual operation of the office had received the lowest rating, called for the continuation of the office with greater power and more local control. Only 4 percent of respondents wished to see the office discontinued.

The three communities that we studied intensively varied according to the leadership emphases on different aspects of ONG's role. There was, however, considerable unanimity across the districts on the need for better ways to communicate with the city administration and a belief that ONG was a useful agency to fulfill this function. One Bushwick respondent expressed what seemed to be a widely held opinion about the office and its continuation by indicating his belief in the positive effects of decentralization combined with skepticism that the improved responsiveness that he desired would be institutionalized:

I was really glad when they came here; it showed the city cared. The people at the office are responsive; it's another question if even they can get the job done. They have only been here a little more than a year; I'll wait and see how many services they make better or bring in. . . . It is easier to get a response from them [than from other agencies] but that is because the people there now are responsive. If those people should change, it could become just another game. That's why I wonder if they have really helped citizen participation, because these gains could be gone if there was a new staff. A person has a right to say something about his destiny—that is a basic individual right. And every citizen should have the same right to get something done; one shouldn't need special contacts. A more permanent form of citizen participation is needed.

Data on leadership evaluation of city services in the district tend to indicate that most respondents shared the view quoted above that ONG had proved itself responsive but had not yet made a major impact on services. While the majority of leaders endorsed ONG and reported contact with the office, a comparison of leadership ratings of services in ONG and control districts shows a similar slight improvement in both between 1972 and 1974 (Table 6-6).

The data in Table 6-6 indicate no differences between experimental and control districts in terms of the perceived extent of service improvement between 1972 and 1974. This finding, however, should not be used as conclusive evidence that ONG had no perceptible effect on service delivery. Two extraneous events occurred during the experimental period that made the comparison between experimental and control less meaningful. One was the introduction of the district service cabinet into two of the three control districts, thereby causing at least one major element of the experiment to be present in the control districts. This factor probably had much less impact than did the second—the transition to a new mayoral administration. Anticipation of a Beame victory in the summer of 1973 followed by a year of uncertainty concerning the fate of ONG meant that after reaching a peak of activity in early 1973 the offices gradually wound down. By the time the second wave of the survey was taken in the spring of 1974, there was little reason to expect that a demoralized ONG could have been having a major effect on city services.

Cynicism toward the city government along with a belief in the greater

Table 6-6
Evaluation of City Services in ONG versus Control Districts

Mean Service Rating	ONG	Control
Wave 1	39.7	42.1
Wave 2	41.3	45.3

Note: Respondents were asked to rate thirteen services including sanitation, fire, police, housing, welfare, recreation, parks, and so forth on a five-point scale. A zero indicated a rating of very bad; a 4 indicated a rating of excellent. Index scores equal the summation of the ratings for each service over the services evaluated divided by four times the total number of services evaluated, with the resulting quotient multiplied by 100. The range of index scores was therefore zero to 100. A score of zero would mean that every service was evaluated as very bad; a score of 100 would mean that very service was evaluated as excellent.

Standard deviations ranged between 11.4 and 12.6.

flexibility and responsiveness of decentralized institutions characterized leaders in both experimental and control districts (Table 6-7).

Relations between ONG and Community Leadership

There was widespread agreement among the leaders that ONG was not well known by the general public and that it should have made greater efforts in that direction. Differences among the districts existed, however, in terms of specific complaints concerning ONG operations and emphases on the type of citizen-participation and service-providing roles it should play. For that reason we now examine the three districts of Bushwick, Crown Heights, and Wakefield-Eden-wald separately in order to describe the particular relationships between ONG and the community leadership structure that developed in each of them.

Bushwick

Of our three districts, Bushwick is the poorest. The drab quality of the streets and the deterioration of its predominantly low-rise housing stock make it easily identifiable to the casual observer as a low-income neighborhood with heavy demands for public service. Only 27 percent of its present population lived in Bushwick ten years ago. The area is characterized by low-wage employment and serious unemployment. Less than 2 percent of the population completed college.

The organizational structure of the neighborhood reflects these patterns. As might be expected in an area of high population mobility with low income and employment, only a few community organizations existed prior to the beginning of the antipoverty programs in 1965. These organizations represented primarily the general concerns of homeowners, long-time residents, or a middle-class membership. In contrast, the most recent organizations, especially the delegate agencies of the Community Corporation, tend to be functionally specific—oriented toward a particular service need among the population. There has been a large upsurge of local or block organizations, and ethnic organizations have started among black, Hispanic and white groups. Hispanic and white immigrants have formed local social clubs as well. Even now, however, despite the growth of organizational infrastructure in the last decade, Bushwick is still remarkably lacking in stable, effective community institutions. As a result, the decision of the city to place an ONG in Bushwick represented a significant addition to the organizational capacity of the area.

The introduction of the Office Neighborhood Government in Bushwick (BONG) produced three types of responses from local leaders. Among the civic leaders, there was a general feeling of satisfaction, even anticipation, that the

Table 6-7

Leaders' Attitudes toward Various Kinds of Representation and Decision Making, 1974

	Percent agreeing with statement among:		
	All Leaders	Minority Leaders	White Leaders
Political parties in area benefit mostly candidates and jobseekers	70	79	65
Neither Republicans nor Democrats represent interests of ordinary people	53	63	47
City services would be better run if most decisions were made by local administrators rather than the central office	77	82	75
A local board should have budgetary power over city agencies	61	74	54
A local board should have the power to hire and fire government administrators	42	49	38
Total Number	201	78	123

presence of BONG signaled a new attitude on the part of the city toward Bushwick. There was hope that a long period of neglect was over and that greatly needed resources would begin to pour into the neighborhood. Those civic leaders who were in contact with the office in its early days were impressed by its management orientation and the promise that any benefits resulting from BONG activity would be distributed in an unbiased manner.

Political leaders reacted somewhat differently. These leaders immediately saw a possible conflict between their traditional functions and the power that was vested in BONG and the district manager (DM). They were determined to watch the office carefully and monitor the tone of its activities. These leaders, while willing to let the DM and his staff implement management programs, were ready to block the office should it become a means of aggregating political power—whether for a staff member, some local leader, or Mayor Lindsay—at their own expense.

No organization, regardless of any change or innovation it may represent, is born entirely free of the reputation of organizations that preceded it. The basis of the third response to BONG, then, was a fear that it represented nothing more than its predecessor, the Urban Action Task Force (UATF). Several leaders stated BONG, like UATF, would be unable to increase participation and effectiveness in dealing with government. Some white and Hispanic leaders were afraid the new office would deal mostly with black groups, as UATF had done, and this anticipation was heightened when they learned the district manager, Sidney Jones, was black. And finally, some organized interests in various service and community action agencies, the Community Board, and the Community Corporation board watched BONG warily as they wondered whether it would undermine or even eliminate their functions.

In this climate of fear and expectation, BONG capitalized very quickly on the favorable predispositions of the civic leaders. By approaching them and offering his help, the district manager gained forums in which to explain the ONG program. By dealing with these leaders and opening a two-way flow of information, by handling their complaints on service delivery as well as forwarding their suggestions to the district service cabinet, and by fulfilling the promise of nonpartisan service management, the BONG staff developed trust and a constituency for the office. In addition, BONG itself increased the civic leadership by promoting the organization of numerous block associations and other groups. This stratum of the local leadership served as the primary constituency for BONG's advisory council (later the town hall meeting), which was established so the district manager could report to the community and hear its suggestions and advice.

BONG followed a conscious policy of working with political leaders and succeeded in not antagonizing them. When both BONG and political leaders worked together on projects, there was no competition for credit. BONG included political leaders in its information network and invited them to participate in its town hall meetings. When they came to these meetings, the district manager provided time for them to speak and to discuss any issue with people in attendance. Political leaders indicated a respect for the working style of BONG and particularly for the professionalism of the district manager.

Immediately upon its introduction in Bushwick, ONG also attempted to reach hitherto neglected groups and include them in its activities. While maintaining the contact with black groups that had been established by the UATF, BONG approached white and Hispanic leaders. The staff worked to help existing organizations reach their goals and supported the efforts of the Community Board and the Community Corporation to serve the neighborhood. With the exception of some leaders in the Community Corporation and its service agencies who were threatened by the demise of the Office of Economic Opportunity (OEO) and the absence of city or state funds, BONG convinced the active leadership that it could be an asset to the existing groups because of its unique structure and relationship to city agencies.

The ONG program design placed great emphasis on the workings of the district service cabinet, but gave little guidance on the issue of community consultation. In order to facilitate contact with community groups, Jones established an advisory council and a steering committee and had himself appointed to the Community Board. The advisory council permitted ONG to gather community ideas and obtain participation in a system of reporting service complaints. It also was a forum for disseminating information on ONG projects and other programs available to the community such as block beautification and block security programs. Moreover, from the start, Jones informally began using his staff to carry out decisions of the Community Board; for example, when the CB wanted to carry out a study on revitalization of a commercial street, Jones provided staff to obtain merchant and community cooperation as well as to explore sources for funds.

The Bushwick ONG was allocated $250,000 in capital funds to be spent on cabinet and community projects for 1974. To decide how this money was to be spent, the DM solicited ideas from the cabinet and presented these to the Community Board and the advisory council for their priorities and approval. Such community approval was not legally required, but ONG sought it as a means of initiating community involvement in government decisions. In the fall of 1973, at Jones' request, the borough president expanded the Community Board by adding members from the ONG advisory council. ONG then dissolved the advisory council and formed a town hall meeting, which was a monthly session at which ONG staff and the community discussed problems, often with elected officials or individual cabinet members. The Community Board responded to this infusion of new energy and began to take a more active role in community issues with a wider range of groups represented. ONG's relationship with the CB, though informal, increased the community's ability to address service problems.

Our interviews with Bushwick community leaders revealed that they saw the benefits of ONG most often in the "hard services" (police, fire protection, sanitation, vacant lot clean-up, street repaving and lighting, abandoned car removal, and water services). Twenty-four of the thirty-six leaders interviewed in 1973 mentioned this improvement as a positive result of ONG's action (Table 6-8). Paradoxically, several leaders said that while they appreciated the improved services, they did not necessarily feel the overall ONG impact was beneficial, either because it institutionalized no direct accountability to the community on the part of the service deliverers, or because handling service deficiencies through complaints tended to favor groups with access to the complaint system. Significantly, only six leaders mentioned coordination of service delivery and a new way of handling problems as an impact of ONG. Thus, this latter effort of the ONG staff, one that met considerable success among the service agencies themselves, was not perceived by most neighborhood leaders.

Some leaders faulted ONG for its failure to touch what they saw as the critical problems of the neighborhood: lack of housing, welfare, unemployment, and poor education. This impatience was tempered in most leaders by a realization that far more resources and perhaps structural changes would be

Table 6-8
Attitude toward ONG of Bushwick Leaders, 1973

Race-Ethnicity	N	Positive	Mixed	Negative	Don't Know
Black	17	9	5	3	0
Hispanic	12	6	2	2	2
White	7	6	1	0	0
Total	36	21	8	5	2
Percent		58%	22%	14%	6%

required than could ever be available to ONG under its present program design. Nonetheless, a critical determinant of the rating given ONG was the respondent's framework of evaluation—that is, those who viewed it within the relatively narrow criteria of its impact on existing city services were more positive than those who viewed it from the perspective of Bushwick's vast social problems.

Only minimal differences existed among racial and ethnic groups in their reactions to ONG. As one leader said, "ONG has in a sense brought the groups together because it takes a stance in the center of three conflicting groups." The office made special efforts to contact Hispanic leaders, since their constituency, while the largest population group in Bushwick, tended to be the least visible. Hispanic respondents expressed disappointment at the lack of Spanish-speaking personnel at ONG, but, as one such leader said:

That is the only thing I can blame them for. Otherwise they are the only government program really trying to reach the Hispanic community.

It is possible to divide the Bushwick leadership stratum into two groups based on their general orientation toward civic activity. The first consists of those who were concerned with general political questions and had a broad strategy they wanted to see followed in order to better the situation in Bushwick. The concerns of this group are summarized in the following statement from one of them:

At first people feared that ONG had come here as an attempt to take over the other agencies, but this fear is disappearing. It is disappearing mostly because ONG has tried to work with and through the agencies and groups that are here.

Another of this type of leader expressed general approval of ONG's strategy as follows:

They have helped to get better street lighting and the sewer lines are getting unclogged. Of course they haven't yet solved the big problems, like housing. But they are working on it.

A third leader echoed this sentiment in describing his dealings with the office:

They have taken a broad approach to housing. That is good, because not only will it help my group, but other groups as well. Also, I've worked with some of their task forces, which cut across department lines to see a problem in its totality and deal with it.

These leaders can be distinguished from a second group of more specialized leaders who were generally less politically oriented and more local in their oulook (they were less likely to subscribe to an overall strategy but often had definite ideas how to improve a specific area or address a particular problem). These leaders usually rated ONG in terms of the outcome of a specific request that was made to the office, although they also exhibited a concern that the office did not touch the "real problems" of education, housing, jobs and welfare. If they rated ONG positively, they were more likely to refer all problems to ONG in the belief that this office could often handle the problems better than they could with their own contacts in city agencies.

In general, there was an unease among both groups of leaders, not so much because ONG failed to do enough, but because there was so much more to be done. They had been grappling at the local level with questions of poor service delivery, some for ten years or more. They had seen programs come and go with no real change in underlying causes of neighborhood deterioration. They were beginning to see a connection between power—not just partisan political power, but institutional and local organizational strength (a type of civic power)—and service delivery. And they recognized Bushwick sadly lacked that power, so they looked to any organization, such as ONG to bridge the gap. One leader said:

We welcomed ONG; we perceived a lack here and hoped ONG could fill it. The lack was an absence of any local vehicle to get to the service agencies, to make them responsive. ONG hasn't yet proved if it is the agency to do it, but before you remove it you better suggest something else to fill that lack. Eventually it should be a more definite form of community control with a representative elected board. ONG is not the only way to reach this, but it has done some good things for the community. It can be the first step in having the community relate to the agencies and to the mayor. That is the start.

Again and again leaders called for the next steps that would create a firm system of community participation in addressing questions of service delivery, and their fear was that ONG would never accomplish this. Leaders, even while praising ONG's successes, seemed to feel its usefulness was bound to be short-lived and that it would turn into another layer of bureaucracy or a politically oriented patronage club.

In spite of having achieved some success through direct action or through cooperation with special programs such as ONG, the leaders were troubled that the major problems were being dealt with in piecemeal fashion, that some groups and interests were still being left out, and that ONG was not institutionalized with a definite role for community involvement. One leader summed this up when he said, "Management is a good word for us now, because we are getting some results. But it could become a shell game."

The leaders believed there were too many boards and agencies dealing with the same kinds of problems and not enough boards dealing with root causes of Bushwick's problems. They recognized that ONG was closest to these causes and had more resources to deal with them, but the lack of a role for themselves in the process, the leaving out of nonvocal interests, and the possibilities of a radical reduction of functions for ONG (which occurred in late 1974) made the leaders uneasy. They therefore called for a basic political reform—that is, a restructuring of their relationship with the city and its authority in allocating service delivery. Their suggestions for a strong community-based ONG as a government vehicle of more local participation and power stemmed from this desire.

The district manager's role was made difficult by the conflicting administrative goals of efficiency and better service delivery and the political goals of citizen participation. Jones clearly recognized that the level of administrative reform that ONG represented was insufficient for dealing with the basic causes of service problems in Bushwick. In an interview on January 29, 1974, Jones stated:

We have gone just about as far as we can go in giving better services and increasing productivity as a result of service integration at the cabinet level. We are now up against the problem of a lack of the equipment and the things needed from the city's capital budget. Bushwick is suffering from years of neglect and these local service chiefs feel the pinch with their outdated and broken down equipment. We really can't address any more of the problems here unless we solve the problem of getting more capital money.

While discussing the fact that the Brooklyn Borough Improvement Board was not acting on a required approval of the spending of $250,000 in capital money allocated to Bushwick by the City Council, Jones touched the heart of the ONG dilemma. ONG was unable to address root causes of Bushwick's problems unless it could deal with a redistribution of capital investment to the area. But this redistribution was a political question, and ONG, as an administrative innovation in government, could not attack the basic political policies of the city.

Jones clearly sought ways to strengthen the organizational base of the community so groups could affect the political process and use community needs as an appeal to citywide allocation decisions. These actions corresponded with the reported desires of community leaders, who not only wanted to see ONG maintained, but who were made more responsive to the community through a formal participation structure. Based on what existed in Bushwick, the leaders judged ONG to represent progress. Measured against what the leaders felt was still needed, however, ONG could only be considered a small step forward.

Crown Heights

Crown Heights has undergone several major shifts in population in the last century. In the mid-nineteen hundreds a relatively prosperous black settlement occupied the area. During the 1920s it became a predominantly Jewish neighborhood, and after World War II it began to attract middle-class blacks who were fleeing the ghetto. The 1960s brought a new group of less-affluent blacks, accompanied by block-busting, rising crime and welfare rates, and other signs of neighborhood instability. Even with the continued presence of a well-to-do black group, the number of very poor families increased significantly.

Despite its recent social transition, Crown Heights has a well-developed organizational infrastructure. There are over 120 block associations, as well as several large civic associations. While the absence of stable tenants organizations is noticeable, short-lived protest groups, usually mobilized to fight central governmental decisions, have successfully pressed their interests on such issues as the placement of day-care centers, drug clinics, urban renewal strategies, and the selection of school personnel. Other, more permanent groups have sought to develop mechanisms for community input to increase resources coming to Crown Heights, and to stimulate neighborhood beautification or the development of recreation facilities. In addition, a number of ethnic associations have been formed by Haitian and Hispanic residents. These have primarily restricted themselves to social functions, although on occasion Black Power groups have sprung up and then lapsed into quietude.

The most powerful and effective ethnic self-help and advocacy organizations in Crown Heights belong to the Hasidim. This sect of Orthodox Jews constitutes a highly visible white enclave in the center of the district. The decision of the Hasidim, numbering between ten and twenty thousand, to remain in Crown Heights was influenced by the members' desire to maintain the synagogues and yeshivas that they had built in the area and by the symbolic meaning of the location there of the world headquarters of the Lubovitcher Movement. The Hasidim have a very hierarchical social structure dominated by a single leader, the Rebbe, and his close associates. The Rebbe has used his religious and secular authority to encourage his people to vote as a bloc for those candidates whom he views as best representing Hasidic interests and to use their organizations to press local politicians and governmental officials. The Hasidim have also developed close ties with people in the central city bureaucracies.

In contrast, Crown Heights' blacks are divided by class and ethnic differences (only about half of the black population was born in the United States; the remainder, drawn from their Caribbean islands, speak different native languages, keep their own customs, and belong to their own social and religious organizations). Lacking a cohesive political identity, crosscut by a number of political jurisdictional lines, and indifferent to the infighting of the activists, many blacks ignore the political process altogether. Low voter turnout and divisions among black voters create a vacuum that the Hasidim have successfully filled. The black or white candidate who can win the support of the conservative Hasidim has a powerful edge in the election. The result has been Hasidic domination of the poverty board and considerable Hasidic influence on the school board, Community Board, and the Democratic club. It is noticeable, however, that those boards with voluntary or appointive membership—such as the precinct council, code enforcement board, health board, and Community Board—have proved to be forums for a broad spectrum of individual people with specialized knowledge in a number of service areas.

Thus, the introduction into Crown Heights of an Office of Neighborhood Government (CHONG) in January 1972 meant the creation of a new institution in an already complex situation. CHONG came as the successor to a previous mayoral experiment, the Neighborhood Action Program (NAP), which had been established in 1970 to provide improved service delivery in transitional neighborhoods. NAP, with $200,000 in capital budget funds to be spent beautifying and maintaining the area, had not been readily accepted by some of the Crown Heights leadership for several reasons. First, since the citywide director of NAP was a Hasidic rabbi from Crown Heights (who had received notice in the mid-sixties when he formed a neighborhood vigilante group, the Maccabees), the local director was of the Jewish faith, and the office was located near the Hasidic center of the district, some black leaders clearly perceived NAP as a mayoral gift to the Hasidim. Second, other groups were suspicious of any move the mayor might make to increase his local political base. They suspected that NAP was a political ploy not designed for their benefit. Conservative groups feared the damage that the stigmatizing designation as a transitional neighborhood might do to their status, land values, and insurance rates.

The NAP director worked to establish the program's credibility with local leaders through various outreach methods: He published a newsletter, attended local meetings, and provided all groups equal access to his office. He established an advisory board of black, Hasidic and non-Hasidic white residents, which developed priorities for capital budget expenditures. In addition, he initiated the precursor of ONG's cabinet by holding monthly meetings of the area's service officers.

ONG's arrival meant additional staff, power, and functions for the existing NAP office, since, in contrast to Washington Heights, the NAP director was appointed as the Crown Heights ONG district manager. In June 1972 the city was awarded a $300,000 federal planning grant to design a program of neighborhood rehabilitation for Crown Heights, with the multi-agency effort to be under the overall direction of the Crown Heights Office of Neighborhood Government. CHONG solicited the advice of a broad range of community groups, the participation of which was formalized in an advisory board to the Crown Heights Area Maintenance Program (CHAMP). With the prospect of millions of dollars for plan implementation in view, numerous elements in the community vied for dominance of the CHAMP board. Eventually a somewhat militant young black leader defeated a leader of the conservative black homeowning element and was elected chairman.

In subsequent months, CHAMP became the full-time preoccupation of the Crown Heights ONG. The program, however, failed to gain federal approval for plan implementation, and the ambitious effort that was initially foreseen became reduced to a city-sponsored neighborhood preservation program. Despite the letdown that followed the denial of federal funds, a new community board was forged out of the remnants of the NAP and CHAMP boards. Called the Crown Heights Board of Community Affairs (CHBOCA), this new entity was intended to preserve the high level of mobilization and diversified representation of CHAMP and to serve as the primary instrument for formal community input into CHONG. Membership on CHBOCA consisted of elected members of the old NAP board, appointed members of the CHAMP board, and additional people who were prominent in the community. Of the seventy-five designated members, however, black conservative homeowners (political rivals of the CHBOCA chairman's brother) and most of the Hasidic representatives never participated in the board's activities, and the remaining Hasidic members dropped out.

The final split between the Hasidim and CHBOCA arose out of an incident on Eastern Parkway, the main thoroughfare of Crown Heights and the location of the Lubovitcher headquarters. The service road in front of the synagogue was blockaded by police on the Sabbath so as to protect the worshippers who congregated on the street before and after services. It was also a tacit acknowledgment of Orthodox Jewish rules prohibiting the operation of motor vehicles on the Sabbath. Residents of the block objected to the barricaded street and persisted in driving their cars past the obstructions. Eventually the car of a black woman driving through was severely shaken, a near riot occurred involving Hasidic and other residents, and several shots were fired. CHBOCA attempted to mitigate the ensuing tensions, but the Hasidim refused to recognize it as a legitimate governmental body and boycotted its meetings.

By the end of the summer of 1973, CHBOCA members had abandoned attempts to encourage Hasidic input. Hopes to create a representative neighborhood board evaporated under the pressure of community hostilities that ONG had not created but that were too deeply held for ONG to be capable of resolving. Despite its formal neutrality, ONG's position among community leaders was affected by the summer's events. Those leaders who were participants in the Board of Community Affairs enthusiastically endorsed ONG; leaders who boycotted CHBOCA felt that ONG was useless, redundant, or biased. Nonetheless, as can be seen from Table 6-9, the great majority of the Crown Heights leadership evaluated ONG positively.

While race was not a particularly good predictor of a leader's attitude toward ONG, organizational and/or religious affiliation proved to be more important. Thus, all the Hasidic leaders and all the blacks associated with the

Table 6-9
Attitude toward ONG of Crown Heights Leaders, 1973

Race-Ethnicity	N	Positive	Mixed	Negative	Don't Know
American black	21	12	3	6	0
West Indian black	5	4	1	0	0
Total black	(26)	(16)	(4)	(6)	
Hispanic	1	0	0	0	1
White hasidic	5	0	3	2	0
White other	8	8	0	0	0
Total white	(13)	(8)	(3)	(2)	
Total	40	24	7	8	1
Percent		60%	17%	20%	3%

Hasidic-controlled Community Corporation had mixed or negative feelings toward ONG. Most of them considered ONG either to be superfluous or dominated by a single element in the community. Many of these leaders had infrequent contacts with ONG and were unable to give an accurate description of its activities. Some leaders of black homeowning groups who were negative toward ONG distrusted it as an example of mayoral interference in the area.

Leaders who were favorably disposed toward ONG came from a wide range of organizations and ethnic backgrounds. Most were connected with groups that had made use of the services provided by ONG, and they felt that the quality of services had improved in the neighborhood since 1972. They liked having an office nearby where they could obtain information and services—one that seemed actively concerned with their interests. As one block association chairman put it:

I'd rather see the office here—or at least something here—rather than have to go downtown or go to political officials. It's a small office that's nearby and you feel you're more at home there. You don't have to go downtown and have problems with taking care of the kids. It's good to have a neighborhood office. I think all agencies could work better if they had local offices.

All but one of the six political officeholders whom we interviewed in Crown Heights favored the office and felt that it performed a needed function.

As in Bushwick, the majority of leaders calling for changes in the ONG structure wished to see it move in the direction of more local power and greater citizen input. Black leaders, clearly fearful of the power of the Hasidim in controlling local elections, sought a governing board consisting primarily of appointed members who would reflect the racial and ideological composition of the community. Many leaders endorsed the hiring of a black district manager and felt that the community should participate in his/her selection. Several leaders urged that ONG increase its public relations efforts so as to become better known among the community at large.

Throughout the two-and-a-half years of its operations, CHONG was distinguished from other ONG offices by the elaborate mechanisms for community input it had developed. There were two major causes for the greater degree of community participation there. First, the personal philosophy of CHONG's district manager created a context for institutional development. Clearly, he believed that some form of political decentralization should accompany administrative decentralization, and he actively sought to create a means for legitimate, balanced community input that would enable all sections of the community to have equal access to the CHONG office. Second, Crown Heights encompassed a divided but sophisticated and competitive leadership that sought formal input into an office with jobs, prestige, and services to offer.

The formation of a community board permitted a system of institutionalized interactions to evolve between the office and community leaders—a pattern that was distinct from the multitude of daily complaint-oriented contacts between community and office. The elements in the system were the district manager, his staff, the cabinet, and CHBOCA. At times the manager brought citizen demands to the cabinet; at other times he and the staff acted as buffers between community and city agencies. Obviously, a major concern of the district manager was to create permanent channels of responsiveness within cabinet agencies so that continued intervention by ONG would not be required. By clearly considering himself to be a professional service manager, CHONG's district manager avoided competition with the area's public officials and did not seek credit for work accomplished in their names, but in return, he expected, and usually received, support from them for ONG projects.

In a divided community the strategy of equal access required a high degree of flexibility and at times ambiguity and diplomacy on the part of the district manager. Despite the policy of impartiality, CHONG was never able to overcome the legacies of the battle to control the aborted area maintenance program and of the intermittent conflicts over the role of the Hasidim. Those who "won" control of CHBOCA—moderate and militant civic activists, both black and white—consistently supported ONG. Those who lost—the Hasidim and the conservative elements in the black community—boycotted the board and widened the chasm between themselves and ONG by closing off communications and publicly challenging its legitimacy. Given the complicated nature of the Crown Heights community, it is doubtful whether any strategy the office could have devised would have satisfied all elements in the district.

Wakefield-Edenwald

The northeast Bronx, of which the neighborhoods of Wakefield and Edenwald form the largest components, is a predominantly middle-income section of the city (although there are wide variations from the mean). Over 50 percent of its residents own their own homes. While the district has been fairly stable in composition since the arrival of a large wave of Italian immigrants in the first part of the century, the last two decades have witnessed a moderate influx of blacks and Hispanics into its southern portion.

The interests of Wakefield-Edenwald's various neighborhoods are articulated by a large number of civic and block associations representing mainly home-owners. The goals of these groups are straightforward if somewhat contradic-tory: improve city services and stabilize or reduce the property tax. The type of city services they desire are directly related to property ownership: well-paved streets, a high level of police protection, and better lighting and sewers. As a rule, the larger civic associations seldom act in concert. Instead, individual associations concern themselves with issues and service problems specific to their own territories. This lack of interaction has been increased by the personalistic character of leadership among these groups.

Wakefield-Edenwald has a variety of ethnic and religious organizations that mainly restrict themselves to social activities. The local chapter of the NAACP tends to concentrate on national issues affecting its parent organization. In 1969 a group of black leaders organized the Coalition of Black Organizations (COBO), which has on occasion acted as a mobilizing agent in the black community.

Another group of community organizations has devoted itself to providing services to neighborhood residents. The oldest of these are concerned with youth employment and recreation. More recently, groups have organized for various service purposes such as assisting senior citizens or planning health programs for the area. Leaders of these service groups tend to be highly specialized in their interests and to restrict their participation in civic activities to the immediate area of their concern.

The foregoing description of Wakefield-Edenwald's organizational structure indicates a rather fragmented system of actors. Civic associations, while sharing similar memberships and goals, are isolated by localized interests and personality conflicts. Quasi-governmental groups such as the Community Board are led by civic leaders but can rarely implement the desires of their constituency. Particular service shortcomings have spawned new organizations whose leader-ship only marginally overlaps with the civic corps. Confounding this situation are the local political clubs. There are three in the 86th Assembly District that emcompasses Wakefield-Edenwald: a Republican and two Democratic (one regular, one reform) clubs. The North Bronx (regular) Democratic Club domi-nates local political activity. The clubs attract a leadership cadre quite separate from that of other local organizations. As had been the case traditionally, the clubs are run by individuals whose occupations allow plenty of time for such activity and may be benefited by it. Lawyers, real estate brokers, and an occasional undertaker are among the leaders. Rank and file membership of the North Bronx Democratic Club remains largely middle-aged or older Italians.

What is most striking about attendance at a club meeting is the decided lack of civic or service delivery leaders.

The root of this separation is the mutual mistrust felt by civic leaders and political activists. The former clearly prefer to think of themselves as unselfish servants of the entire community and regard politicians as primarily motivated by personal interest. Party members do not express the same antipathy for civic leaders; and in fact, they often claim to be seeking the same things as the civics—that is, community stabilization and better city services. Club members, however, privately ridicule the civic leaders for their supposed pettiness and general ineffectiveness. While the personal culpability civic leaders ascribe to club members is overdrawn, the goals of the clubs—that is, election of members to public office, retention by the leadership of attractive city jobs, and the maintenance of the organization as an effective election-winning device—have little direct relationship to civic goals.

Two groups of people are largely unrepresented by the existing organizational framework. These are the area's large minority of tenants and the small group of Hispanic residents. In general, tenants comprise the district's poorest and most transient group. Some tenants organizations exist, but membership is thin, and few exhibit a coherent program. Even the Edenwald Tenants Association (serving a large public housing project) with a potential membership of over two thousand families is scarcely active. While the interests of tenants and homeowners are not necessarily contrary, homeowners tend to distrust renters as people with no real stake in the community. In fact, the bylaws of some block/civic associations preclude membership for nonhomeowners residing in structures housing more than a certain number of families.

A rare convergence of sentiment among all types of leaders in Wakefield-Edenwald greeted the location of an Office of Neighborhood Government in the district by Mayor Lindsay's administration late in 1971. Clearly, neither civic leaders nor politicans felt their interests would be markedly furthered by ONG. Local homeowners expected the agency to concentrate its efforts on the less desirable, transient portion of the local population, while neglecting its stable, property-owning element. Club members feared ONG would be a repeat of the little city halls, an effort to institutionalize grass roots political support for Mayor Lindsay. ONG's first task was to undermine these negative preconceptions.

ONG's official mandate was as a purely management mechanism. Obviously, John Sanderson, the first Wakefield-Edenwald district manager, perceived the need, however, to sell his organization to local residents, and neither he nor his staff felt management reorganization would strike a particularly responsive chord in the community. Consequently, the Wakefield-Edenwald ONG staff spent most weekday evenings in early 1972 attending the meetings of local civic groups, explaining their program, seeking out the membership's complaints, and promising to work on serviceable requests. ONG clearly wanted to show community leaders that it could deliver to them many of the services they desired. In its early months this was just the kind of work ONG was most capable of handling—the short-term, hard service project such as pothole fixing or street sign placement. Sanderson had clearly decided that the real measure of ONG as a street level management reform would turn on its ability to coordinate those services demanded by the populace.

At the same time as ONG was getting to know the community and vice versa, Sanderson was also exploring his more directly mandated role. This effort involved creating a district service cabinet composed of the local directors of all the city agencies working in Wakefield-Edenwald. Without line authority over cabinet members, the district manager was limited to suggesting problem areas where horizontal cooperation among local agency chiefs could improve service output. The willingness of local directors to participate varied considerably. Some, coming from agencies with a tradition of centralization and/or clear superior-subordinate relationships among vertically differentiated officers, were wary of making interagency initiatives. Others felt that ONG might be a threat to their own authority. However, through the two and a half years of the cabinet's existence, Sanderson and his successor as district manager, Robert House, brought the cabinet along by never threatening its members and playing to their strengths and resources.

Sanderson and House (initially the deputy district manager) were discovering a role for the district manager in these early months that would become a hallmark of the program. First, by going to the community and determining what services were lacking or inadequately delivered, ONG publicized its presence, indicated concern for community needs, and gave people a place to go when making complaints or seeking information. Although it was not within the power of ONG to solve every problem, the office did possess resources useful to local citizens. Among these were a knowledge of where to go in the city bureaucracy with specific complaints and a staff with the time and skill to research and write proposals for local action. Similarly, ONG performed services useful for cabinet members. With its ties to the community it was able to obtain more easily feedback on the impact of certain agency activities, and once ONG became established in the community, people began going to it with complaints rather than flooding the phones of their respective agencies. ONG shared contacts with both local residents and agency personnel, and its very position between these two sets of actors gave it considerable power.

Sanderson was moving toward a view (that was fully articulated by House) of the district manager as an "integrator." Clearly, in the analyses of Sanderson and House the potential of the manager rested not in any powers the position commanded but in its unique connections with both community and administration. ONG had found many community residents who were willing to play an active role in improving local services and related activities but who lacked an understanding of city government (to say nothing of federal programs) and the resources to take care of basic administrative work. With a staff at hand ONG could provide information, do paperwork, and in several other ways "channel the energy" of local people. ONG could become the link between local residents and city agencies. By bringing together community energy channeled in constructive directions with administrators seeking to provide services, ONG could make the jobs of these bureaucrats easier. Projects could be tailored to voiced community needs by agency personnel working both with community residents and across agency lines. Not only would the chance of success be higher, but also much of the groundwork would be laid by citizens. Thus, ONG could build the self-esteem and sense of efficacy of residents and administrators. Moreover, a long-run output would be the establishment of regular but informal lines of communication.

In contrast to the supportive civic leaders, elected officials and clubhouse activists seemed less pleased with ONG. They clearly feared that by providing a complaint service (traditionally performed by club leaders and city councilmen) ONG could undermine their political influence. The situation of the regular Democratic Party in the North Bronx differed from that in Crown Heights and Bushwick. The stability of the population had meant that the party could hold on to its traditional constituency among the descendants of the European immigrants. Political leaders continued to be predominantly Italian. Thus, whereas in Brooklyn the old linkage systems had largely been shattered as a result of population changes, in the Bronx the political clubs continued to be a meaningful framework for political mobilization, at least for those individuals associated with them. Thus, while ONG could assist the Brooklyn political leaders in establishing new communications networks to replace the old ward system, in the Bronx, ONG represented a competing system (unless it could be integrated into the existing mode of political domination). In fact, once the election of the Beame administration indicated renewed influence for the regular Democrats at the city level, the Wakefield-Edenwald ONG was immediately overhauled to correspond to the wishes of the Democratic organization.

To counteract the resentment of local politicians, Robert House often verbalized a policy of "red carpet treatment" for officials from both parties— that is, ONG would respond as best it could to any elected official's legitimate request. In practical terms, this policy seemed to mean favors in the nature of placing this or that teenager in a summer job program. However, ONG was almost inevitably the victim of suspicion from one side or the other that inordinate concessions were being made to the opposition. The often tenuous support rendered by elected officials led ONG to look elsewhere for supportive constituencies.

It did so by stressing adaptability. Rather than marshalling most of its resources behind a few ongoing projects, the office attempted to create a more general system of encouraging local actors to carry out their own initiatives. One of ONG's primary early objectives was to create among community leaders a feeling that city government was interested in their needs. At the same time a quick-response citizen complaint service was organized. The objective was to accept local complaints, bring them to the attention of the proper agencies, insure action, and follow-up with the citizen within a week or so. Similarly, the effort to build feelings of efficacy among community leaders led to some lengthy conferences about specific problems. The Shoelace Park project was particularly beneficial to ONG's prestige because a long-standing eyesore was brought to ONG's attention by a community leader during a walking tour of part of the district. ONG worked with the leader in developing a plan for renovating an abandoned roadway of the Bronx River Expressway and managed to get a commitment from an agency (the highways department), which had previously appeared none too friendly to innovative programs, to aid in laying out the park. It was an unprecedented joint effort by residents and city agencies.

ONG's ability to bring together hard service agencies in coordinated efforts to upgrade the physical appearance of Wakefield-Edenwald was among its notable successes. More subtle issues, such as youth problems or improved social services in the Edenwald public housing project, brought a different response from ONG. Instead of directly orchestrating interagency efforts, it seemed to prefer to stand in the background by aiding but not leading community initiatives. Clearly, this strategy was in part directed at building permanent local institutions and in part at avoiding becoming overly associated with controversial projects. Realizing the distrust that marked relations among homeowners, tenants, Italians, and blacks, ONG stressed "coalition building"—the creation of program-oriented organizations crossing ethnic and class lines.

The North Bronx Health Council was an example. This group's goal was the establishment of a health maintenance organization (a subscriber-supported prepaid health service) in Wakefield-Edenwald. Benefits from such a program would mainly accrue to large, lower-income families, but membership would not be limited in any way. ONG aided the health council by handling some clerical tasks, putting out a newsletter, and making contacts in city government.

Riskier, but still fairly well-accepted, were ONG's efforts in the summer job field. Again, its goal was to create working relations among potentially antagonistic interests by stressing mutually beneficial interaction. Bringing to the community as many summer jobs as possible had been a prime concern of all types of local leaders. For years, city agencies provided funds to pay teenagers working for various youth programs in the community. Competition among directors of these programs for job slots had often been severe. In 1972, ONG stepped into this situation, advising the two best known youth directors in the community (one Italian, the other black) that open negotiations in allocating the jobs would be preferable to hostile lobbying. The result was that the Youth Services Agency positions were disseminated to several more community programs than was the norm, and in 1973, ONG itself received two hundred job slots from the Human Resources Administration.

ONG's early and continued stress on hard services had a marked effect on the thinking of our sample of leaders. When asked to describe their contacts with ONG, the most common response was that they had made calls to complain about potholes, abandoned cars, and like irritants. The typical accompanying statement was: "With ONG we finally have a place to go in the community that will listen to us." Improvements in sanitation, traffic control, and street maintenance were frequently mentioned as coinciding with ONG's local presence. The sample expressed much less knowledge of other ONG mandates. For instance, agency coordination was an ONG role rarely discerned by community leaders—despite their awareness of projects such as Shoelace Park and summer job allocation, both of which were engineered by ONG's intervention with several local groups and agencies. Likewise, an increase of the local information flow was seldom noted as an ONG achievement.

The most consistent criticism of ONG emerged from those leaders whose own contacts with it were limited. ONG's community penetration was seen as shallow. The average resident, critics contended, was not touched by ONG at all. A second line of criticism concerned which groups within the community were best served by the office. As one person put it, "ONG pays too much attention to the screamers." Generally, those making such statements would not identify exactly to whom they referred. When names were disclosed, a sense of jealousy and/or organizational competition was usually evident. However, several respondents more favorable to ONG recalled the period when the office was grasping for community acceptance without knowing the district well. At that time it seemed that "screamers" did have an advantage in gaining ONG's attention. These respondents intimated that this situation improved noticeably with ONG's increased familiarity with Wakefield-Edenwald.

Table 6-10 reflects some of the differences between the black and white leadership groups in the district. White leaders, as a rule, had been residents of the area for longer than their black counterparts. Wakefield-Edenwald's white leadership interacted through sets of established institutions, some of which (notably the North Bronx Democratic Club) were not within the reach of black leaders. Consequently, black leaders who were not so assimilated to the

Table 6-10
Attitude toward ONG of Wakefield-Edenwald Leaders, 1973

Race	N	Positive	Mixed	Negative	Don't Know
Black	15	10	2	2	1
White	27	12	7	4	4
Total	42	22	9	6	5
Percent		52%	21%	14%	12%

established information-influence networks naturally found ONG a welcome innovation.

As in Crown Heights and Bushwick, civic leaders who participated in a variety of organizations and did not limit their interest to a particular issue area constituted the group most favorable to ONG. Such a respondent commented: "I wear a number of hats in the community and this causes me to run into ONG all the time." The president of one of the largest civic associations in the district felt that ONG had made a discernible positive impact on the quality of service delivery. He added:

It's gotten to the point where you almost take them for granted. . . . They've given us a ready access to city agencies. It's hard to distinguish what they've done for us from what they have made easier for us to do.

Even leaders who did not give ONG a positive evaluation supported its continuation. They were pleased that a local office of the city government existed in what they regarded as "the forgotten borough." One respondent went to some length in minimizing ONG's achievements, characterizing it as another bureaucratic burden on the community, and wondering why it had never done anything for him. But when asked whether ONG should remain in Wakefield-Edenwald, he exclaimed, "Hell yes, without any doubt. I like the idea of bringing city government into the community." A more positive response could hardly have been expected from someone who was satisfied with ONG's job.

Leaders were unwilling to make many recommendations in terms of modifications for ONG. Clearly, the precise nature of its original mandate was not a matter of utmost importance for them. Seldom were references made to ONG as a management innovation. Instead, as our earlier comments indicated, most leaders looked upon ONG as a complaint service that somehow persuaded city agencies to do what they should be doing anyway. In line with this, several leaders spoke of ONG's acquiring authority over local agency directors, an idea Wakefield-Edenwald's district managers frequently disavowed. In regard to citizen participation, Wakefield-Edenwald leaders were supportive of local boards. Many, in fact, cited the need for an advisory council for ONG. However, the consensus was that local boards should be restricted to advisory status. Only a few people supported increased power for local boards, such as budget approval, broader zoning authority and/or capital budget approval.

Determining what difference ONG made to Wakefield-Edenwald demands an eye and ear for how people behave as much as a simple tabulation of successes and failures. Numerous physical reminders of what ONG did are present: Shoelace Park, a town hall housing a half-dozen or so local agency offices, and several capital budget items requested by agencies. In addition, ONG altered the views of local residents concerning how city government could be approached and their own role in working with it. Two effects were noticeable.

First, many civic leaders learned about places in city government where they could take complaints and suggestions, and they discovered how to deal with service agency bureaucrats. It no longer seemed impossible for private citizens to improve agency service delivery. Second, these people expressed a belief in the idea that only professional managers should be running service agencies. ONG's staff consistently claimed it accomplished the job it did because of its professional background. The civic leadership's agreement was most evident from its public protests when Robert House and his two deputies were fired by Mayor Beame.

The Survival of ONG

Despite ONG's success in gaining the verbal support of both the community leadership and the service cabinets, it was unable to survive intact the transition from the Lindsay to the Beame administration. The Beame administration decided, after more than a year's deliberation, to keep the cabinet structure and expand it to the rest of the city, but to eliminate the district manager's position and centralize staffing through a new Office of Neighborhood Services (ONS).[b] The history of ONG therefore raises two important political questions: Why was ONG able to generate positive response from potentially hostile elements in both the community and the city bureaucracies? And, why, if ONG had such a supportive, and presumably influential constituency, did its transformation from a device enhancing local access to city government into another remote city agency occur with little opposition?

ONG's positive endorsement by community leaders and cabinet officials can be attributed to the structure of the program, the caution with which it proceeded, and the energy of the district managers. ONG's structure developed from an assessment of previous decentralization efforts in New York and perhaps substantiated the proposition that public officials can learn from experience. Its supporters within the city government had participated in school decentralization and had learned that a decentralization policy that generated issue polarization was foredoomed. Further experience in setting up the Mayor's Urban Action Task Forces (little city halls) and Neighborhood Action Programs in some neighborhoods provided sensitivity to possible pitfalls. Three major lessons came out of the efforts of the past: (1) the need for careful management at the center; (2) the necesssity of soft-pedalling community control as a goal; and (3) the desirability of avoiding overidentification with the mayor's political ambitions.

[b]Needleman and Needleman, *Guerillas in the Bureaucracy*, assert that the role of community planner, which strongly resembles that of district manager, "contains a built-in self-destruct mechanism" (p. 295). They continue: "Ironically, it seems that through its very success, the community planning program creates the condition for its own suppression by external pressure on its parent bureaucracy" (ibid., p. 335).

The role of the central Office of Neighborhood Government was critical to the development of the neighborhood offices. ONG central constituted part of the mayor's office, and an executive order commanded the various city bureaucracies to treat directives of ONG as having the authority of the mayor. Yet, ONG avoided using this mandate to provoke conflict with city agencies and attempted, rather, to deal with the various commissioners and agency heads as diplomatically as possible. Central ONG concerned itself with monitoring information relevant to the program's interests, coordinating the efforts of the field offices, assisting the offices in developing programs, and selling the experiment to those in decision-making positions.

ONG personnel, both at the center and in the neighborhoods, clearly sought to avoid direct confrontations with bureaucrats and city officials. Although they were concerned with increasing neighborhood power, and sometimes did bring pressure on recalcitrant agency people, their rhetoric stressed ONG's role in improving service delivery. ONG, moreover, avoided becoming a real threat to the bureaucracies in part because of its very weakness. It had no command authority over agency personnel, nor did it attempt to acquire any. It did not involve itself in questions of recruitment or promotion. Its job of coordination could be viewed as an effort to enhance bureaucratic power rather than to undermine it. And while ONG did not significantly threaten the interests of the agencies as bureacratic wholes, it probably advanced the interests of many district-level officials.

The district managers in particular had to toe a thin line, as they occupied a pivotal position between community residents and bureaucrats and frequently had to act as if they were in sympathy with both. To the extent that their activities created a genuine communality of interest between the agencies and the community, their capacity to maintain the peace represented a substantive achievement. In some instances, however, it arose from their ability to frame agendas and limit information, particularly in relation to community residents who had to rely on the manager to provide them with an arena for participation.

The perception of the district managers that they should minimize any appearance of confrontation with the civil service was largely shared by community leaders. Although the managers manipulated the community to some degree, most leaders whom we interviewed also felt that strikes, boycotts, picketing, and other protest tactics were a last resort, since they tended to precipitate massive retribution—"we've gone that route and it doesn't work." Many minority leaders now had years of experience in dealing with city bureaucracies and had become accustomed to using inside channels of influence rather than outside pressure. A number occupied administrative positions themselves. In fact, what made the management of decentralization possible was the relative lack of initiative from "below"—from the neighborhoods themselves. The one district where an organized effort by community residents brought in ONG—Maspeth, Queens—had a white and politically conservative population.

Thus, there was no spectre of black power and the end of the civil service. If there had been a popular upsurge in a place like Crown Heights, ONG would have had to choose sides between bureaucracies and nonwhite community, an event that would surely have transformed managed innovation into political battleground.

ONG's tact in dealing with potential opponents extended also to political officials. Here the history of previous efforts at little city halls left its mark. Many elected officials, including councilmen and borough presidents, clearly regarded the little city halls as a ploy aimed at establishing a Lindsay political machine in the neighborhoods that was ready to provide patronage and mobilize for the next election. In order to evade accusations of this sort, ONG sought to tie itself into the administrative rather than the political structure of the city. None of the district managers had a background of political activism; they largely allied themselves with civic organizations rather than political clubs; they did not discriminate among community leaders on the basis of political affiliation; and they went out of their way to give credit to elected officials for neighborhood achievements where ONG provided staff work. Most of the elected officials in ONG districts viewed the district managers and their professional staffs as an administrative device for performing constituency duties that they themselves had been forced to neglect. The fact that the district managers usually were bureaucratic types rather than community leaders, and that none tried to parlay his office into a political career, seemed to have allayed the fears of most local officials.

A structure that placed the district manager in the pivotal position between the central office and the district, on the one hand, and the community and the cabinet on the other made the manager the key figure in the experiment. The original managers brought to this role considerable commitment to the program, a desire to innovate, and the energy to follow through on program initiatives. Their activities focused the program and caused it to elicit enthusiastic rather than merely indifferent responses from its attentive public. It was, however, precisely their position that was eliminated when the Office of Neighborhood Government became the Office of Neighborhood Services. We must therefore examine why this critical element in the program was destroyed.

The advent of a regular Democrat, Abraham Beame, to the mayoralty meant that the Democratic political clubhouse acquired a renewed importance in New York City politics. Lindsay had attained his second term of office as an independent and thus had no permanent local political organization; decentralized agencies such as ONG took on some of these linkage functions. Once Beame was elected, it would seem to many Democratic politicians that ONG's function became redundant and that the local clubhouse as the locus of community representation was preferable. The alliance the district managers had forged with local civic associations became valueless as a basis of support once influence within city government shifted to the regular Democratic organization. Moreover, the usefulness of ONG as a patronage device became increasingly obvious. Thus, even during New York City's most severe budget crisis, patronage appointments to ONG, now reconstituted as the Office of Neighborhood Services, continued.[c]

As a vehicle for representation of the interests of civic associations, ONG seemed capable of mobilizing endless demands that a city strapped for funds could not easily meet. The managers, in developing their popular base in the communities, had succeeded in translating individual complaints into more coherent policy interests that were presented through channels outside the partisan political process. In fact, this development of new modes of communication for previously excluded organizations was ONG's most important achievement. To an administration that was not sympathetic with such a goal, however, the district manager experiment would not seem worth saving.

The phasing out of the district managers did not go entirely unnoticed. *The Village Voice, New York Magazine, The New York Times*, and other citywide media condemned the attenuation of the experiment, particularly in light of the endorsement it had received from the New York State Charter Commission. In Wakefield, citizen rallies were held to protest the removal of the district manager. But the lengthy period in which ONG slowly faded away meant that the local offices ceased to function long before they were officially terminated; by the time their fate was made clear, they had lost their public.

The popularity of ONG with community leadership did not prove that ONG was necessarily a worthwhile institution. It seemingly went unnoticed by the public at large, and showing that it had a discernible impact on service delivery is difficult. Nonetheless, our findings demonstrate quite clearly a felt need on the part of community leaders for a local branch of the city government with a staff capable of responding actively to their demands. The reconstitution of ONG as the Office of Neighborhood Services did not result from the demands of neighborhood leaders, the great majority of whom favored greater administrative decentralization. It arose instead in response to pressure from partisan political organizations. While a revitalization of the party at the grass roots may indeed prove to be an equally effective means of channeling community demands, it necessarily means the limiting of access for civic leaders who find partisan activity distasteful. As of this writing, the city planned to continue the service integration functions of ONG. These, however, while popular with cabinet members meant little to the leadership stratum. And it remains to be seen whether a cabinet operating without the presence of a district manager to energize, coordinate, and follow-up will continue to function in a meaningful way.

---

[c]In an article headlined "Patronage Jobs Allotted Despite City Fiscal Crisis," *The New York Times* quoted ONS director John Carty as defending". . . the hiring of politically connected workers in the office. 'Our job is to work with communities,' he said. 'And we need workers with ties to those communities,' " See *The New York Times*, June 13, 1975.

7

**Local Operating Officials'
Responses to the
Experiment: Service
Integration, Agency-
Community Relations,
and Overall Attitudes**

John M. Boyle

Introduction

The effectiveness of the experimental ONG program depended on the response of local operating officials in the many city agencies working in the districts. In this chapter, we consider four issues.

1. Since the demonstration program did not succeed in increasing the autonomy of local officials through "command decentralization," as noted in earlier chapters, was it possible to improve service integration within the existing administrative structure? This issue will be explored by examining the extent to which the two variables, autonomy and awareness of interdependence, are independently related to amount of interagency communication at the local level.

2. Did the presence of a district manager or a district cabinet increase the field administrators' awareness of interdependence and, hence, their stake in interagency cooperation?

3. Did the experiment improve the level of service integration? More specifically, was exposure to a district manager or a district cabinet associated with more frequent contact among field services, better cooperation, fewer interagency problems, and more efficient conflict resolution, as reported by field administrators?

4. Did the experiment improve the relationships of operating agencies to the community and its organizations, as reported by local officials?

5. Did local officials themselves perceive the ONG as contributing to interagency and agency-community communication and cooperation?

6. What was the overall attitude of local officials toward the ONG program?

The issues raised in the first three questions can be represented by a somewhat more detailed section of the overall "flow chart" of the theoretical effects of the program (Figure 7-1), which is based on Figure 1-1 in Chapter 1. A similar chart could be made for the effects on agency-community relationships.

Research Methods

The purpose of this chapter is to measure the effect of two components of the experiment, the district manager and the district service cabinet, on local service integration. How does one measure the interaction that occurs among urban

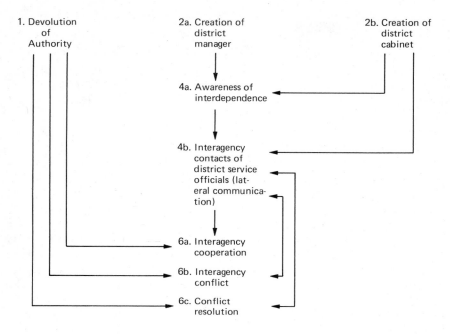

Figure 7-1. Hypothetical Effects of Experimental Program on District Service Officials' Attitudes and Behavior.

field services? The most desirable method would be for outside observers to count the number of interactions between agencies, and categorize their outcomes, over an extended period of time. Given the number of field offices that we would have had to observe to achieve a representative sample and time frame, such an approach was not feasible. Therefore, we used a survey of local field administrators to report on the actual behavior of their offices and the relationships between their offices and other city agencies. By asking the sanitation district superintendent how often his office is in contact with the Police Department, rather than actually logging the number of contacts ourselves, we give up some measure of accuracy. By asking him to characterize the degree of cooperation and of conflict in that relationship, we rely on the field official's judgment rather than use "objective" standards applied by outside observers. However, we did standardize the questions asked of everyone and have no reason to suspect any particular bias in the reporting that would affect the relationships analyzed here. Moreover, the survey approach allows us to elicit perceptions as well as behavior that is relevant to service integration. We can find out how important the field official considers interagency contacts and cooperation, and how this attitude relates to his behavior.

In conducting the survey, one of our first concerns was drawing a sample that would reflect the impact of the experiment on urban field administration. We selected the district-level administrator of urban field services (e.g., precinct commander in police, district superintendent in sanitation, and so forth) since this was the level in the city administration at which the experiment was primarily aimed. The two questions that we had to answer in constructing the sample were from which *agencies* and which *districts* should these officials be drawn.

We decided to exclude borough-level agencies from our sample, despite their occasional interaction with the experiment, because it would be impossible to measure differences across districts. We also excluded the powerless coordinating offices that were represented on some district cabinets because they had no control over operating services, the target of service integration. These exclusions left us with fifteen major field services that operated at or near the district level. These were: Police Department; Department of Sanitation; Office of Code Enforcement (Housing); Department of Parks; Department of Recreation; Department of Highways; Fire Department; Bureau of Child Health; Bureau of Community Health; Youth Services Agency; Office of Income Maintenance (IM); Office of Community Services (OCS); elementary schools, high schools, and community schools. (Note that the cabinets that we studied added the Fire Department and representatives of the community school board to the list of original participating agencies; usually the high school principal in the area also participated.)

We were unable to include three of these fifteen district-level services because we could not obtain agency permission to interview their field officials: parks, recreation, and highways departments. Since these three agencies were involved in the experiment, their exclusion from the sample may weaken some of the correlations between experimental influence and indicators of service integration. We do, however, have measures of the frequency and quality of interaction reported by the *other* field services with these three. Only in the case of the highways department does there appear to be any interesting relations.

There may also be some question about our inclusion of three agencies that were not directly represented on the district service cabinets: Office of Code Enforcement, Bureau of Child Health, and elementary schools. We included these three for two principal reasons. First, since our purpose was to measure the effect of the experiment on service integration in urban field administration, we felt that all district-level services should be included in the sample. If the designers of the experiment failed to include these agencies on the service cabinets and if this failure to include them reduced the impact of service integration, this problem is one of experiment design, not evaluation design. Second, the program did seek to influence some of these offices through intermediary coordinating offices, such as the area housing director in the case of the Office of Code Enforcement and the district health managers in the case of the Bureau of Child Health. Since we do not measure the influence of the experiment on the powerless intermediary, it is important to measure the influence that he is supposedly passing through to the operating service itself. In order to allay any fears that this decision might be biasing the findings of the evaluation, we have run all of the tests of associations reported in this chapter with these three agencies excluded. The exclusion of these three agencies has only minimal effects on the correlations—that is, by slightly increasing them for the most part, while reducing sample size. It has no effect on the direction of the associations. Consequently, we have left them in the analysis.

In our analysis, we attempt to evaluate the hypothesis advanced in Chapter 2, that the district manager, not the district service cabinet, had the most effect on local service integration. As Heginbotham has noted, New York City was actually involved in two separate experiments. In the first districts selected for the program, service integration was dealt with through both a district manager and a district service cabinet. These were the fully experimental districts. Later, a number of "expansion districts" were added to the experiment. These expansion districts possessed district service cabinets but no district managers. We can measure the effects of these two different elements in the experiment by creating two dichotomous variables. "District manager-non-district manager" cuts our sample into two groups: those field officials who operated in a fully experimental district with a district manager and those who were not in fully experimental districts. "District service cabinet-non-district service cabinet" cuts our sample into two different groups: those field officials who operated in a district with a district service cabinet, whether a fully experimental or expansion district, and those who did not have a service cabinet in their district. The test of the hypothesis that the district manager was more important in local service integration than the district service cabinet is accomplished by comparing the strength of the associations between the two measures of experimental influence and the indicators of service integration. (It should, however, be kept in mind that the district manager had been operating for two years, while the "Cabinet only" version had been in operation only one year.)

The choice of districts was dictated by the two variables with which we were most concerned: exposure to the district manager and exposure to the district service cabinet. We needed to include field administrators in our sample who were exposed to the district manager form of the experiment. Consequently, we selected the first four fully experimental districts of the experiment, which had been in operation since early 1972. We matched these districts with three expansion districts and three control districts, which approximated the social-demographic composition of the fully experimental districts. The expansion districts had had operating district service cabinets since early 1973. The number of control districts was cut from three to two after we entered the field, because we learned that one of the control districts although not classified as an expansion district had had an operating service cabinet for two years. It was reclassified as an expansion district in the analysis. The selection of twelve agencies and ten districts for our sample produced a target sample of one hundred and twenty respondents. We completed one hundred and seven interviews, which represents a completion rate of 94 percent of the filled positions. The survey was conducted in the summer and fall of 1974, when the fully experimental districts had been in operation for two years and the expansion districts for at least one year.

Given the number of associations that are tested in this chapter, it is impossible to illustrate more than a few in tabular form. For the most part, we have simply reported the association between two variables as a correlation coefficient.[a]

Throughout the chapter we use causal language—that is, we speak of "explaining" variation in dependent variables and of "effects" or "impacts" of some variables on others. Since the data reported in this chapter were all gathered at one point in time, and since we are not comparing groups that were assigned on a strictly random basis to be exposed or not exposed to the "independent variables," this language is an overstatement of what we actually know, which is simply that these variables are correlated with each other at the time of the study. We cannot be sure of the *direction* of the causation in the relationship, for instance, between frequency of lateral communication and awareness of interdependence between agencies; a plausible case can be made that the causation goes either way or both ways at once. In comparing manager-non-manager and cabinet-non-cabinet districts, we also have the problem that we don't know whether the districts all started off identically in interagency relationships or whether for some reason these differed beforehand between experimental and nonexperimental districts. The experimental programs were not randomly assigned, and in any case there are so few districts that random or historical differences might have existed already.

What will be reported in this chapter, therefore, are correlations that *may* indicate causal relationships or "impacts" of variables. The causal language is used for two reasons. First, it is convenient, compared to attaching a set of qualifications to each statement of a relationship. Second, we believe (although we cannot prove) that it is realistic and that the alternative hypotheses that the causation went in the opposite direction (from what we have labelled the dependent to the independent variable) or that the correlation is due to some other common factor is less likely than the causal interpretation we propose. However, the reader may want to substitute the language "is associated with" for the language of "had the effect of" in this chapter.

---

[a]We have reported the aggregate variables in terms of Pearson's product moment correlation since there is some justification using this statistic in these cases and the reader is more likely to be familiar with it. Most of our data, however, do not exhibit the minimal properties that make this a suitable statistic. Since these variables are measured as ordinal variables with a limited number of categories (four or five), Kendall's tau seems the most appropriate choice. Tau b will be reported for square tables, while tau c will be reported for rectangular tables.

Does Service Integration Require Greater Local Autonomy?

The most prominent element in the 1971 statement of the Program for the Decentralized Administration of Municipal Services in New York City Communities was the delegation of authority and responsibility to the district level of the city's administrative structure. This element was also one part of the program design that was never effectively implemented (see Chapter 2, pp. 35-36). The district managers were left to improve the level of service integration and quality of public service delivery within the existing framework of city administration. The importance attributed to command decentralization by the Lindsay administration in this program was based upon the assumption that it was critical to local service integration:

Even more detrimental to the functioning of effective government, local agency officers have been unable to work fully with each other at the district level. Each must seek approval for his individual actions from his own superiors in the chain of command before proceeding in joint actions with other city agencies.[1]

When it became clear that no major command decentralization was going to occur within agencies, the Office of Neighborhood Government had to proceed on the assumption that it was possible to improve local service integration without it. Before we can evaluate the impact of the experiment on local service integration, it is critical that we know which assumption was more accurate. If the mayor was correct in the initial assumption that greater delegation of authority was the sine qua non for local service integration, then the program would have to fail. But if the later assumption that significant improvements in local service integration could be accomplished without greater delegation was valid, then further evaluation of the successes and failures of the program is necessary. Indeed, an experiment in local service integration without a greatly increased delegation of authority may be of more value to other potential users than an experiment with such decentralization. Other governmental units are far more likely to undertake innovations that do not require major restructuring of administrative authority.

We can test these assumptions with the data collected in the survey of field administrators by using the existing variations in autonomy between different departments and districts and seeing whether or not they relate to integrative behaviors of the officials such as direct communication with other agencies at the local level.

The field officials whom we interviewed were asked to report the relationships between their office and other city agencies operating in their districts. One prerequisite for service integration is lateral communication with other agencies. If further command decentralization is necessary before local officials can deal directly with their opposite numbers in other field services on matters of mutual concern, then we should find the degree of centralization in their agency closely related to the frequency of lateral communications. If, on the other hand, field officials are already able to deal with each other when they perceive a mutual concern, then we would expect that the perception of mutual concern would be the prime determinant of interagency behavior.

We ran a series of multiple regressions of various indicators of these two types of variables on the frequency of lateral communications. The final regression, which is reported in Table 7-1, includes only those measures that contribute independently to the explanation of the frequency of lateral communications.

We found that the perception of mutual concerns with other field services, particularly the extent and importance attributed to interdependence with other agencies, explains most of the variance in lateral communications. The extent of perceived overlapping responsibilities and concerns with other field services accounts directly for more than 40 percent of the variance in lateral communications. The frequency of perceived problems-conflicts with other agencies and the importance attributed to the most salient issue of interdependence also have an effect. Four structural variables indicating local autonomy do have some effect

Table 7-1

Multiple Regression of Indicators of Awareness of Interdependence and Autonomy on Frequency of Interagency Communication

Independent Variables	Dependent Variable: Frequency of Interagency Communication	
	Correlation Coefficient	Standardized Regression Coefficient
Awareness of interdependence:		
Extent of overlapping responsibilities	.736	.650
Frequency of problems	.438	.161
Importance of interdependence	.093	−.173
Autonomy vs. centralization:		
Span of control (large span implies autonomy)	−.200	−.149
Specificity of review (high specificity implies centralization)	−.224	−.109
Decision-making autonomy	.412	.172
Capital budget influence (implies autonomy)	.325	.098

Note: $R^2 = .69$.

$F = 28.26$ with 7 and 89 degrees of freedom.

on the frequency of lateral communications: (1) span of control; (2) specificity of review; (3) decision-making autonomy; and (4) influence over capital budget items affecting the respondent's district.

The findings in Table 7-1 suggest that the autonomy granted to the local official does have some impact on his willingness or ability to engage in joint activities with other officials. The one structural variable that does not operate in the expected direction is "span of control"; the greater the span of control of the superior to whom the local official reports (and hence presumably the less close the supervision), the *less* likely the local official is to contact other field administrators. We have no explanation for this result, but can point out that span of control does not have any significant relationship one way or the other with the other three indicators of autonomy, which do correlate positively with one another.

It is likely that autonomy acts as a screen between the local official's perception of mutual concerns with other agencies and contacts with these agencies. Consequently, further decentralization should improve the quality of interagency interactions at the district level. But the major determinant of those interactions is not the extent of autonomy allowed to the local official but, rather, his perception of a mutual concern with other agencies.

This explanation suggests that the failure of the command decentralization element in the program for service integration had some negative effects on the potential of the experiment, but that this failure would not preclude the improvement of local service integration. On the contrary, it seems likely that the greatest potential for improved service integration lies within the current powers of the field official. If the local official perceives a need for coordination with other local agencies—that is, an area of shared concern or a mutual problem—he is likely to act on that need. Consequently, the job of the district manager-district service cabinet would be to promote awareness of a need for coordination, to direct that need to its proper locus, and to manage the cooperation and conflict resolution evoked by the need.

This assumption was the one under which the district manager experiment evolved. The district service cabinet was a forum where mutual concerns among the line officials in the district could emerge, be discussed, and their resolution be planned and executed. The district manager was appointed to manage the complex task of identifying common problems in service delivery, establishing their priority among the local service chiefs, planning and directing their solution, and managing the problems they might evoke.

The strategies adopted by the various district managers often differed, as Chapter 2 has discussed in some detail. But all were aimed at the same objectives: to identify areas of common concern between the local operating officials; to find some basis for securing their cooperation on these issues; to direct and support their efforts to provide the necessary services or solve the particular problem; and to manage the problems among the local service officials that emerged from the process. Despite the many approaches to the selection of problems and the method of securing cooperation, the basic task of the manager remained the same. Given the nature of interdependence in urban field administration, it was possible for the experiment to have improved local service integration in some measure.

Is the Presence of the Manager or the Cabinet Related to Awareness of the Need for Service Integration?

The Program for the Decentralized Administration of Municipal Services in New York City Communities in both its district manager and district service cabinet forms sought to improve the quality of urban services by improving coordination among the provider agencies. It was, as Heginbotham points out in Chapter 2, the imposition of a geographic framework on a functionally organized administration. Unlike territorial administration in European and colonial systems, however, the areal integrator was given no authority to coordinate the functional agencies. The district manager was not a prefect. He was given the responsibility for improving local coordination, but not the power to compel it. Both the district manager and the district cabinet depended on the interest of the local official in interagency coordination and his willingness to provide the necessary cooperation to achieve it. Consequently, the experiment sought to enhance the local official's perception of the need to cooperate with other agencies to improve local service delivery.

In order to measure the perceived need for interagency cooperation and the importance attributed to it by local field administrators, we asked our respondents a number of questions about their dependence upon the cooperation of other city agencies. First, we asked them whether any areas that fell within the responsibilities or general concern of their office also fell within the responsibilities or general concern of other city agencies. To root their answers in an operational reality, we asked them to provide examples. We found that virtually every field administrator in our sample could identify at least one area of operational responsibility that his office shared with another city agency. Most could provide a number of such cases. To achieve a more sensitive measurement of the extent of perceived interdependence with other city agencies, we asked them to specify the extent of their office's interdependence with each of the other sixteen major urban field services. Would they say that their office shared many areas of overlapping responsibility and common concern, some areas, few areas or no areas with the Police Department? What about the Department of Sanitation? And, so on for each of the sixteen other agencies. We found that, in general, the field administrators reported intense interdependence (many areas of overlapping responsibilities) with only one or two other agencies. Less-intense interdependence, however, was reported with many of the other field services.

We also asked our respondents whether their office ever needed the assistance of each of the sixteen other field services. We found that virtually all of the field administrators reported needing the assistance of at least one other agency. Most of the sample reported needing the assistance of at least five other field services. The number of agencies from whom the field administrator needed assistance was somewhat less than the number with whom interdependence was reported. The explanation for this difference was volunteered by several respondents with the comment: "They need us but we really don't need any assistance from them."

We also used a number of indicators to attempt to measure the importance the field administrators attributed to interdependence for the operation of their office. Two of these indicators sought to measure the official's perception of the loss and gain to his office's performance that could be attributed to interagency cooperation. First, we asked the respondents what percentage of the total performance of their office would be lost, if any, if other agencies stopped cooperating with them? Second, we asked them if cooperation from other agencies improved from what it was now to the best that could reasonably be expected, how much improvement would they expect in their office's performance? Only a handful of the field administrators felt that the behavior of other agencies had no actual or potential impact on the performance of their office. Most felt that the cooperation received from other agencies had a substantial effect on the total performance of their own office.

These findings suggest that not only does substantial operational interdependence exist among urban field services at the district level, but that the local field administrators are well aware of this interdependence. This awareness of interdependence with other city agencies has a number of behavioral ramifications. We have already noted that a very strong relationship exists between the perception of overlapping responsibilities with other city agencies and the extent of lateral communications with other agencies. Furthermore, we would expect that the perceived need for coordination under conditions of operational interdependence would provide a good basis for cooperative integration. The question that we now raise is what effect the experiment had on these perceptions of interdependence. Did the field official's experience in a district service cabinet district increase his sense of interdependence with other agencies? Was the district manager able to expand the number of agencies or issues on which the field administrator perceives a need for assistance? This was certainly one of the major objectives of the experiment, since the willingness of the local official to cooperate in service integration should be tied to his perception of its advantage for the performance of his office.

To evaluate the effects of the experiment on the perception of local field administrators of the extent and importance of interdependence with other agencies, we tested the association between exposure to both the district manager (fully experimental versus all other districts) and the district service cabinet (fully experimental and expansion districts versus control districts) and four indicators of perceived interdependence (Table 7-2).[b] The first two indicators of extent of interdependence are aggregate measures constructed across the respondent's answers for each of the sixteen other field services. The second two measures simply indicate the percentage of office performance the respondent attributed to the loss or gain in cooperation from other city agencies.

We find no significant association between the exposure of the field official to either experimental variable and any of the measures of the official's perception of his office's interdependence with other city agencies. If the district manager or district service cabinet increased the field official's sense of interdependence with other city agencies, we should have found a positive association. (Not only are there no significant positive associations but there is no pattern of generally positive relationships.)

We can also investigate the effect of the experiment on the field administrators' perception of their relationships with particular city agencies. As we noted earlier, the overlap and assistance variables reported in Table 7-2 are aggregate scores across sixteen other agencies. We can disaggregate these scores to see whether or not either of the experimental variables had any effect on either the official's perception of the extent of overlapping responsibilities with a particular agency or his perception of whether the assistance of that agency is needed. Although the experiment clearly had no effect on the general level of

Table 7-2
Perceived Interdependence with Other City Agencies

Dependent Variables	Experimental Variables		
	District Manager	District Cabinet	N
Extent of overlapping responsibilities	.0392	−.0097	107
Number of agencies whose assistance is needed	−.0141	−.0324	107
Potential loss without cooperation	−.0266	−.0880	102
Potential gain with cooperation	−.0360	.1086	99

Note: Figures show Pearson's r for relation of four measures of field officials' perceptions of interdependence with other agencies and the two experimental variables: presence or absence of a District Manager, and presence or absence of a District Cabinet. No relationships significant at .05 level.

[b]An ordinal measure of experimental influence was also used in the initial analysis, along with the two dichotomous measures. It is not reported here because few associations appear to be monotonic across the three categories: fully experimental, expansion, and control.

interdependence with other city agencies, it may have had some effect in regard to selected agencies. A positive relationship would indicate a higher sense of interdependence with an agency associated with the experiment. A negative relationship would indicate a lower sense of interdependence with an agency associated with the experiment.

We find a limited experimental association with the level of perceived interdependence with four agencies: housing police, fire, sewers, and the Department of Community Development (DCD) (Table 7-3). Respondents from both fully experimental and expansion districts reported more overlapping responsibilities and more need for cooperation from the Department of Community Development than did respondents from control districts. At the same

Table 7-3
Perceived Interdependence with Specific City Agencies

Agency	Correlation of Manager and Cabinet with Perceived Overlap of Own Agency with Various Other Agencies		Correlation of Manager and Cabinet with Perceived Need for Assistance of Own Agency from Other Agencies	
	District Manager	District Cabinet	District Manager	District Cabinet
Police				
Sanitation				
Housing police		−.1855[b]		−.1699[a]
Fire			.1499	
Recreation				
Highways				
Traffic				
Sewers				.1627[a]
Code enforcement				
Health				
Hospitals				
Schools				
DCD		.1464[a]		.1485
Youth services				
Income maintenance				
Community services				

Note: Figures show Kendall's tau for relation of two measures of field officials' perceptions of interdependence with specific agencies and the two experimental variables. "District Manager" dichotomizes sample into fully experimental districts versus expansion and control districts. "District Cabinet" dichotomizes sample into fully experimental plus expansion districts versus control. Relationships are reported only when they exceed .1000.

[a]Significant at .05 level.

[b]Significant at .01 level.

time, the cabinet influence appears to have reduced the extent of overlapping responsibilities and need for assistance from housing police. This pattern makes a good deal of sense. The Department of Community Development was a nontraditional field service that was represented on the district service cabinets, while the housing police were not represented on the cabinets. We also find that exposure to the district service cabinet is associated with a need for assistance from the sewers department, another nontraditional district level service that was represented on the district service cabinet. We also find a slight relationship between the exposure to the district manager form of the experiment and a more frequent perception of the need for assistance from the Fire Department. The local fire batallion chiefs were not originally part of the experimental design, but were brought on to cabinets by the district managers in fully experimental districts.

These findings suggest that the experiment was successful in increasing and/or expanding the local official's sense of interdependence with certain select agencies. Two factors help to explain why these effects on the perception of interdependence with particular agencies do not produce an association between exposure to the experiment and the general level of perceived interdependence. First, the experiment produced only relatively slight changes in the degree of perceived interdependence with only a few of the many field services. Second, the direction of experimental influence was both positive and negative, depending on the agency. Exposure to the cabinet apparently increased perceptions of interdependence with some of the agencies represented on the cabinet (fire, community development, sewers) while it reduced the sense of interdependence with some of those agencies not represented on the cabinet (housing police). Individual correlations operating in opposite directions tend to reduce the aggregate effect on the experiment. By examination of the interagency relations on an agency-by-agency basis, we do find that the experiment had at least a limited effect on improving the field administrator's perception of the stakes of cooperation with a limited number of agencies. This effect is not limited to the fully experimental districts; but is found in all districts with service cabinets.

The perception of mutual advantage in interagency cooperation, indicated by the awareness of interdependence and the need for assistance, is one source of the willingness of field administrators to cooperate in service integration. Another potential source of interagency cooperation is the perception that coordinating interagency relations is a part of the local field official's function. Like "community relations" this is a broader definition of the field administrator's responsibilities than the narrow functional specialization of his agency duties. Presumably, normative pressures that develop from a sense of responsibility for interagency coordination might produce cooperative behavior from an official, even in a situation where no mutual advantage is perceived.

We did not ask the field administrators whether they felt a responsibility for interagency coordination. Rather, we asked our respondents to describe the more important functions of their position. A little less than one-fifth of the sample volunteered "coordinating interagency relations" as one of the more important functions of their job. We would expect that the experiment would have had some effect on this perception. The relationship would not necessarily be very strong since this was a volunteered response. Nevertheless, we would expect to find a positive relationship between exposure to the experiment and a sense of responsibility for local interagency coordination. We present the relationship in tabular form in Table 7-4, which allows us to see the difference in effect across the three types of districts.

Our findings suggest that the experiment did have an effect on the local official's perception of interagency coordination as a function of his job. But the effect of the experiment on this attitude appears to have existed only in the fully experimental districts, where a district manager as well as a district service cabinet existed. Almost one-quarter of the respondents from fully experimental districts volunteered "interagency coordination" as an important function of their position, as compared to less than 10 percent in control districts. In expansion districts, however, very little difference exists between the local official's perception of interagency coordination as a job function and that of officials in control districts. Only 12 percent of the respondents from expansion districts volunteered this function, as compared to 9 percent in control districts. It seems evident that this perception was a product of exposure to the district manager form of the experiment, rather than exposure to the district service cabinet alone.

Our findings suggest that the experiment did have a limited but positive effect on the field administrator's perception of interdependence with other field services and his sense of responsibility for interagency coordination. Both of these effects should have increased the willingness of local personnel to

Table 7-4

Officials' Perceptions of Interagency Coordination as Important Function of their Job (Volunteered)

Type of District	Percent Mentioning Interagency Coordination as Important Function	Total N
Fully Experimental	23.8	42
Expansion	11.9	42
Control	9.1	22
Total	16.0	106

Note: $\text{Tau}_c = .1324$
Significance = .04

cooperate in service integration at the district level. The weaker form of the experiment, the district service cabinet in the expansion district, had no effect on the officials' sense of responsibility for interagency coordination. It did, however, have a modest effect on the perceived interdependence with certain other agencies in the district.

The only question that remains to be answered about the impact of the experiment on attitudes supportive of a cooperative service integration program is why the effects were so limited. We suspect that the answer lies in the existing level of perceived interdependence with other city agencies. The program began with the implicit assumption that local service chiefs were unaware of the actual and potential interdependence between their agencies and other local field services. The district manager and district service cabinets were supposed to make the service chiefs aware of this interdependence and to use this awareness as the basis for securing cooperation. We find, however, that most local officials were not only aware of interdependence with other agencies, but reported both intense and extensive relationships with other agencies. So, one of the reasons for the limited effect of the experiment on perceptions of interdependence is the fact that such perceptions were well developed in field administration prior to the inception of the experiment. This factor was not detrimental to the experiment. On the contrary, a basis for local cooperation in mutual advantage was already established prior to the experiment. Rather than devote most of their limited resources to establishing a basis for cooperation, the managers and cabinets were able to begin exploiting that resource for service integration almost immediately.

Is the Experiment Related to the Perceived Levels of Service Integration?

The primary purpose of the program was to improve the quality of interaction among urban field services in the delivery of public services. In the words of Mayor Lindsay:

At present, on too many problems and in too many communities, the most effective integration of service delivery between the different departments is carried out by elected officials or local groups, who are too often the only local 'bridge' between two or more operating city departments on a particular problem. The creation of District Service Cabinets establishes a governmental mechanism to fill this vacuum and will significantly ease this pressure on local groups.[2]

A number of facets to interagency interaction directly impact on service integration. First, no integration of operating city agencies for service delivery is possible without communications between those agencies. Second, problems or conflicts that develop between city agencies can reduce the quality of both individual and joint service delivery. Third, the degree of cooperation that exists between city agencies will determine to a substantial degree the quality of joint service delivery efforts. Fourth, the ease with which problems or conflicts can be resolved between the field services mitigates the impact of interagency problems on the quality of service delivery. These four aspects of interagency interaction are the basis of the presumed effects of service integration on the quality of urban service delivery.

The district manager experiment was designed to improve interagency interaction in these areas. The local service chiefs met at least monthly in the district service cabinets and more frequently in the issue-oriented task forces. This interaction provided at least a minimal opportunity for interagency communications. The district managers reported their belief that these formal arrangements for interagency communications would stimulate further informal communications; the increased communications should lead to improvements in service integration. The institutionalization of interagency integration through the district service cabinet should reduce the number of conflicts between city agencies, at least in the long run, and improve the ease with which these problems could be resolved in the short run. The district managers also believed that using the cabinet and task force meetings to involve the local agency chiefs with one another at both professional and personal levels would improve the quality of their cooperation.

These considerations produced four hypotheses about the effects of the experiment on local service integration. First, it should increase communications. Second, it should reduce conflict. Third, it should improve cooperation. Fourth, it should improve satisfaction with the quality of conflict resolution.

In order to establish measures of communications, conflict, cooperation, and conflict resolution, we asked the respondents about their office's relations with each of the sixteen other field services in each of these areas. 1. "How often, over the past year, has your office contacted each of the following agencies: never, infrequently, monthly, weekly, or daily?" 2. "How willing do you find each of the following agencies to cooperate with your office when you need their assistance: very willing, somewhat willing, sometimes willing and sometimes resistant, somewhat resistant, very resistant?" 3. "In general, how often would you say that some sort of problem or difficulty occurs between your office and each of the following agencies: often, sometimes, rarely, never?" 4. "When problems and difficulties have occurred between your office and each of the following agencies, how often were the difficulties resolved to your satisfaction: always, often, sometimes, rarely or never?" The question of the degree of cooperation was limited to those agencies from whom assistance was needed, while the question of conflict resolution was limited to those agencies where a problem was reported. In constructing the aggregate variable from individual agency responses in these two areas, the number of agencies where the quality of cooperation or conflict resolution was reported was used as the denominator.

In considering the effects of the experiment on the general level of communications, conflict, cooperation and conflict resolution, we find no confirmation of any of our four hypotheses (Table 7-5). In only one case, however, do we fail to find a significant association between exposure to the experiment and the indicator of service integration. Exposure to the experiment apparently had no effect on the frequency of interagency communications. This finding is not very surprising, since we already know that the perception of interdependence tends to determine lateral communications among field services and exposure to the experiment had little effect on perceptions of interdependence, at the aggregate level. What is surprising is that there are significant associations between exposure to the experiment and the general levels of conflict, cooperation, and conflict resolution. Our hypotheses are not confirmed because these associations do not exist in the predicted direction. Exposure to the district service cabinet produced a positive association with the frequency of conflict and negative associations with the quality of cooperation and conflict resolution. Thus, officials in fully experimental and expansion districts reported more problems, poorer cooperation, and less-satisfactory conflict resolution than did officials from control districts.

The findings in Table 7-5 could be interpreted to mean that rather than improving service integration in urban field administration, the district manager-district service cabinet experiment actually impaired service integration. If we assume that the associations are indicators of a causal relationship then it would appear that the presence of a district service cabinet, both in fully experimental and expansion districts, would increase interagency problems, reduce cooperation, and impair conflict resolution. Before making any such assumption, we must first analyze the individual relationships between experimental exposure and the level of service integration with individual field services that compose

Table 7-5
Level of Service Integration Among Field Services

	District Manager	District Cabinet
Frequency of contact	.0136	.0066
Frequency of problem-conflict	−.0020	.1646[a]
Degree of cooperation	.0933	−.2034[a]
Degree of conflict resolution	−.0525	−.1595[a]

Note: Figures show Pearson's *r* for relation of four measures of service integration among field services and the two experimental variables: presence or absence of a District Manager, and presence or absence of a District Cabinet.

[a]Significant at .05 level.

these aggregate variables. Perhaps this analysis will help in our understanding of these seemingly inexplicable findings.

When we consider the association between the experiment and the frequency of communications with particular agencies, we find little difference between the individual agency relationships and those of the aggregate variable (Table 7-6). We find only two marginal relationships between exposure to the experiment and the frequency of communications with city agencies. Exposure to the cabinet is negatively associated with the frequency of communications with the housing police. This finding is apparently a product of the fact that housing police were not represented on district service cabinets. Consequently, field officials in fully experimental and expansion districts contacted housing police less often than did those in control districts. We also find a negative relationship between the strict managerial form of the experiment and the frequency of contact with the Office of Income Maintenance. The explanation

Table 7-6
Level of Service Integration with Specific City Agencies

Agency	Correlation of Manager and Cabinet with Frequency of Contact with other Agencies		Correlation of Manager and Cabinet with Frequency of Problems with other Agencies	
	District Manager	District Cabinet	District Manager	District Cabinet
Police				
Sanitation				
Housing police		−.1604[a]		
Fire			.1583[a]	.1304[a]
Recreation				
Highways			.1377[a]	
Traffic				
Sewers			.1149[a]	.1153[a]
Code enforcement				
Health				.1290[a]
Schools				
DCD				
Youth services				
Income maintenance	−.1405		−.1475[a]	
Community services				

Note: Figures show Kendall's tau for relation of two measures of reported relationships with other agencies with the two experimental variables, presence or absence of a District Manager, and presence or absence of a District Cabinet. Only relationships greater than .1000 are reported.

[a]Significant at .05 level.

for this relationship is less obvious. Clearly, however, neither the district service cabinet nor the district manager increased the general frequency of interagency communications at the district level. As in the case of the perception of interdependence, this finding is probably a product of the rather well-developed pattern of interagency relations that predated the experiment. The monthly cabinet meetings had little effect on the rather frequent lateral communications among field offices.

On the other hand, we find a rather strong pattern of relationships between exposure to the experiment and the frequency of problems and conflicts in urban field administration. The pattern of individual relationships, however, indicates several interesting items that are lost in the aggregate measure. First, the fully experimental form of the experiment with the district managers has a number of significant associations with problems-conflict in individual agencies that are not reflected in the aggregate measure. The reason is that some of the associations are positive, while others are negative. Consequently, they wipe out any correlation on the aggregate measure that assumes unidirectional effect. In reality, more problems with the Fire Department, for instance, were found in fully experimental districts than other districts, while fewer problems with the Office of Income Maintenance were found in the fully experimental districts than in others. The effect of the more general form of the experiment, the district service cabinet, was one directional. Consequently, the correlation between exposure to the district service cabinet and the frequency of problems with individual agencies is also found in the general measure.

The second interesting finding in the relationship between exposure to the experiment and the frequency of problems with individual agencies relates to those agencies where positive associations exist. As in the case of the perception of interdependence, most of these are the agencies that are normally less involved in district-level field administration. The highways and sewers departments were brought into interaction with other field services at the district level through the district service cabinet. The Fire Department, although it is outstationed at the district level, normally would not interact with most other field services at this level. Its presence on the service cabinet, particularly in fully experimental districts, apparently affects its relations with other agencies. The only field service that exhibits a positive relationship between experimental exposure and more frequent problems-conflicts and does not fit this "outsider" pattern is the health department.

Does this pattern of association suggest that the experiment increased the level of conflict in urban field administration? Not necessarily. It may be of particular importance that the higher frequency of reported problems seems to be descriptive of relationships with "outsiders" to traditional district-level interactions. That field officials discovered problems and difficulties with agencies with whom they had little in common in the past is probably a normal part of the process of emerging interagency relationships. Moreover, awareness of interagency problems is also a reflection of a perception of interdependence. (There is a correlation of .3816 between extent of overlapping responsibilities and frequency of conflict.) An increased awareness of problems with another agency may have been positive advantage to the program, since it increased the stakes of cooperation for those agencies that recognized new areas of interdependence.

We find a similar pattern in the individual agency relations that comprise the aggregate indicators of the *quality of cooperation* and *conflict resolution* (Table 7-7). Once again, we find that the general effect of the fully experimental district, alone, on the general measures is wiped out by individual correlations

Table 7-7
Quality of Cooperation and Conflict Resolution with Specific City Agencies

Agency	Correlation of Manager and Cabinet with Perceived Cooperation from other Agencies		Cooperation of Manager and Cabinet with Conflict Resolution with other Agencies	
	District Manager	District Cabinet	District Manager	District Cabinet
Police				
Sanitation				
Housing police		−.1944	.4444	
Fire		−.1533		
Parks				
Recreation			−.5185[a]	
Highways		−.2045		−.2188[a]
Traffic				
Sewers				
Code enforcement	−.2663			
Health		−.1663[a]		
Hospitals	.1658			
Schools	−.1828	−.2213[a]	−.4012[b]	
DCD				
Youth services	.1578	−.1894		−.2344[a]
Income maintenance				
Community services		−.1893[a]		

Note: Figures show Kendall's tau for relation of perceived cooperation with other agencies and of conflict resolution with other agencies and the two experimental variables, presence or absence of a District Manager and presence or absence of a District Cabinet.

Number of cases is considerably smaller than total sample size because the cooperation and conflict resolution questions were only asked with regard to other agencies from whom assistance was needed or with which problems were reported.

[a]Significant at .05 level.

[b]Significant at .01 level.

operating in opposite directions. In fully experimental districts, we find poorer cooperation from the Office of Code Enforcement and the public schools than we do in other districts. But we find better cooperation from hospitals and the Youth Services Agency than we find in expansion and control districts. We find better conflict resolution with housing police in the fully experimental districts than we find in other districts, but we find poorer conflict resolution with the recreation department and public schools. In the more general form of the experiment, the district service cabinet, all positive associations disappear. We find only poorer cooperation and poorer conflict resolution than exists in the control districts. This one directional effect of the experiment allows a correlation to develop between exposure to the district cabinet and the general measures of cooperation and conflict resolution.

What does this pattern of relationships mean? It seems likely that some measure of the poorer cooperation and conflict resolution reported in experimental districts is a product of higher expectations and more active integrative programs than in control districts. But this answer is not enough to explain the universally negative relationships produced by the cabinet form of the experiment, while the addition of the district manager produces some positive relationships. This seems to make sense only if we assume that the cabinet had one effect and the manager had another, different effect. Consequently, we offer the following hypothesis: The interaction produced among urban field services by district service activities increases awareness of interdependence, perceptions of assistance needed from other agencies, awareness of problems with other agencies, and greater expectations for service integration. Awareness of interdependence and problems that need solution, by itself, however, need not produce the desired results. There may be no mutual advantage in a particular case of interdependence, leading one agency to demand cooperation while the other is reluctant to provide it. The more complex problems of interdependence that agencies attempt to deal with in new structures of service integration may prove less tractable than easier problems to which earlier attempts were limited. Higher expectations about cooperation from another agency may limit the types of outcomes that field administrators consider as satisfactory after they gain some experience in the district cabinet.

Any number of explanations for the negative impact of exposure to the district service cabinet are possible. The only likely explanation of the occasionally positive impacts of the more-developed form of the experiment with the district managers is that the manager mitigates some of these "growing pains" of service integration. He can try to find a basis of mutual advantage among field officials who have to cooperate to solve a problem. He can try to limit service integration projects to those with the highest potential for success. He can soothe the often difficult service relationships that develop from the different perspectives of the individual agencies. We know that all of these strategies were undertaken by district managers in the fully experimental districts. The positive associations between the official's exposure to this form of the experiment and cooperation and conflict resolution with some agencies would seem to reflect this effect.

We do have one final indicator with which to test this hypothesis. We asked the field administrators in our sample about the general quality of issue resolution in areas of operational interdependence with other city agencies. We asked them, "In general, do you feel that problems and issues that occur in areas of overlapping responsibility or mutual concern between your office and other city agencies are dealt with much better, somewhat better, about the same, somewhat worse or much worse than issues that come up within areas of exclusive responsibility?" Almost one-quarter of the respondents from fully experimental districts felt that interagency issues were dealt with better than single agency issues (Table 7-8). Only 8 percent of the officials from expansion districts felt that interagency issues were dealt with better than single agency issues, which is slightly less than the 10 percent from control districts. At the other end of the spectrum, only a quarter of the officials from the fully experimental districts felt that interagency issues were dealt with any worse than single agency issues. Almost half of the respondents from both expansion (46.1 percent) and control (47.6 percent) districts felt that interagency issues were dealt with worse than single agency issues. This seems to suggest that the district service cabinet, per se, had no effect on the quality of resolution of interagency issues. There are only minimal differences between the quality of resolution of interagency issues in expansion districts and control districts. There is a substantial difference between both of these types of districts and the fully experimental district with its district manager. The presence of a district

Table 7-8
Reported Quality of Resolution of Interagency Issues

In Comparison to Issues of Exclusive Responsibility, Interagency Issues are Resolved:	Type of District (Exposure to Experiment)			
	Fully Experimental Percent	Expansion Percent	Control Percent	Total Percent
Much better	15.4	5.1	9.5	10.1
Somewhat better	7.7	2.6	0.0	4.0
About the same	51.3	46.2	42.9	47.5
Somewhat worse	20.5	33.3	38.1	29.3
Much worse	5.1	12.8	9.5	9.1
	100.0	100.0	100.0	100.0
Total Number	39	39	21	99

Note: $Tau_c = .1928$
Significance = .01

manager in a district is associated with reports of better resolution of inter-agency issues. This tends to support our hypothesis that the efforts of a district manager are an integral part of a successful service integration program.

Is the Experiment Related to Community-Agency Relations?

The local urban service delivery network is not limited to the public agencies of city government but also embraces many non-public provider agencies. This is clearly the case in the fields of public health and social services where the efforts of private organizations complement and supplement the work of city depart-ments. It is also true in the environmental and regulatory services where the efficient delivery of these services is often aided or supplemented by the activities of community organizations. The field administrator in New York City is well aware of his dependence upon the cooperation of individuals and organizations outside of the bureaucracy for the effective performance of his work. For instance, 96 percent of our respondents reported that the attitudes of the community towards their office had an impact on the performance of their work. Moreover, 83 percent of the sample could cite at least one example in the past year when they needed the active support of community organizations on a concrete issue.

The field administrators' examples of issues requiring community support can be classified into four general categories: political, volunteer, information, and general compliance. Political needs involved community organizations in getting additional program resources or in protecting and maintaining the present level in the district. These ranged from getting additional office space or equipment for the field office to active demonstrations against the closing of a local office or the abandonment of an existing program. Volunteer services included a range of more traditional supplementary services provided by community organizations, such as auxiliary police, clean-up campaigns, sponsor-ing health fairs, and so forth. Community organizations were also needed as a means for gaining needed information about the community and a means for disseminating information to the community. These organizations were those that could provide information about the availability of local resources and community priorities in service delivery, as well as informing the public about changes in eligibility requirements or whom to contact about specific problems. Finally, the needs of some field administrators for community activity seemed to be limited to simple compliance with their operating procedures, such as putting out refuse at the proper time, providing access for building inspections, refraining from calling in false alarms, and not causing disturbances in welfare centers.

The district manager experiment was created with a strong sense of the importance of community organization in the process of local service delivery.

Nevertheless, the formal experiment was not designed to involve any close contact with community organizations. Rather, the development of a district-level administrative system was viewed as the necessary precondition for a system with greater community influence over service delivery. But, as Hegin-botham has pointed out in Chapter 2, the district managers soon developed a strong community component as a modification of the original design of the experiment. They had two strong incentives for creating linkages to local community organizations that were eventually formalized in community advisory boards. First, community organizations were local service providers who should be integrated into a local service delivery system for maximum efficiency. If the volunteer services of private organizations could be coordinated with the services of public agencies, one might expect a substantial improvement in the quality of urban service delivery. Second, there were strong political reasons for securing community support for the program. Initially, community organization support was sought to neutralize potential hostility to the program. But after 1973, when it became clear that the program would become a political football, the managers clearly sought to counterbalance the political threat to the program through community support.

These circumstances lead us to certain expectations about the impact of the program on field administrators' attitudes and behavior towards community organizations in their districts. First, one would expect that the experiment would have an impact on some aspects of the relationship between the field administrator and community organizations in his district. Second, one would expect that the managerial rather than the cabinet form of the experiment would have a greater impact. Third, one would expect at least some politization effect.

All three of these expectations are borne out when we study the relationship between exposure to the experiment and the field administrator's need for community support (Table 7-9). A substantial and significant association exists between exposure to the managerial form of the experiment and need for political support from the community. More surprisingly, there is a slight negative association with the need for volunteer services from the community. This finding is hardly evidence of a major politicization of the field administration, but it does suggest that the experiment had an impact on how local bureaucrats perceive community organizations. They were somewhat less likely to view the organizations in the traditional paternalistic manner or as being capable of little more than maintaining litter baskets and sponsoring educational drives. Rather, the experiment appears to have demonstrated some of the more substantial benefits that good community relations can provide: a new fire house, more office space, additional equipment, protection of an endangered school or health station.

It is also clear from our findings that the increased importance attributed by field administrators to political support from community organizations is

Table 7-9
Field Administrator's Perceived Dependence on Community Support

Type of Community Support	District Manager	District Cabinet
Political	.2140[a]	.0293
Volunteer	−.1399	−.1272
Information	−.0577	.0973
Compliance	−.0812	−.0239

Note: Figures show Kendall's tau for relation of perceived dependence on four types of community support with the two experimental variables, presence or absence of a District Manager, and presence or absence of a District Cabinet.

[a]Significant at .01 level.

exclusively a product of the fully experimental form of the program. This is consonant with the development of the community orientation in the experiment due to managerial activities. By itself, the district service cabinet does not lead to a more activist perception of community resources as the district manager form apparently does. There does appear to be some evidence, however, that the volunteer service need declines with exposure to the cabinet form just as it does with exposure to the fully experimental form.

The impact of the experiment on the frequency of contact with particular community organizations and the importance the field administrator attributes to maintaining good relations with them is limited but suggestive (Tables 7-10 and 7-11). Exposure to the experiment increased the importance attributed to good relationships with local political clubs but reduced the importance of poverty organizations. It also increased the frequency of contact with political clubs and ethnic organizations, while it reduced contact with tenant associations and poverty organizations. It would appear that this is further evidence that the experiment increased the local field administrator's awareness of the political aspect of his work, since the most substantial effect of experimental exposure was to increase the importance attributed to the political club and the frequency of contact with it.

Local Officials Direct Perceptions of Effects of ONG

The most important consumer of the services directly provided by the district manager-district service cabinet experiment was the local field administrator. His evaluation of the usefulness of the program is a necessary and important part of the general evaluation of the impact of the program on local service integration. In many ways, however, this element is the most problematic measure of the

Table 7-10

Perceived Importance of Good Working Relations with Community Organizations

Type of Organization	District Manager	Service Cabinet
Block association		
Tenant association		
PTA		
Church group		
Senior citizen group		
Community council		
Ethnic organization		
Political club	.1366	
Poverty organization	−.1017	
Civic association		

Note: Figures show Kendall's tau for relation of perceived importance of good working relations with various types of community organizations and the two experimental variables, presence or absence of a District Manager, and presence or absence of a District Cabinet.

All correlations of .10 or higher are reported; no correlations are significant at .05 level.

Table 7-11

Contact with Community Organizations

Type of Organization	District Manager	Service Cabinet
Block association		
Tenant association	−.1352	
PTA		
Church group		
Senior citizen group		
Community council		
Ethnic organization	.1020	.1027
Political club	.1279	
Poverty organization	−.1439	
Civic association		

Note: Figures show Kendall's tau for relation of contact with various types of community organization and the two experimental variables, presence or absence of a District Manager, and presence or absence of a District Cabinet.

All correlations of .10 or higher are reported; no correlations are significant at the .05 level.

impact of the experiment. What we are measuring is not clear when 50 percent of the field administrators in the district rank the district manager-district service cabinet as "very useful" in interagency communications. We may be recording the field administrator's enjoyment of the monthly service cabinet meeting or his affection for the manager or his unwillingness to criticize a fellow civil servant. Even if the evaluation is strictly based on his perception of the program's usefulness in interagency communications, what the evaluation means is still not clear. Does it mean a quantitative increase in communications or a qualitative improvement in the level of communications? Perhaps it reflects only a single instance of better communications that particularly impressed the respondent. Consequently, we are skeptical about the utility of such a measure when presented outside of the context of other indicators of program impact.

On the other hand, this more general measure is very useful as a supplementary indicator of program impact. For one thing, it may include a number of factors that were unmeasured by our earlier indicators. Although we find no evidence that the experiment had any impact on increasing the frequency of communications between field services, the experiment could have facilitated a few very important contacts. Likewise, in the areas of cooperation and conflict resolution, the experiment could easily have put off cooperation and conflict resolution on a number of minor matters while it improved the resolution of some very critical issues. For these reasons, considering the consumers' evaluation of the program is important as is considering that of the researcher who is concerned with "harder" measures of program impact.

During the course of the interviews, the respondents were asked to rank the importance of a number of offices, both within and outside of their agency, in improving service integration between their office and other parties in their district. These questions were asked about the four areas of service integration that we have been most concerned with: (1) "promoting or facilitating communications between your office and other city agencies in this district"; (2) "promoting cooperation on matters of overlapping responsibility between your office and other city agencies in the district"; (3) "resolving conflicts between your office and other city agencies in this district"; and (4) "establishing and maintaining good working relationships between your office and community groups in this district." To avoid response set, we asked each of these questions at different points in the interview schedule. Respondents were asked to rank the importance of each of the offices mentioned—including the district manager-district service cabinet—as very important, somewhat important, little importance or no importance.

Three-quarters of the field administrators serving fully experimental districts, half of those in expansion districts, and less than 10 percent of those in control districts attributed at least minimal importance to the district manager-district service cabinet in promoting or facilitating interagency communications in their districts (Table 7-12).[c] Two things appear fairly clear in the contingency table. First, field administrators from fully experimental districts gave a relatively satisfactory evaluation to the experiment with 40 percent of them

[c]The two cases attributing importance to the experiment in a control district both represent contamination. In one case the respondent had just transferred from an experimental district, while the other had been in contact with an Office of Neighborhood Government from an adjoining district.

Table 7-12

Evaluation of Importance of District Manager-District Cabinet in Interagency Communications

| | Type of District (Exposure to Experiment) | | | |
	Fully Experimental (Percent)	Expansion (Percent)	Control (Percent)	Total (Percent)
Very Important	39.5	11.9	0.0	20.6
Somewhat Important	25.6	21.4	9.1	20.6
Little Importance	9.3	16.7	0.0	10.3
No Importance	25.6	50.0	90.9	48.6
	100.0	100.0	100.0	100.0
Total Number	43	42	22	107

Note: Tau_c = .4447

Significance = .0001

ranking it as very important in interagency communications. Second, there is a substantial difference in the evaluation given to the experiment in fully experimental and expansion districts. Only 12 percent of the respondents from expansion districts considered the experiment as very important, as compared to 40 percent in fully experimental districts. Likewise, fully half of the field administrators in expansion districts considered the experiment to have no importance in local interagency communications, as compared to one-quarter of the respondents in fully experimental districts. We can only conclude that while an expansion approach to service integration was considered an improvement over no approach, the fully experimental model with the district manager was thought to be considerably more important in facilitating interagency communications at the district level.

In the area of promoting cooperation among city agencies on matters of overlapping responsibility, we find a very similar pattern (Table 7-13). In every category, there is at least a slight decline in the importance attributed to the experiment in interagency cooperation as compared to interagency communications. Another 5 percent of the field administrators from fully experimental districts and 10 percent of those from expansion districts considered the experiment to have no importance in this process. Although there is a general decline in the importance of the experiment, it is more pronounced in expansion districts than fully experimental, which thus increases the distinction between the two approaches. Thirty-seven (37) percent of the service chiefs from fully experimental districts considered the experiment to be very important in interagency cooperation as compared to 2 percent of those from expansion districts; 70 percent of those from manager districts felt the experiment had some importance as compared to 40 percent from expansion districts.

Table 7-13

Evaluation of Importance of District Manager-District Cabinet in Interagency Cooperation

	Type of District (Exposure to Experiment)			
	Fully Experimental (Percent)	Expansion (Percent)	Control (Percent)	Total (Percent)
Very Important	37.2	2.4	4.5	16.8
Somewhat Important	20.9	28.6	0.0	19.6
Little Importance	11.6	9.5	0.0	8.4
No Importance	30.2	59.5	95.5	55.1
	100.0	100.0	100.0	100.0
Total Number	43	42	22	107

Note: Tau_c = .4365

Significance = .0001

It would appear that the importance of the district manager-district service cabinet steadily declines with the difficulty of the service integration task (Table 7-14). Sixty-four (64) percent of the agency chiefs from fully experimental districts still considered the experiment as having some importance in resolving conflicts, but only 28 percent of them ranked it as very important in the process. Once again, the decline in experimental importance is even steeper in expansion districts than in fully experimental ones. Only 32 percent of those from expansion districts attributed any importance to the district service cabinet in resolving interagency conflicts. Fully half of those attributing any importance to the experiment in expansion districts only considered it of little importance.

The experiment is ranked as somewhat less important in community relations than in interagency communications, approximately equally useful as in interagency cooperation, and more important than in conflict resolution between city agencies. All in all, field administrators from fully experimental districts tend to attribute a great deal of importance to the district manager and district service cabinet in establishing and maintaining good community relations between the respondents' office and groups in the community (Table 7-15). Thirty-seven (37) percent consider the experiment as very important in this area. Once again, we find that there is a very strong distinction between the two forms of the experiment with much less importance being attributed to the expansion form which lacks a district manager.

These findings suggest that the consumers of the program's services, the local service chiefs of city agencies, considered the experiment did make substantial contributions to all of the major areas of service integration: communications, cooperation, conflict resolution, and community relations. The impact of the experiment seems weakest in the area of conflict resolution, but it

Table 7-14

Evaluation of Importance of District Manager-District Cabinet in Interagency Conflict Resolution

| | Type of District (Exposure to Experiment) | | | |
	Fully Experimental (Percent)	Expansion (Percent)	Control (Percent)	Total (Percent)
Very Important	27.8	5.3	0.0	12.8
Somewhat Important	25.0	10.5	0.0	13.8
Little Importance	11.1	15.8	5.0	11.7
No Importance	36.1	68.4	95.0	61.7
	100.0	100.0	100.0	100.0
Total Number	36	38	20	94

Note: Tau_c = .4091

Significance = .0001

Table 7-15

Evaluation of Importance of District Manager-District Cabinet in Community Relations

| | Type of District (Exposure to Experiment) | | | |
	Fully Experimental (Percent)	Expansion (Percent)	Control (Percent)	Total (Percent)
Very Important	37.2	11.9	4.5	20.6
Somewhat Important	18.6	14.3	4.5	14.0
Little Importance	7.0	14.3	0.0	8.4
No Importance	37.2	59.5	90.0	57.0
	100.0	100.0	100.0	100.0
Total Number	43	42	22	107

Note: Tau_c = .3556

Significance = .0001

is substantial even there. This is especially significant since those interviewed were not given any indication that an evaluation of the Office of Neighborhood Government was any part of the purpose of the survey. Indeed, these were the only four questions about the experiment that were asked and they were in the context of many other local offices. Consequently, there is no reason to believe that the field administrators did not give us their actual perceptions of the importance of the experiment in these matters.

The most interesting finding drawn from these questions is the importance attributed to the experiment. It tends to counterbalance the weak or negative effects that our "harder" indicators report. Two conclusions seem possible. First, the experiment may have produced a sense of its own importance that is not strongly reflected in actual changes in behavior. Second, the experiment may have produced improvements in service integration that alter the quality of service integration but not the general level, as measured by our indicators.

The second important finding of the consumer's evaluation is the really substantial difference in experimental importance in service integration processes between fully experimental and expansion districts. There appears to be strong support for the creation of a district manager along with the district service cabinet in order to produce a substantial impact. A difference is clearly produced by the district service cabinet itself, but it is not nearly as extensive as that produced by the fully experimental form.

A Survey of District Service Cabinet
Members Attitudes toward ONG[d]

Another source of information on the attitude of local service officials to ONG was a separate survey that covered all local officials who actually participated in district cabinets in the five original ONG districts (Bushwick, Crown Heights, Rockaways, Wakefield-Edenwald, and Washington Heights) and was carried out in 1973 in conjunction with the community leadership survey. The results of this survey are along the same lines as the responses to the questions on the importance of ONG in promoting contact, cooperation, and communication reported in the previous section.

Despite the possible drawbacks that might have accrued to the local service agency chiefs from the intervention of a new layer of bureaucracy, cabinet members turned out to be even more enthusiastic than the community leadership group in their endorsement of the experiment. Almost 80 percent of these cabinet members rated the ONG district manager as effective or very effective (Table 7-16). An even higher percentage (83 percent) called the monthly cabinet meetings useful or very useful (Table 7-17). Although the districts differ in social composition and physical amenities, the responses were almost equally favorable, with the exception of Washington Heights, where as we have seen the district manager encountered serious problems in dealing with pre-existing mechanisms of neighborhood representation that had hope to control the appointment of the manager. Even there, the majority of the cabinet members gave the manager and the cabinet meetings a positive evaluation.

The extent of unanimity of registered support for ONG might be the result of several factors. First, of course, it could simply be a product of the effectiveness of the organization and its genuine contribution to municipal

[d]This section was written by Susan Fainstein and Fran La Spina Clark and is based on data collected by the leadership study component of the project.

Table 7-16
Rating of District Manager in Five Districts by Cabinet Members, 1973

	Rockaways (J. Langsam) (N) (%)	Crown Heights (R. Duhan) (N) (%)	Bushwick (S. Jones) (N) (%)	Washington Heights (D. Middleton) (N) (%)	Wakefield-Edenwald (R. House) (N) (%)	Total N	Total %
Very effective	6 } 88	7 } 79	10 } 75	3 } 64	9 } 82	35	43 } 79
Effective	8	8	2	6	5	29	36
Hardly effective	0	0	1	0	0	1	1
Ineffective	0	0	0	2	0	2	2
Detrimental	1	0	0	1	0	2	2
No response[a]	1	4	3	2	3	13	16
Total	16	19	16	14	17	82	100

Note: The question read as follows: "If you were to rate the performance of the district manager on a five-point scale, according to his impact on the quality of city services in the district, where would you place him?"

[a]No response indicates the respondent was either too unfamiliar with the style or personality of the district manager or unwilling to rate him/her.

Table 7-17
Rating of ONG District Service Cabinets in Five Districts by Cabinet Members, 1973

Response	Rockaways (N)	(%)	Crown Heights (N)	(%)	Bushwick (N)	(%)	Washington Heights (N)	(%)	Wakefield-Edenwald (N)	(%)	Total N	Total %
Very useful	6 ⎫	94	6 ⎫	95	8 ⎫	81	5 ⎫	57	12 ⎫	82	37	45 ⎫ 83
Useful	9 ⎭		12 ⎭		5 ⎭		3 ⎭		2 ⎭		31	38 ⎭
Hardly useful	0		0		2		0		1		3	4
Not useful	0		0		0		3		0		3	4
Detrimental	0		0		0		1		0		1	1
No response	1		1		1		2		2		7	9
Total	16		19		16		14		17		82	100

Note: The question was worded as follows: "Have you attended ONG Cabinet meetings? If yes, how would you rate their usefulness?"

administration. Before ONG, these neighborhoods lacked any direct contact with the general city administration and no agency whatever existed to act as a communications link among the various city services that operated within them. ONG provided a link between the public and the city, and within the city among the various service providers. The district managers went out of their way to perform these communication functions tactfully. To the extent that service fragmentation and lack of responsiveness were the result of insufficient information and lack of institutional structure, ONG offered a method of overcoming these barriers where none other existed.

A second reason for the positive response of agency officials could be the boost to their morale provided by the existence of local institutions. While a sanitation district supervisor might be very far down the hierarchy of the Environmental Protection Agency, he was the equivalent of a commissioner within the district; as a member of the service cabinet he was treated in the latter status. The effort made by the district managers to urge on and praise the cabinet officials contributed to the heightened morale. Many individuals within the agency pyramids found that their efforts went unrecognized by superiors far from the scene. ONG offered encouragement and the assurance that job performance would not pass unnoticed.

Third, it is possible that the support expressed for ONG by our respondents represents a cautious bureaucratic reaction to the interview situation. Agency personnel might have felt that they could stay out of trouble by giving interviewers the responses that they wanted to hear. We have no assurance that this was not so in the case of those who simply stated that ONG was effective. Many of the representatives interviewed, however, were highly enthusiastic about the experiment. Moreover, one would expect that those who thought the move toward decentralization was harmful or threatening to agency prerogatives would take the opportunity offered by the research to attempt to block the agency's future.

The support evidenced for ONG among cabinet members meant that although ONG had to rely primarily on voluntary agency compliance, it could draw on a reservoir of good will in seeking cooperation. Whether increased authority for ONG and the community that it represented, if it resulted in either control over agency budgets or evaluation power over agency personnel, would have produced greater disaffection remains an open question. Most of the agency representatives expressed satisfaction with ONG as it was. In the words of a Wakefield cabinet official: "ONG should remain as it is—much has been accomplished. In the beginning I had my doubts as to what could be done, but I have totally reversed my thinking." While proposals for modifications pointed in the direction of greater local power, the implementation of such measures, especially if it proceeded rapidly or passed beyond increased community "input" to community oversight, would probably have provoked a negative reaction.

In all five areas studied, suggestions for possible improvements in ONG were strikingly similar, although there were variations on a number of themes. Those most commonly repeated among all five cabinets follow:

Coterminous boundaries for all involved government agencies;
Guidelines for cabinet members to follow in their dealings with ONG:
Definition of the limit of the district manager's authority;
A full-time, impartial district manager, knowledgeable of, but not necessarily a resident of the neighborhood and familiar with workings of city government;
Increased citizen participation on the advisory level;
Continuity of the ONG concept, which includes expansion to more controversial neighborhoods;
Increased budgetary responsibility on the local level.

In general, cabinet members wanted to feel free to enter into local projects without fear of supervisory reprimand. ONG, they maintained, could not hope to be effective without total commitment on the part of city administrators; those in a position of power should allow their local offices the flexibility to perform for the good of the neighborhood, not for the good of the agency.

Conclusions

What do we conclude from the data presented in the preceding pages about the impact of the district manager experiment on service integration among the components of New York City's local service delivery system? The most basic question that we set out to answer is whether or not the experiment improved the quality of interagency coordination. Our evidence indicates that there was no perceived general improvement in the level of service integration in experimental districts, as compared to control districts. There were only slight improvements in integration with regard to a few specific agencies—those least likely to have developed informal integration through frequent district-level interaction. But this finding has to be qualified by the consumer's evaluation of the experiment's impact on the processes of service integration. A substantial number of field administrators felt that the district manager-district service cabinet played a very important role in these processes. A few even considered the experimental mechanism the most important office in the coordinative processes between their office and other city agencies, more important than even their offices or the heirarchy of their agencies. Furthermore, a survey of Cabinet Members in five fully experimental districts showed strongly favorable attitudes toward the ONG program and support for its continuation.
Effects of structural change on interagency coordination ideally should be

studied by observing the behavior of officials in typical operating situations with and without the structural change. In practice, we have tried to use the district-level officials as informants as to:

Their attitudes toward interagency coordination and community-agency cooperation (awareness of their importance);

Their self-reported behavior in very simple terms—contacts with other agencies and with community groups;

Their perceptions of very complex relationships—degrees of cooperation and conflict between agencies and with the community.

Several methodological limitations on these data should be noted:

1. We have rather few interviews in the pure control areas, and in general the differences have to be rather large to achieve statistical significance. However, this factor does not help to explain the frequency of negative effects; we do not even find a "pattern" of positive but nonsignificant effects.

2. Respondents in experimental areas include both those directly participating in cabinets and those whose agency is represented through a "coordinator," whose effectiveness we know to be low. We are also lacking data from the parks, highways, and recreation agencies, which we know were actively involved in the experimental program. This factor weakens the possibility of positive effects being found, although again it does not explain why negative effects turn up.

3. Evaluations of interagency relationships may be influenced by changing levels of *expectations* as well as by differences in the actual performance of the agencies in dealing with one another; changed expectations may counterbalance or even outweight objective improvements. This factor is a possibility to be considered, but it is also a typical excuse for getting null or negative results on an evaluation; ways need to be found to measure expectations to test this argument.

4. The experimental period covered the *early stages* of trying to develop new interagency relationships, which may have been a period of strain that would work itself out in the longer run. On the other hand, the district managers deliberately tried to pick acceptable projects for interagency cooperation, precisely to avoid this problem.

A possible substantive explanation of the seemingly inconsistent findings is that the experiment achieved in each district a few examples of successful interagency cooperation (in particular "projects" as described earlier), which impressed local service chiefs with the *potential utility* of the mechanism. At the same time, the political limitations under which the program labored, the shortness of time it operated, and the declining level of political support that it enjoyed in its second year prevented it from substantially altering the *general levels of integration* between the agencies, which are what the officials responded to in the evaluations obtained in the comparative study. The program therefore may have failed to produce practical results on a large scale, while it succeeded as a "demonstration" to the local officials of the potentials of interagency cooperation.

Furthermore, if the perceptions of local officials can be taken as accurate, a good deal of interagency interaction already existed in all districts, whether or not a district manager or district cabinet was established. The existence of informal integrative channels reduces the possibilities for dramatic improvements in service integration through creation of a formal mechanism. The nature of the already-existing interactions needs to be taken into account in designing new mechanisms to improve service delivery.

Would there have been a significant positive effect on perceptions of interagency and agency-community cooperation, if the program had been given more high-level support and more time to develop and implement its projects? Or would a more sustained and serious effort to coordinate services at the district level have produced more conflict between the priorities and procedures of the different specialized agencies and between the agencies and the community? The significant *negative* effects of the "cabinet only" version of the program on some relationships, and the occasional significant negative effects of the full district manager version, suggest that there is a potential for conflict and complaint as well as cooperation in these efforts to integrate services. Confirming this suggestion is something we cannot do on the basis of the district manager-district cabinet experiment as implemented during the Lindsay administration. The fact that the city charter was revised by referendum in November 1975 to mandate a citywide district manager program along the lines of the ONG suggests that we may have the opportunity to find out.

If we were being asked for advice on how to design the best possible district government program, we would suggest at least two things.

First, the program should encompass all the field administrators within the district. The ONG program omitted certain agencies such as code enforcement and child health, due to the weakness of the "coordinator" role created to represent fundamentally separate branches of the superagencies in health, housing, and human resources. Had the experiment brought all the chiefs of operating services in the district into the cabinet, we believe that it would have had a more favorable impact.

A second question of importance is the relative merits of the full-time district manager versus the cabinet only approaches to service integration. The cabinet only approach appears to be substantially less effective in local service integration than does the fully experimental approach. Indeed, there does not even seem to be an ordinal relationship between the two forms of the experiment. Without the district manager, the district service cabinet may have a negative effect on measures of local service integration. It would appear that the sine qua non of cooperative integration among local service chiefs is a person who can exploit the potentials of the district service cabinet by finding common interests and mutual objectives and reducing the frictions produced by inter-action through soothing techniques. The district service cabinet, which brings together city officials with different goals, responsibilities, interests, powers and status, has as much potential for hostility as cooperation. The success of coordinative integration rests on the ability of the district manager to increase one while reducing the other.

Notes

1. Mayor John Lindsay, *Program for the Decentralized Administration of Municipal Services in New York City Communities*, Office of the Mayor, City of New York, December 1971, (reproduced as Appendix to this volume) p. 265.

2. Ibid., p. 267.

8

The Quality of Big-City Life in 1972

Theresa F. Rogers
and
Nathalie S. Friedman

Introduction

Underlying most proposals for urban reform is the assumption that our cities are in a state of crisis. Rising crime and addiction rates, congested and inadequate mass transit systems, littered streets and polluted air, poor schools, and deteriorating housing characterize big city-life. Further, it is assumed that municipal service agencies charged with alleviating these problems are cumbersome, fragmented, overlapping, and unresponsive to citizen needs. Urban residents, it is said, feel powerless and are becoming increasingly alienated.

Negative judgments about the "facts" of the urban condition are hardly new. During the 1920s and 30s, urban sociologists of the "Chicago School" decried the inability of cities to provide a healthy social life, and the tendency of urban living to create segmentalized personalities and social disorganization.[1] The 1950s and early 60s countered these pessimistic analyses by calling attention to the vitality of urban communal structures and the positive individual and group adaptations to high-rise living, but in the late 1960s, cities again came under attack as centers of poverty, segregation, and inadequate municipal services.[2]

Periodic polls and surveys confirm that citizen alienation has been increasing. In 1973, for example, 37 percent of city residents in a national sample felt that compared to five years ago they had less confidence in local (city) government.[3] Similarly, in 1975, a Harris poll found only 14 percent of a national sample of urban residents expressing confidence in municipal government, compared with 43 percent a decade previously.[4]

Most surveys of citizen attitudes toward government, however, are national in scope, and "government" generally refers either to the federal system or to "government in general." Relatively unexplored are citizens' perceptions of *city* government and the factors underlying varying levels of alienation and powerlessness. Proponents of decentralization, including those responsible for New York City's experiment in administrative decentralization, assume a high level of citizen alienation and argue that such alienation will be substantially reduced through implementation of a decentralization program. The reasoning is fairly straightforward: Decentralization, by reducing organizational scale and devolving authority to the local level will make government more responsive to neighborhood needs, ensure improvement in the delivery of services, and increase citizen participation in neighborhood institutions.[5] At question, however, are the actual

185

level of alienation among New Yorkers and whether such alienation is, in fact, related to the problems of city life and to frustrations with municipal service agencies.

The assumption that New Yorkers have become increasingly alienated from city government and more dissatisfied with the quality of service delivery was explicit in the proposal, announced by Mayor Lindsay in June 1970, to create a new system of neighborhood government throughout the city for the purpose of:

Improving the delivery of municipal services by making city agencies more responsive and accountable at the neighborhood level, and

reducing the alienation and distance that citizens feel toward a remote city government.[6]

Lindsay's proposal goes on to note:

Proliferation of governmental bodies and offices at the local level has . . . led to duplication and, at times, self-defeating confusion. A *citizen concerned about a local issue* often cannot be sure where to go to have his voice heard; a *citizen with a complaint* against a city agency sometimes finds it hard to pinpoint which governmental official is responsible for serving that area; a *community suffering from inadequate services* still has no certain means of exposing the failure of government.

It is this fragmentation of citizen involvement in governmental decision-making *and the frustration of citizen ability to make government accountable* that we want to change now [emphasis added].[7]

The answer in part was the Office of Neighborhood Government (ONG). The survey component of the study was designed to pick up whatever measurable impact there might be on individuals from this experimental program by interviewing samples of the public at the beginning of the program and after two years.

It should be noted that many discussions of "the public" in relation to government are really concerned with what we have in this study called "local community leaders," or with a small stratum of active community participants who belong to organizations, contact public officials, and involve themselves in politics. In the present study we are trying to look at all three groups: local community leaders (through the leadership study), active participants in community affairs (a group that may be pulled out of the general public survey), and the great majority of the public that is relatively inactive, except for periodic voting, and that includes many nonvoters (the bulk of the general public sample). When we refer to "the public" we mean our representative sample of the entire adult population of the districts studied.[a]

---

[a]The districts selected for the ONG experimental program (and consequently, the control areas) include neither the city's wealthier white neighborhoods nor the hard-core, low-income ghetto areas. See Table 1-3.

Samples of 240 residents were drawn in each of four experimental districts and three socioeconomically similar "control" districts: a total of 1,683 people. They were selected in clusters of 10 on each of 24 blocks in each of the seven districts. The first wave of interviews was conducted in the summer of 1972, after the ONG program had been underway just six months. In the spring and summer of 1974 the original respondents who could be located were reinterviewed, including those who had moved out of their neighborhood but still lived in the New York-New Jersey metropolitan area.[b]

Respondents were questioned about problems of living in New York City, neighborhood ties and satisfactions, evaluations of city services, political activities and attitudes, and personal and family characteristics such as income, ethnicity, education, and family composition. In addition, 1970 census data were collected for each census tract containing a sample block. This information on racial composition, median family income, and other tract characteristics provided a context within which individual perceptions and attitudes could be assessed.

The 1972 base-line data provide information about the setting in which the program began: the public's problems, their evaluation of city services, their knowledge of where to go with complaints, and their general attitudes toward city government in different types of neighborhoods. In this way it is possible to discern whether the assumptions underlying the inception of the program—namely, that New Yorkers are frustrated with the municipal service delivery system and alienated in general from city government—are in fact valid. At the same time, the analysis of citizen problems and complaints in different neighborhood settings can serve to point up what kinds of demands a local service system would confront.

Who Wants to Live in the City?

It is an old American tradition to negate city living and to extol the virtues of country life. Over the years, national polls have documented the consistent tendency of residents of large cities to opt ideally for life in a suburb, small town, or farm. A 1971 Gallup poll, for example, showed that among residents of cities of one million or larger, more than seven out of ten would choose noncity living if they could.[8]

Citizen complaints and their attitudes toward *city* government in our study must similarly be seen in the context of an overall negative attitude toward the city, and a strong preference for living outside the city. Fully 63 percent of the residents of our seven neighborhoods, for example, would like to live in the

---

[b]At the same time, we also interviewed the "inmovers"—people who had moved into the housing units which first-wave respondents had vacated. The interview completion rate in 1974 for both the original respondents and the inmovers was 75 percent for those respondents who could be located. In sixty-three instances, where an original respondent had died, moved away, or could not be questioned for some reason, a substitute member of the household was interviewed.

suburbs, a small town, or on a farm; only 37 percent prefer city living.[c] Couple with this the finding that 54 percent of the respondents in 1972 expressed the desire to *move* from their particular neighborhood and, in fact, 30 percent of them actually did move between 1972 and 1974. While New York City is in some way "very much alive," a majority of respondents would rather not be living there.[9] Even among those who express a desire to stay in the neighborhood, or who give the neighborhood a relatively high rating, the *ideal* is suburban or small town living. With this information as background then, we examine the problems of city living, how citizens rate municipal services, and what their attitudes are toward city government.

Problems of Urban Residents

The respondents in the study were presented with a list of twenty items and asked whether each was a great problem, somewhat of a problem, or no problem at all for them or their families. Table 8-1 presents their responses to the full array of problems. Clearly, in 1972 fear of crime was troubling New Yorkers more than any other problem. In fact, only about one in four reported that fear of crime was no problem at all for them or their families. Concern about safety is hardly a new phenomenon in large cities, including New York, as a recent account of the last four decades of the nineteenth century notes:

New York was known as the world's center of crime, earning the title with an extravagant toll of murders, assaults and robberies. . . . "Each day" as a New York weekly observed, "we see ghastly records of crime . . . murder seems to have run riot and each citizen asks . . . who is safe?"[10]

Environmental issues occupied second place among respondents' problems. Both air pollution and dirty streets and sidewalks were reported by one in four as great problems, and about two in five said these constituted somewhat of a problem. Six items—lack of play areas for children, housing, addicts in the neighborhood, low pay or not enough money to live on, noise, and lack of good schools—were cited by between 15 and 20 percent of the sample as great problems. Three of these, however (addicts, low pay, and noise), seemed to be critical, since close to one-third said they were somewhat of a problem and only about half reported them to be no problem at all. The remaining eleven items were of lower priority. For more than two-thirds of the sample these constituted no problem at all, and only between 5 and 11 percent cited them as great problems. However, these items should not be dismissed as being of no concern

[c]The preference for noncity living was highest among the blacks in the sample (70 percent), while 38 percent of the whites and 44 percent of the Hispanics opted ideally for residence in the city.

Table 8-1
Problems of Residents of the Seven Districts, 1972

Problem	Great Problem (Percent)	Somewhat of a Problem (Percent)	No Problem at All (Percent)	N
Fear of crime	35	39	27	1683
Dirty air or pollution	25	40	35	1677
Dirty streets and sidewalks	25	36	39	1681
Lack of play areas for children	20	24	56	880[a]
Housing	19	21	61	1681
Drug addicts	18	31	51	1673
Low pay	18	33	50	1681
Noise	17	30	53	1683
Lack of good schools	15	19	67	871[a]
Lack of teenage recreation	11	20	68	1662
Lack of parks	10	22	68	1680
Cheating or overcharging	10	24	65	1671
Lack of adult recreation	9	19	71	1676
Childcare	8	12	81	863[a]
Unemployment or layoff	7	12	81	1678
Fires	6	16	78	1683
Teenage gangs	6	20	75	1672
Lack of good medical care	5	13	81	1680
Garbage collection	5	17	78	1682
Lack of transportation	5	11	84	1678

[a]Only asked of respondents with a child under eighteen in the household.

to residents since several of them (cheating or overcharging by local merchants, lack of parks, lack of teenage recreation facilities, and teenage gangs in the neighborhood) were reported to be at least somewhat of a problem by more than one in five respondents.

Residents, then, were clearly bothered by a number of problems. While few were seen as great problems by large proportions of respondents, many were moderate problems for them or their families. These problems are critical to document, for city government must continually deal not only with the "great problems" faced by urban residents, but also the many of "moderate salience" because these too undermine the quality of life.

New York City, of course, is comprised of neighborhoods that differ widely, both ethnically and economically. Common sense suggests that the incidence, range, and salience of residents' problems will vary from one neighborhood type to another. An examination of these variations can serve to alert city officials to the different—and possibly competing—needs of different types of neighborhoods and can aid in the process of tailoring municipal services to meet local needs. Accordingly, using 1970 census data for the 146 tracts from which respondents were sampled, we identified six "neighborhood types," ranging from poor minority to white middle-class areas.

An alternative perspective from which to consider the problems of residents is that of the city's racial and ethnic diversity. Although there are numerous ethnic groups, it has become a convention to characterize New York in terms of its "newer" and "older" racial-ethnic groups. In the areas studied, this means attention to the responses of blacks and Hispanics, the "newer" arrivals, and to those of white ethnics, who in our sample are overwhelmingly (75 percent) Irish, Italian, or Jewish.

In Table 8-2 the problems of residents are seen from the companion perspectives of where they live and the racial-ethnic groups to which they belong. The data are presented only for those twelve issues cited by at least 10 percent of the respondents as a great problem.

An interesting pattern evident in Table 8-2 is that the reported frequency of some problems is fairly consistent across neighborhood types, while that of other problems fluctuate from one type of neighborhood to another. For example, fear of crime, air and noise pollution, and dirty streets were reported as great problems at fairly similar rates in each type of neighborhood. In contrast, the problems of lack of play and park facilities, addicts, low pay, and cheating or overcharging by local merchants were reported at three, four, or even five times as high a rate in poor neighborhoods as in working- or middle-class areas. (See column in Table 8-2 showing the ratio of the highest to the lowest reported frequency for each problem.) In other words, some problems appear generic to city living and will have to be dealt with by all local service delivery systems. Others are neighborhood-specific and will have to be faced primarily by service agencies in poor areas, particularly those with a large minority population.

Turning to the reported frequency of these problems by ethnicity, we find that the *generalized* fear of crime was more likely to trouble whites than either blacks or Hispanics. In contrast, the *specific* problem of drug addicts in the neighborhood was cited at a higher rate by the two minority groups than by the majority whites. Economic problems (housing, low pay, and cheating or overcharging by local merchants) were reported at their highest rate by blacks. Lack of good schools and environmental problems (dirty air, noise, dirty streets) were clearly concerns of the whites in the sample.

In sum, the problems of city residents are not uniformly experienced by blacks, whites, and Hispanics. An understanding that this is the case can alert service officials to the fact that the ethnic composition of a neighborhood must be taken into account in considering the nature of the demands that will be placed on a local service delivery system.

Table 8-2
Great Problems by Neighborhood Type and by Ethnicity, 1972

Great Problem	Type of Neighborhood							Ethnicity		
	Minority Poor (Percent)	Mixed Poor (Percent)	Minority Working Class (Percent)	Mixed Working Class (Percent)	White Working Class (Percent)	White Middle Class (Percent)	Ratio of Highest to Lowest Percent	Black (Percent)	Hispanic[a] (Percent)	White (Percent)
Fear of crime	37	36	29	36	32	34	1.3	35	22	42
Dirty air or pollution	25	27	23	26	26	26	1.2	23	17	31
Dirty streets and sidewalks	29	32	20	21	27	19	1.7	25	16	29
Lack of play areas for children[b]	25	25	19	7	18	19	3.6	22	10	24
Housing	29	25	16	11	16	11	2.6	24	19	14
Drug addicts	32	18	15	13	14	9	3.6	21	21	15
Low pay	28	21	20	13	11	9	3.1	26	17	12
Noise	20	18	13	13	15	18	1.5	14	14	21
Lack of good schools[b]	15	12	14	10	20	16	2.0	15	7	21
Lack of teen recreation	15	13	12	9	8	10	1.9	12	8	13
Lack of parks	16	12	8	5	6	10	3.2	11	10	10
Cheating or overcharging	20	7	9	8	4	6	5.0	18	9	6
Total Number	457	179	205	265	216	361		498	398	712

[a]Two-thirds of the Hispanic respondents (68 percent) are Puerto Rican, 13 percent Central or South American, 12 percent Dominican, and 7 percent are Cuban.

[b]Only asked of respondents with a child under eighteen in the household.

Problem Salience, Contact, and Blame

Some concerns, particularly acute financial problems, clearly lie beyond the scope of ONG action.[d] But many of the items cited as great problems by residents are amenable to neighborhood treatment and lie within the province of municipal agencies responsible for service delivery at the local level. For these agencies to respond effectively to citizen needs, assessing the salience of residents' complaints is important in order to suggest priorities for action. Accordingly, respondents were asked which of their "great problems" constituted the *most important problems* for them or their families.

Table 8-3 shows that fear of crime was far and above everything else the most salient problem for residents; it superceded even the problems of inflation and recession. Almost six out of ten of those for whom fear of crime was a great problem cited this as their *most important problem*. Similarly, more than one in three (37 percent) who reported addicts in the neighborhood to be a great problem said this was their most important problem. On the other hand, although environmental concerns such as dirty streets and sidewalks were great

Table 8-3
Great Problems, Most Important Problems, and Agency Contacts about Most Important Problems

Item	Those for Whom Item Is a Great Problem		Those for Whom Great Problem Was Their Most Important Problem[a]		Those Who Contacted an Agency about Their Most Important Problem[b]	
	(%)	(N)	(%)	(N)	(%)	(N)
Fear of crime	35	(1683)	59	(581)	24	(343)
Dirty streets and sidewalks	25	(1681)	23	(415)	30	(99)
Housing	19	(1681)	42	(310)	67	(128)
Drug addicts	18	(1673)	37	(304)	23	(113)
Low pay	18	(1681)	39	(294)	25	(114)

aPercentages based on those for whom the given item was cited as a great problem.

bPercentages based on those for whom the given item was cited as the most important problem.

dIn fact, community leadership expressed dissatisfaction and frustration with ONG's inability to deal with the critical problems of an economically depressed neighborhood. See Chapter 6, pp. 127-130 of this volume.

problems for large proportions of residents, these were not top priority concerns for more than about one in five persons who cited them as great problems.

Not surprisingly, housing was rather high on the salience scale. More than two in five (42 percent) for whom this was a great problem said this was their most important problem. Further, compared with all the other items, people were most likely to call, write, or visit an agency about a housing problem. Fully 67 percent for whom housing was the most important problem contacted someone about their problem, while this was true for only about one in four persons overall.

Why was the contact rate so low? When asked why they did *not* contact an agency about their problem the most frequent answer was "it wouldn't help" (27 percent), which was followed by lack of knowledge about whom to call or where to go (20 percent).

To obtain a better assessment of the public's awareness of places to go for help, we asked whether they knew of any place, or group, or particular person in the neighborhood who helped people deal with city offices and services. Only one in five did know of such a place or person and, as Table 8-4 indicates, such knowledge was not evenly distributed. It was highest for whites (25 percent), slightly lower for blacks (22 percent) while only 12 percent of the Hispanic respondents knew of such a place or person in the neighborhood. Similarly, while problems are particularly burdensome for those living in poor neighborhoods (Table 8-2), it was the residents of the middle-class and white working-

Table 8-4
Percent Who Knew Place in Neighborhood that Helps People Deal with City Agencies

	Percent	*N*
All Respondents	20	1671
Ethnicity		
Black	22	497
Hispanic	12	398
White	25	709
Neighborhood Type		
Minority poor	16	454
Mixed poor	11	178
Minority working class	26	204
Mixed working class	14	264
White working class	21	216
White middle class	28	355

class areas who knew of places in the neighborhood where people could get help in dealing with city agencies.[e]

The 1972 survey did not specifically ask residents who they thought was to blame for the conditions they cited as their most important problems. This question was asked, however, of everyone interviewed in 1974. Table 8-5 presents their responses and shows that, except for lack of recreation facilities, citizens were less likely to blame city services or the *city* government than to attribute their frustrations with urban life to other factors. More than half, for example, blamed the state and federal governments for their financial woes, while most of the remainder felt that the overall state of the economy or general inflation was to blame. For dirty streets and sidewalks, almost three out of five placed the blame on *people* who litter the neighborhood and just one in four said that the fault lies with the unsatisfactory performance of the Department of Sanitation. Similarly, regarding fear of crime or addicts in the neighborhood,

Table 8-5
The Attribution of "Blame" for Most Important Problem in 1974

Most Important Problem	Who is to blame for most important problem?					
	City Services (Percent)	City Gov't. (Percent)	State-Federal Gov't. (Percent)	People (Percent)	Other (Percent)	N[a]
Fear of crime	23	12	17	33	43	281
Housing	11	34	17	6	56	64
Dirty streets and sidewalks	21	19	2	58	19	81
Low pay	3	9	49	3	49	149
Dirty air	2	11	7	19	81	54
Addicts in neighborhood	26	16	23	26	44	70
Lack of recreation for young people	5	52	9	24	35	85

Note: This table presents the responses of 973 of the "original" respondents interviewed in 1972; 63 "substitute" respondents from the same household who were interviewed in those instances where the original respondent had died, was ill, or otherwise unable to be interviewed; and 252 respondents who had moved into dwelling units vacated by the original respondents.

aPercentages total more than 100 percent since respondents could attribute blame to more than one source.

---

[e]Interestingly, when asked where or to whom a citizen could go for such help, more than one in three mentioned a political party organization or club. Perhaps the political party has not lost its traditional function of intermediary between the public and the city bureaucracies. See R.K. Merton, *Social Theory and Social Structure* (New York: Free Press, 1968), pp. 126-36.

only one in five faulted the police, even fewer blamed the addiction services, and most seemed to think that these problems stemmed from the frailties of *people*, such as insufficient parental supervision, lax law enforcement, or more generally the low level of morality in the nation.

Evaluation of City Services

Although residents did not single out city services as the cause of their problems, their views of the functioning of these services are important to understand better how they assess city living. For the purposes of this study, residents evaluated the quality of fourteen city services—police, sanitation, schools, recreation, and so forth—by indicating whether they thought each of these services was excellent, good, fair, bad, or very bad. As may be seen in Table 8-6, respondents found essential city services wanting in their neighborhoods. With the exception of fire protection, at least one-third and as many as two-thirds found various services no more than "fair" in their estimation.

In Table 8-6 the reader should also take note of the last column that shows the differential ability of residents to evaluate each of these services. Although 1683 New Yorkers were in the sample, the number who felt capable of rating

Table 8-6
Ratings of City Services

City Service	Excellent/Good (Percent)	Fair (Percent)	Bad/Very Bad (Percent)	N
Fire protection	84	14	2	1593
Health	65	26	9	1242
Subway and bus	62	25	13	1631
Sanitation	60	30	10	1662
Police	57	31	11	1610
Welfare	49	32	19	783
Public schools	46	33	21	1291
Parks	44	28	28	1467
Rent control	41	32	28	1124
Public housing	39	35	26	968
Housing inspection and code enforcement	37	31	31	1144
Services for treating drug addicts	34	30	36	605
Street repairs	33	29	38	1568
Recreation for teenagers or children	31	30	39	1157

each service varied from 605 to 1,662. More than one-half, for example, had either no knowledge or insufficient knowledge to judge addiction or welfare services while almost everyone assessed sanitation, police, and fire services.

The inability of citizens to evaluate certain services in their neighborhoods raises a question for survey researchers whose efforts are directed toward answering policy-related problems. Mandates for action are risky to extrapolate from survey results when large numbers of people may lack either the cognitive skills or a level of motivation necessary for valid responses. As Douglas Scott notes:

... much research devoted to obtaining citizen evaluations and preferences places the 'evaluative horse' before the "cognitive cart," if the latter is considered at all.[11]

Several implications follow from the finding that large numbers of residents do not judge the quality of some local services. To begin with, the researcher, when presenting findings that may be utilized in the planning process, must be explicit about the base upon which results have been calculated. For example, when the total sample of 1,683 are used as the base for determining citizen evaluations of welfare and addiction services, we find that ratings of excellent/ good are assigned by 23 percent and 12 percent, respectively. When the base for calculating ratings of these services is reduced to those assigning a rating, the figures rise to 49 percent and 34 percent. (Table 8-7). At the other end of the evaluation scale, using the full 1,683, welfare and addiction services received ratings of bad or very bad from 9 percent and 13 percent, respectively. These figures rise to 19 percent and 36 percent when restricting the analysis to those who actually rated the service.

Obviously, there is a difference between concluding that half (49 percent), rather than less than one-fourth (23 percent) of the residents of a neighborhood think that welfare services are excellent or good. Action based on citizen evaluations of municipal services, accordingly, must be predicated upon a clear understanding of the proportion of the population that has evaluated the various services.

Even more critical is the fact that there are significant differences between those who do and do not rate these services. Analysis of those with few, as opposed to many, "don't know" responses shows that the latter tend to be older people, whites, childless, relatively "problem-free" and—more importantly— unlikely to have had any contact with a city agency, or public official, to have participated in a neighborhood protest, or to have discussed either local conditions or national political questions with their neighbors.

In other words, the policymaker who is concerned about improving service delivery at the local level must bear in mind that a large contingent of residents are not prepared or able to make judgments about the quality of many services

Table 8-7
Citizen Evaluation of Welfare and Addiction Services

	Entire Sample (Percent)	Those Rating the Service (Percent)
	(N = 1683)	(N = 793)
Welfare services		
Excellent/good	23	49
Fair	15	32
Bad/very bad	9	19
Don't know	53	–
	(N = 1683)	(N = 605)
Addiction services		
Excellent/good	12	34
Fair	11	30
Bad/very bad	13	36
Don't know	64	–

in their neighborhoods. While this relatively passive group is not likely to oppose change in the method of delivering services, neither will they be likely to react at the perceptual level to such change. Further analysis of the number of "don't know" responses tends to confirm a basic premise underlying the administrative decentralization program—namely, that the remoteness of urban service bureaucracies is associated with a sense of powerlessness or alienation among residents. Expressions of powerlessness or distrust of city government were most evident among those in our sample with the highest number of "don't know" responses. (A more complete analysis of citizen attitudes toward city government can be found in a later section of this chapter.)

Clearly, if the ultimate objective of an administrative decentralization program is to increase citizen satisfaction with city services and to reduce levels of alienation, considerable resources will be required to reach that large body of residents who neither have information about services in their neighborhoods nor feel capable of exercising influence upon city government.

One may also explore ratings of municipal services by comparing respondents for whom the service is essential with those who have no direct need for the service. We did this for three services—welfare, public schools, and recreation facilities for young people (Table 8-8). In the case of welfare—putting to one side those who did not rate the service—we find that welfare and nonwelfare recipients viewed the service similarly. The same pattern holds for ratings of public schools. Those who had children under eighteen years of age and those

Table 8-8
Ratings of Three City Services by Whether Service is Relevant to Their Needs

	Percent Rating Service Excellent/Good	
	(%)	(N)
Welfare		
Recipient	51	(181)
Nonrecipient	48	(587)
Public schools		
Respondents with one or more children	45	(743)
Respondents with no children	48	(550)
Recreation for young people		
Respondents with one or more children	28	(635)
Respondents with no children	35	(522)

who did not were alike in their appraisal. One recreation for young people, those with no children were slightly more likely to make a favorable judgment of the service. A total of 35 percent of these people said the service was excellent or good in contrast to 28 percent of those with no children. Clearly, disparities in ratings are not to be found by simply comparing respondents for whom the service is intended with the wider public.

Differences in ratings become more meaningful when one considers the kinds of neighborhoods in which respondents live and their ethnic backgrounds. In general, the ratings from one neighborhood type to another show no consistent pattern but rather differ depending upon the particular service. Three services, for example (subway and bus transportation, welfare, and street repairs) were rated as harshly in the wealthier white neighborhoods as in the other five types of areas. The data do suggest, however, that people living in poorer neighborhoods—especially those dominated by ethnic minorities—were least likely to rate essential city services as excellent or good.

Of particular interest is the comparison between residents in white versus minority working-class neighborhoods (Table 8-9). On eleven of the fourteen services, a higher proportion of those living in white working-class neighborhoods than in minority working-class neighborhoods rated city services favorably, which thus suggests that minority neighborhoods suffer even when their residents are relatively well off financially.[f]

[f]The 1970 census tract data showed no difference at all in the median family income of white and minority working-class neighborhoods: white working-class, $9,375; minority working-class, $9,378.

Table 8-9
Percent Rating City Services Excellent or Good by Type of Neighborhood and Ethnicity

City Service	Type of Neighborhood						Ethnicity		
	Minority Poor (Percent)	Mixed Poor (Percent)	Minority Working Class (Percent)	Mixed Working Class (Percent)	White Working Class (Percent)	White Middle Class (Percent)	Black (Percent)	Hispanic (Percent)	White (Percent)
Fire protection	75	78	83	86	93	93	74	86	91
Health	60	56	58	68	69	75	58	70	67
Subway and bus	60	72	57	65	65	59	57	74	59
Sanitation	57	49	63	63	62	63	55	69	57
Police	41	49	61	57	75	67	48	61	61
Welfare	45	46	53	57	60	37	39	60	47
Public schools	39	45	53	45	39	57	43	56	42
Parks	29	38	45	55	58	47	38	47	46
Rent control	35	40	35	40	54	47	30	44	47
Public housing	25	31	49	46	50	59	31	45	45
Housing inspection and code enforcement	27	36	42	39	40	50	30	39	43
Addiction services	29	25	29	42	40	40	25	41	35
Street repairs	31	29	29	40	39	31	27	49	28
Recreation for teens or children	22	20	33	32	41	39	26	34	33
Total Number	212-454	67-177	71-203	85-256	82-213	88-359	204-497	182-387	194-704

Note: Percentages are based on the number of respondents in each category who evaluated each service. This number varied from service to service, and the Total Number column indicates the range of this variation.

The ratings of city services by blacks, whites, and Hispanics varied somewhat with blacks least likely and Hispanics most likely to rate these essential services favorably.[g] Interestingly, however, all three groups seemed to agree that the five services least liable to criticism were fire protection, health, transportation, sanitation, and the police. At the other end of the scale, housing inspection, addiction services, street repair, and recreation services received low ratings from all three groups, with the one exception of the Hispanics who rated street repair services more favorably than did either blacks or whites.

Although where one lives and one's ethnic background have something to do with judgments of municipal services, the strongest link is to perceived problems. We saw that people did not explicitly "blame" poor service delivery for their problems (Table 8-5) but the consistent and statistically significant findings in Table 8-10 show that the greater a neighborhood problem was perceived to be, the more harshly respondents rated the related city service.[h] For example, the more troubled people were about the lack of recreation facilities, the more critical they were of city recreation services. The pattern is uniform for every item in Table 8-10, and the differences in the last column are all positive, thereby demonstrating that service ratings are harsher when the related problem is the more aggravated. As may be noted, the differences are particularly great for school problems and public school ratings, recreation needs and services, financial problems and welfare services, and for housing problems and ratings of housing-related services. On the other hand, there is a noticeable failure of the public to downgrade police and sanitation services, even when crime, addicts, and dirty streets were perceived as great problems.

Neighborhood Satisfaction and Stability

Perhaps more critical than the relationship between problem perception and service ratings is the finding that residents' irritations about both problems and services strongly color their overall perceptions of, and readiness to remain in, their neighborhoods. Table 8-11 shows that people with five or more great problems were considerably more likely than those reporting no great problems to assign a poor rating to the neighborhood and to express a desire to move. Similarly, the harsher respondents' judgments of city services, the more likely were they to see their neighborhood as an unsatisfactory place to live and to say that they would like to move. The relationships are strong and statistically significant at the .001 level.[i]

[g]Although the data are not presented here, "other Hispanics" rated these services even more favorably than Puerto Ricans, probably because the Puerto Ricans tend to live in the poorer neighborhoods, while other Hispanics are largely located in working- or middle-class neighborhoods where services received generally higher ratings. (See Appendix Table 8A-1).

[h]One problem is not neighborhood-based, that of low pay.

[i]See Appendix Table 8A-2 for ethnic and neighborhood differences in neighborhood rating and the desire to move. While neighborhood ratings are somewhat lower for blacks than

Table 8-10

Percent Rating a Municipal Service Bad or Very Bad by Rating of Related Problem

Services and Related Problems	Those Rating Service Bad or Very Bad When Related Item Is:						Total N	Percent Difference[b]
	A Great Problem		Somewhat of a Problem		No Problem			
	(%)	(N)	(%)	(N)	(%)	(N)		
Recreation services and problem of lack of recreation for young people	90	(159)	45	(279)	25	(705)	1143	+65
Public schools and problem of lack of good schools	69	(121)	18	(158)	11	(489)	768[a]	+58
Welfare services and problem of low pay or not enough money to live on	68	(184)	15	(260)	13	(327)	771	+55
Housing inspection services and problem of housing	58	(241)	42	(266)	17	(636)	1143	+41
Addiction treatment services and problem of drug addicts in neighborhood	58	(160)	37	(202)	21	(242)	604	+37
Rent control services and problem of housing	53	(299)	33	(243)	16	(278)	1123	+37
Sanitation services and problem of dirty streets and sidewalks	23	(413)	9	(610)	2	(637)	1660	+21
Police protection services and problem of drug addicts in neighborhood	23	(296)	14	(507)	6	(792)	1595	+17
Police protection services and problem of fear of crime	18	(560)	9	(628)	6	(416)	1604	+12

[a]Statistics based on respondents with a child under eighteen in the household.

[b]All differences are significant at the .01 level or better.

Hispanics or whites, the three groups express the desire to move at the same rate (55 percent). Favorable neighborhood ratings range from 24 percent in poor minority areas to 62 percent in white middle-class neighborhoods and the desire to move correspondingly drops from 64 percent in the poor minority to 44 percent in the white middle-class neighborhoods.

Table 8-11
Problems, Service Ratings, and Neighborhood Satisfaction and Stability

	Those Rating Neighborhood Bad/Very Bad		Those Who Want to Move	
	(%)	(N)	(%)	(N)
All respondents	17	(1672)	55	(1674)
Number of great problems				
None	6	(465)	31	(470)
One	11	(320)	52	(320)
Two	14	(239)	56	(239)
Three or four	19	(303)	67	(302)
Five or more	37	(345)	79	(343)
Gamma	.42		.48	
Number of services rated bad/very bad				
None	4	(468)	34	(470)
One	10	(327)	45	(329)
Two or three	20	(446)	65	(448)
Four or more	32	(431)	75	(428)
Gamma	.41		.46	

Clearly, citizen problem perception and ratings of public services have critical implications for overall neighborhood satisfaction and stability. Residents' dissatisfactions affect their attitudes toward their neighborhood and are components of the general desire to move to another area.

Rational and consistent public policy is difficult to design and implement in the face of the kaleidoscopic character of neighborhood life in the city with populations in a constant state of flux. We have seen that poverty and ethnicity are associated with high problem rates and a critical stance toward municipal services and that these, in turn, create a general dissatisfaction with the neighborhood and a desire to move. Any attempt to cut into this cycle must be predicated upon an understanding of the *relative* effects of those variables which may be manipulated by public policy.[j] Accordingly, this section pulls together the various neighborhood contexts, individual attributes, problem ratings, and service evaluations in an attempt to determine the independent effects of these factors on neighborhood ratings and stability.

[j]It is also important to recognize that some of these variables may lie outside the realm of public policy. For a discussion of the distinction between causal and policy analysis, see James Q. Wilson, "Crime and the Criminologists," *Commentary* 58, No. 1, July 1974.

Regression analysis is probably the most economical way to make this attempt and at the same time to indicate the amount of the total variance in neighborhood ratings and stability that can be explained by these factors.

Four categories of variables are considered:

1. *Census data describing the neighborhood*: median family income of the tract; percent of the population that is black; percent of the population that is Puerto Rican.
2. *Respondent attributes:* age; number of children in household; renters versus owners; family income; ethnicity.
3. *Problems:* safety-related (fear of crime and addicts in the neighborhood); environmental (dirty streets and sidewalks and air pollution); housing.
4. *Service ratings:* child-related (schools, parks, recreation services); uniformed services (sanitation, police, fire); housing inspection and code enforcement.

The dependent variables in the analysis are the neighborhood rating based on a five-point scale ranging from "very good" to "very bad" and a dichotomous (dummy) stability variable—preference to remain in the neighborhood.

We know that there is a good deal of intercorrelation among the four categories of variables—problem incidence and service ratings, ethnicity and problem incidence, and so forth. Simple correlations cannot assess the independent effect of the variables in each category on the dependent variables; nor can they tell us how much of the total variance in neighborhood satisfaction and stability is explained by the four categories of variables. The regression analysis provides this information.

The Tables 8-12 and 8-13 are almost identical, but in Table 8-12 the separate problems and services comprising each scale have been entered into the regression, while in Table 8-13 these have been scaled. We did this to highlight the relative importance of the services or problems within each scale. For example, a quick comparison of the beta weights in the two tables shows that *police* is the strongest determinant in the uniformed services scale as is *public schools* in the child-related services scale. The problems of fear of crime and addicts in the neighborhoods contribute about equal strength to the safety-problems scale. The problem of dirty streets and sidewalks however, has a higher beta weight by itself ($-.10$) than when combined with air pollution in the environmental scale ($-.07$).

Having noted the independent effects of the *separate* problem and service ratings upon neighborhood rating and stability, we turn to Table 8-13 to determine effects of the four *categories* of independent variables on the two dependent variables. Quite clearly, the variables we have selected explain a larger proportion of the total variance in neighborhood rating (33 percent) than in the desire to remain in the area (21 percent). Obviously there are many personal factors involved in the decision to move, and while this question might be an

Table 8-12
Predictors of Neighborhood Rating and Readiness to Stay in the Neighborhood in 1972

Predictors	Neighborhood Rating			Desire to Stay		
	r	Standard Beta	F Ratio	r	Standard Beta	F Ratio
Services						
Sanitation	.27	.06	*	.17	.00	*
Police	.34	.12	13.4	.19	.01	*
Fire	.15	−.01	*	.10	.01	*
Parks	.27	.03	*	.21	.04	*
Public Schools	.33	.16	24.0	.22	.06	*
Recreational services	.27	.04	*	.24	.07	3.8
Housing inspection services	.30	.03	*	.26	.03	*
Problems						
Fear of crime	−.25	−.10	11.2	−.20	−.08	5.9
Addicts in neighborhood	−.34	−.12	14.7	−.26	−.07	3.8
Dirty streets and sidewalks	−.31	−.10	8.4	−.27	−.11	9.8
Air pollution	−.15	.02	*	−.19	.03	*
Housing	−.27	−.06	*	−.31	−.14	15.1
Census Data[a]						
Median tract income	.32	.21	48.0	.18	.07	4.0
Respondent Attributes						
Age	−.01	−.15	26.2	.21	.11	10.7
Renter	−.18	−.12	15.7	−.17	−.09	7.9
Number of children	−.13	−.09	9.4	−.14	−.05	*
Black	.01	.05	*	.02	−.01	*
Hispanic	.02	−.04	*	.03	.03	*
r^2		.35			.22	

Note: $N = 1683$.

[a]Three variables (family income, percent black, and percent Puerto Rican in the census tract) have been eliminated from this analysis since preliminary regression analyses showed their explanatory power to be virtually zero when entered into the equation with the other variables. See Appendix Table 8A-3.

*Nonsignificant at the .05 level.

Table 8-13

Predictors of Neighborhood Rating and Readiness to Stay in the Neighborhood in 1972 (Services and Problems Scaled)

Predictors	Neighborhood Rating			Desire to Stay		
	r	Standard Beta	F Ratio	r	Standard Beta	F Ratio
Service scales						
Child-related	.33	.17	34.8	.26	.13	17.0
Uniformed	.34	.15	26.5	.22	.03	*
Housing inspection	.30	.04	*	.26	.04	*
Problem scales						
Safety	−.36	−.20	50.0	−.28	−.12	15.3
Environmental	−.28	−.07	5.7	−.27	−.11	12.9
Housing	−.27	−.06	*	−.31	−.14	20.2
Census data						
Median tract income	.32	.21	64.9	.18	.07	5.7
Respondent attributes						
Age	−.01	−.15	32.2	.21	.11	14.0
Renter	−.18	−.12	20.7	−.17	−.09	9.7
Number of children	−.13	−.09	11.4	−.14	−.05	*
Black	.01	.07	*	.02	−.01	*
Hispanic	.02	−.06	*	.03	.03	*
r^2		.33			.21	

Note: $N = 1683$

*Nonsignificant at the .05 level.

interesting one to explore, it was not a primary research question. We were more concerned with the ingredients of the neighborhood rating, especially those factors that might be amenable to public change.

While there is some convergence, the factors that account for variations in overall neighborhood rating are not necessarily strong determinants of the desire to remain in the neighborhood. For example, the highest and most significant beta is between median tract income and overall neighborhood satisfaction (.21), but the beta between neighborhood income level and the desire to stay is .07, which thus suggests that preferences to move or stay cut across the income levels of neighborhoods. Housing problems, on the other hand, which are hardly related to neighborhood rating (−.06), have the strongest and most significant negative relationship (−.14) to the desire to stay in the neighborhood.[k]

The *problem* complex with the strongest contribution to overall neighborhood satisfaction is that of safety—that is, fear of crime and drug addicts in the neighborhood. While these items apparently play a strong role in residents' attitudes toward the locality as a whole, they are not as highly related to the desire to move. The *service* measures that are significant determinants of neighborhood ratings are the child-related and the uniformed service scales. The former also have a strong independent effect on the desire to move.

Even after all of the problem scales and service ratings have been taken into account, the median income of the tract retains a strong independent effect on neighborhood satisfaction with a standardized regression coefficient of .21, which is higher than that of any of the other variables included in the regression. The income level of the neighborhood, while strongly related to the quality of public services and to problems, must, in addition, be measuring a complex of other factors related to satisfaction.[l]

Among respondent attributes, age and renting (rather than owning) play a key role in explaining overall satisfaction and neighborhood stability. The elderly, after all other variables have been taken into account, are negative about their neighborhoods, but are not prepared to move. Renting, as contrasted with ownership, has a strong independent negative relationship both to neighborhood rating and the desire to remain in the area. And finally, neither the simple correlations nor the beta for blacks and Hispanics are significant determinants of the dependent variables.

In sum, people's satisfaction with their neighborhood is significantly linked with their perceptions of municipal services—particularly the *police* and the *public schools*—and to perceptions of safety and child-related problems. While this finding may not constitute a mandate for action, it certainly suggests a point of leverage for public intervention.

Attitudes toward Government

Underlying the creation of ONG was the premise that New Yorkers are alienated from and disaffected with city government and that such alienation and

[k]This finding parallels that in a recent study of residential mobility. See Sandra Newman, *The Residential Environment and the Desire to Move*, Institute for Social Research, University of Michigan, Ann Arbor, 1974.

[l]Allen Barton has suggested that "tract income stands as a surrogate for a set of qualities not measured in our direct questions but related to income—particularly the characteristics of people in the neighborhoods, and aspects of the environment beyond those caught by our questions about housing and dirty streets, such as 'suburban' qualities." See Allen H. Barton, "Observations on Neighborhood Satisfaction in New York City," paper delivered at Conference on Subjective Indicators of the Quality of Life, Social Science Research Council, Cambridge, England, September 1975.

disaffection might be reduced by decentralizing the administration of municipal services and coordinating the delivery of these services at the local level. We have seen that residents were troubled by a number of problems at the time that ONG was implemented in the experimental districts. While they tended not to blame city services explicitly for these problems, the more acute their concerns, the more they downgraded related municipal services. Furthermore, high problem rates and a critical stance toward city services explain a considerable amount of the variation in neighborhood satisfaction and stability. Still to be explored is whether residents did, in fact, feel powerless and whether their attitudes toward city government were related to their problems and their perceptions of municipal service agencies.

That a widespread sense of powerlessness existed among residents sampled in 1972 is evident in Table 8-14. About seven in ten felt that influence was necessary in order to get results from city government and that there was little or nothing they could do to stop the city from passing an unfair law. Almost as many—six in ten—did not think that a person who was treated unfairly by the city could do much about it. Moreover, residents were aware of the lack of local mechanisms for citizen influence, for two-thirds agreed that the residents of their neighborhood had little or no influence on the way city services in the area were run. In contrast, almost half felt that residents *should* have a lot of influence over local service delivery.[m]

Table 8-15 presents the results of regressing an index of disaffection (using the first five items in Table 8-14) on the same independent variables used to analyze neighborhood satisfaction and stability (Table 8-13).

Looking first at the zero-order correlation coefficients, we find that the strongest correlates of disaffection are respondents' evaluations of three different categories of city services: The higher the ratings of these services are, the lower the level of disaffection. However, as the standardized regressions and F-ratios indicate, only the uniformed and housing inspection services exert a statistically significant independent influence on the disaffection index.

The problem scales show smaller bivariate relationships with the dependent variable and only one of them—the economic complex—is significant when the other independent variables are held constant. As the reader will note, the relationship is positive, thereby indicating that the more severe these problems, the more the disaffection. Unlike the strong independent effect that median-tract income exerted on neighborhood satisfaction (Table 8-13), the income level of the neighborhood has no predictive power on the dependent variable. Among the individual attributes, only ethnicity is even a minimally significant predictor of disaffection, and the results show that minority residents are less disaffected than whites once problems and service ratings are held constant.

[m]Only in white middle-class neighborhoods did residents express confidence in their ability to exercise influence at the *local* level. Almost half agreed that people had at least some influence on the way city government services were run in their area, in contrast to one in five who live in ethnically mixed, poor neighborhoods. Attitudes toward city government were relatively stable across ethnic lines.

Table 8-14
A Sense of Powerlessness among Residents of the Seven Districts

	Percent	N
Influence is necessary to get results from city government	71	1521
A person can do little or nothing about an unfair city law	69	1589
Can do little or nothing about unfair treatment by city agencies	61	1573
New Yorkers have little or no influence on how city government is run	51	1543
People in neighborhood have little or no influence on how services in area are run	67	1439
People in neighborhood *should* have a lot of influence on how services in the area are run	47	1571

Finally, not much of the variance in the disaffection index (r^2 = .07) is explained by the independent variables included in the analysis.

A search for the determinants of disaffection is beyond the scope of this chapter. Our purpose has been to describe the quality of life as perceived by the public at the time the ONG experiment began and to learn whether in fact disaffection with city government in general is linked to citizens' neighborhood problems and their appraisals of service delivery.[n] Our analysis suggests that dissatisfaction with neighborhood services rather than perceived problems is a contributor, albeit small, to overall disaffection with city government.

At the time that the administrative decentralization program was being implemented in several experimental districts the problems of living in these districts were clear and compelling. Crime, addicts, poor housing, dirty streets, and air and noise pollution combined to make everyday life a trial. Further, the municipal services charged with addressing the problems of city residents were found lacking, especially among those plagued by service-related problems. In turn, criticism of municipal services had a small association with the sense of powerlessness and disaffection with city government.

This then is the context within which the ONG experiment began. After

[n]A dissertation in progress is analyzing the determinants of disaffection with city government for various subgroups in our sample. See Kenneth H. Andrews, "Political Beliefs and Political Experiences: Efficacy, Trust, Participation, and Governmental Treatment," dissertation in progress, Department of Political Science, Columbia University, Ithaca, N.Y.

Table 8-15
Predictors of Political Disaffection in 1972 (Services and Problems Scaled)

Predictors	r	Standard Beta	F Ratio
Service scales			
Child-related	−.16	−.06	*
Uniformed	−.20	−.15	13.3
Housing inspection	−.17	−.10	5.7
Problem scales			
Economic	.12	.08	5.0
Safety	.13	.04	*
Environmental	.12	.00	*
Housing	.11	.02	*
Census data			
Median tract income	−.02	−.04	*
Respondent attributes			
Age	.05	.05	*
Renter	.04	.02	*
Number of children	−.04	−.03	*
Black	−.01	−.10	6.2
Hispanic	−.11	−.13	12.1
r^2		.07	

Note: $N = 1683$.
*Nonsignificant at the .05 level.

almost two years, citizens were again interviewed in order to determine whether the experiment in administrative decentralization had effected any impact on residents' problems, service ratings, contacts with local agencies and feelings of powerlessness and disaffection with city government. The next chapter presents the results of these second interviews.

Notes

1. John D. Kasarda and Morris Janowitz, "Community Attachment in Mass Society," *American Sociological Review* 39, no. 3, June 1974, p. 328.

2. John Walton, "The Structural Bases of Political Change in Urban Communities," a paper prepared for presentation at the 68th Annual Meeting of the American Sociological Association, New York, August 27-30, 1973.

3. Subcommittee on Intergovernmental Relations of the Committee on Government Operations, U.S. Senate, *Confidence and Concern: Citizens View American Government* (Washington, D.C.: U.S. Government Printing Office, 1973), p. 217.

4. *The New York Times*, July 8, 1975, p. 19.

5. Robert K. Yin and William A. Lucas, "Decentralization and Alienation," *Policy Sciences* 4, 1973, pp. 327-8.

6. Mayor John V. Lindsay, "A Plan for Neighborhood Government for New York City," Office of the Mayor, City of New York, June 1970.

7. Ibid., p. 2.

8. *The Gallup Opinion Index Report*, no. 74, Summer 1971.

9. Eli Ginzberg and the Conservation of Human Resources Staff, *New York is Very Much Alive: A Manpower View* (New York: McGraw-Hill, 1973).

10. Otto L. Bettman, *The Good Old Days—They Were Terrible* (Random House: New York, 1974), p. 87.

11. Douglas Scott, *Citizen Evaluations of Local Government Services: Some Measurement Questions.* The Institute of Government and Public Affairs, University of California, Los Angeles, 1974, p. 19.

Appendix 8A
A Summary of Factors Associated with Neighborhood Satisfaction and Stability

Table 8A-1
Type of Neighborhood in which Respondents of Different Ethnicities Live

Type of Neighborhood	Ethnicity			
	Black (Percent)	Puerto Rican (Percent)	Other Hispanic (Percent)	White (Percent)
Minority poor	52	46	24	4
Mixed poor	4	20	4	13
Minority working class	24	5	11	7
Mixed working class	15	14	30	14
White working class	1	8	15	22
White middle class	3	6	16	40
Total Number	498	275	123	712

Table 8A-2
Neighborhood Satisfaction and Stability by Ethnicity and Neighborhood Type

	Percent Rating Neighborhood Very Good/Good	Percent Who Want to Move	N
All respondents	38	55	1672
Ethnicity			
Black	31	55	478
Hispanic	40	54	343
White	40	55	811
Neighborhood type			
Minority poor	24	64	454
Mixed poor	29	61	178
Minority working class	38	49	202
Mixed working class	29	55	263
White working class	43	54	214
White middle class	62	44	361

Table 8A-3

Percent Rating Neighborhood Very Good or Good and Percent Who Want to Stay, by Four Categories of Items, 1972

Selected Items	N	Rate Neighborhood Very Good/Good (Percent)	Desire to Stay (Percent)
Neighborhood contexts			
Median Tract Income			
Under $7000	393	20	31
$7000-7999	339	31	44
$8000-9999	475	36	47
$10,000 or more	466	58	55
Percent Blacks in Tract			
Less than 5%	534	51	51
5-19.9%	370	36	44
20-39.9%	241	26	41
40-59.9%	216	27	38
60% or more	313	33	45
Percent Puerto Ricans in Tract			
Less than 3%	491	57	52
3-4.9%	261	39	49
5-9.9%	269	34	49
10-19.9%	260	30	40
20% or more	393	20	34
Respondent attributes			
Residence Status			
Renter	1258	34	49
Owner	393	49	60
Family Income[a]			
Low	272	28	41
Medium-low	331	37	44
Medium	290	36	44
Medium-high	290	37	44
High	279	46	46
Child in household			
Yes	830	33	36
No	844	42	53
Age			
Under 40 years	847	38	37
60 years or older	367	39	61
Ethnicity			
Black	494	31	44
Hispanic	395	40	47
White	675	39	44

Table 8A-3 (cont.)

Selected Items	*N*	Rate Neighborhood Very Good/Good (Percent)	Desire to Stay (Percent)
Problem scales[b]			
Safety-related problems			
High problem score	462	17	26
Medium problem score	890	40	47
Low problem score	320	61	65
Environmental problems			
High problem score	506	20	27
Medium problem score	815	41	48
Low problem score	350	56	62
Housing Problem			
High problem score	310	19	20
Medium problem score	347	27	32
Low problem score	1013	47	57
Service rating scales[c]			
Uniformed services			
Low score	350	16	28
Medium score	524	31	42
High score	798	52	55
Child-related services			
Low score	553	20	29
Medium score	432	40	44
High score	684	50	58
Housing Maintenance			
Low score	357	16	23
Medium score	354	33	44
High score	424	51	55

[a]Index combines annual family income and number of persons in household.

[b]High problem score represents high problem incidence.

[c]High service score represents favorable service ratings.

Decentralization and the Public

Nathalie S. Friedman
and
Theresa F. Rogers

**Part One: The Impact of the Administrative
Decentralization Experiment on the Public**

*Introduction: Measuring the Effects of the
ONG Experiment upon the Public*

A principal objective of Lindsay's administrative decentralization program was to effect changes in the delivery of municipal services at the local level so that service delivery could be more responsive to the different needs of neighborhoods with varying population mixes. The base-line data of the public survey indicated that problems and priorities did in fact differ from one type of neighborhood to another, thereby suggesting the need for greater flexibility in the deployment of the resources of municipal service agencies.

In this chapter we address ourselves to two major questions. First, did the ONG experiment exert any measurable impact on the public? Second, whether or not the answer is yes, how ready and able is the public to endorse some form of local government?

The assumption underlying the quasi-experimental design of the public survey (before and after interviews in experimental and control districts) was that if the ONG program was successful, the people living in areas with an ONG district manager and cabinet would report:

Reduction in the number of problems;
Greater knowledge of where to go with a problem;
Increased satisfaction with the handling of problems brought to agencies;
Higher evaluation of municipal services;
More positive attitude toward the neighborhood and toward city government in general.

These changes should appear in experimental, but not in control districts.

Broad social programs, such as ONG, are designed to effect large numbers of people, but by relatively small amounts. Few people expected, for example, that within two years, a large majority of those living in neighborhoods under ONG's aegis would become problem-free, satisfied, efficacious citizens; causal sequences designed to bring about social change work along highly intricate paths, and the longer and more complex the path, the weaker the anticipated effect on the dependent variable, whether it is children's reading scores, cleaner streets, or more favorable attitudes toward city government. Moreover, the causal chain required to explain, say, the dollar-cost of hauling away a ton of garbage,[1] a task in itself, is still far less complex than that required to explain attitudes toward city government with *visibility* of improved service delivery as a crucial intervening variable.

Schematically, the model of the causal chain to test the effect of ONG on citizen perceptions of city government would look something like the diagram in Figure 9-1. In neighborhoods with an ONG district manager and district service cabinet, there would first have to be objective improvement in service delivery. Then, the public would have to perceive the positive effects of this improvement and alter their service evaluations, problem count, or satisfaction accordingly. Finally, increased satisfaction, reduced problems, higher evaluations would presumably result in more favorable attitudes toward the neighborhood and toward city government.

Figure 9-1 identifies the sequence of variables needed to test the effect of ONG on the public, but the complexity of these variables and the measurement problems require some explication. If ONG had effected, say, a 10 percent improvement in service delivery between 1972 and 1974, it would have been remarkable. Even a social program many times the size and scope of ONG could not be expected to achieve such an impact on performance in so short a period of time. Under optimum conditions, then, the observed differences in citizen attitudes are likely to be quite small.

Further, our basic concern is that the public *perceive* improvement in service delivery and that their perception then be registered in a more positive appraisal of city government. But a number of factors can intrude on citizen observability of service delivery. To begin, objective improvement in service delivery may go unnoticed,[a] or if perceived, it may raise citizen standards and expectations so that the net result is a higher complaint rate and dissatisfaction with the neighborhood and city government. Second, citizens are more likely to

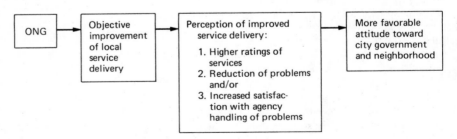

Figure 9-1. Model of Causal Chain.

---

[a]See Chapter 8 for a discussion of inability of considerable numbers of residents to evaluate services in their neighborhood.

take note of the diminution of services than the augmenting of them. For example, if the garbage is not removed by the accustomed hour, they'll remember this more readily than that it was collected three hours earlier. Third, the interval between actual improvement in service delivery and querying the public about it may pose a problem. The public may perceive a change immediately, but a year later when asked about the quality of service delivery, they may have little or nothing to say. Finally, the attitudes of New Yorkers toward government in general may have been adversely affected by the Watergate scandals that peaked in 1974 at just the time we were reinterviewing the public. Every poll taken during this period showed an increase in citizen distrust of and cynicism toward government.

It almost appears, then, that even before the study began, analysis of ONG impact on the public would have little chance of producing significant results. The linkages between objective improvement in service delivery and citizen visibility of that improvement can be confounded in any number of ways and unwittingly minimize, if not obscure, measurable differences before and after the introduction of the ONG program.

We were mindful of these problems that beset any study intended to measure the impact of an experimental program on a specified public. We monitored the program throughout the study period to document: (1) relations of ONG field staff with local service officials and with community leaders; (2) alterations in the decision-making structures of local service agencies; and (3) changes in the patterns of local service delivery as reflected in actual projects initiated under the program. (These data are reported in earlier chapters.) These efforts serve, not only as evidence of the strengths and weaknesses of the program but also as sources for interpreting the data on the impact of ONG on the public.

With respect to the public survey, we took care to include a range of items that would serve to identify citizens who were more or less alert to and knowledgeable about neighborhood conditions. Second, we sought explanatory information about their actual experience with neighborhood groups and city government as well as their orientation to local citizen issues. Third, we attempted to ascertain the quality of life in their neighborhoods and their commitment to the neighborhoods as a place to live. The analysis that follows interrelates these data beginning with the impact of ONG on the public.

Experimental-Control District Comparisons: How
Comparable Are They?

Three districts in which the district manager-district cabinet experimental program was established were matched, using available Census and City Planning Commission data, on socioeconomic status, ethnicity, and homeownership, with three "control" districts in which no such decentralization measures were planned. Comparison of the samples interviewed in these two sets of districts in 1972, at the start of the experimental program, shows that they were indeed very similar on most socioeconomic variables (Appendix Table 9A-1). Incomes, percent on welfare, family stability, and percent with children were virtually identical. Race, homeownership and age were within 2 to 4 percent. The largest difference was the greater number of people who had lived less than three years in the neighborhood. This number was 9 percent greater in the control districts as a whole and largely reflected one control district in which ethnic turnover from whites to minorities was much more rapid than the moderate shifts in the other districts.

Further indication of the close similarity of the basic experimental and control districts is provided by the attitudes and perceptions of their residents at the time of the 1972 survey (Appendix Table 9A-2). The proportion reporting various "great problems" for themselves and their families—crime, housing, low pay, schools, and recreation—was very close, with the greatest difference being that 6 percent more reported "drug addicts" as a great problem in experimental districts. Likewise, the average rating of fifteen public services was within 2 percent in the two sets of districts, the proportion of households victimized by crime was within 1 percent, and general neighborhood satisfaction levels were within 2 percent. All this suggests that the three basic experimental districts and the three control districts started from almost the same social composition and set of local problems; the main exception was that one control area was in more rapid transition.

A fourth experimental district was also studied for which no matched control district was available due to its special composition; it had a strongly organized experimental program in which the city and the researchers were especially interested. This was Crown Heights, almost three-quarters black but not as poor as the hard-core ghetto districts, with a strongly organized Jewish minority group. On most social characteristics other than ethnic composition, Crown Heights was very similar to the other experimental and control districts. The largest differences were 7 percent less homeownership than the three basic experimental areas combined and 7 percent higher membership in two or more organizations, thus reflecting the greater organization of both its black and white populations. For purposes of simplifying the tables in this chapter, in which the emphasis is on *change* between the 1972 baseline and 1974 in experimental districts as compared with control districts, we have *included* this supplemental experimental district with the three basic experimental districts in the figures labeled *Experimental*. This makes the match between the experimental and control districts as a whole less good in terms of race, but not in other characteristics. In an appendix to this chapter we present the experimental-control comparisons for *only* the three matched experimental and three control districts, so that the reader can see that none of the conclusions of this chapter would be different if Crown Heights were omitted from the experimental-control comparisons of changes (Appendix Table 9A-3).

One additional warning has to be repeated here: Two of the "control" districts were, in the second year of the experimental program, "contaminated" by a watered-down version of the administrative decentralization program consisting of a district cabinet without a full-time district manager that met under the guidance of a city official with other major administrative responsibilities. To the extent that the "expansion cabinets" succeeded in improving services, resolving local problems, and increasing public access to the bureaucracy during their year of operation in the two control districts, they will have diminished the measurable impact of the program as revealed by experimental district-control district comparisons. Examination of the results district by district, and analysis of the actual activities of these additional cabinets without full-time Managers, (see especially Chapter 7) suggests that they could not have had much effect during their period of operation. It should also be noted (see Chapter 7) that even the remaining "control" district had a quasi-cabinet in the form of interdepartmental meetings initiated by a previous mayoral program, the Urban Action Task Force. This quasi-cabinet was less active than the "expansion cabinets" during the period of the study.

The experimental-control district comparisons clearly apply to assessing any impact of the *presence or absence of the district manager*, as a full-time local coordinator appointed by the mayor and assisted by the central Office of Neighborhood Government in working with both the local officials and the community leadership. The impact of *cabinets* as such, without managers, is much more weakly measured by the experimental-control comparisons, since the cabinet was present in two of the three control districts for about half the period of the experiment, and a similar interdepartmental group had functioned earlier in the third district.

Impact of ONG on Citizen Appraisal of Service

The first step in the causal path assumes that an improvement in service delivery would be reflected in citizen evaluations of municipal services, that is, any improvement in ratings between 1972 and 1974 would be more marked in experimental districts, any decline less marked. Table 9-1 shows that, in fact, services were more harshly appraised in 1974 than two years previously and that the decline in ratings was somewhat more severe, on the average, in the *experimental* than in the control districts.[b] Welfare, parks, and recreation were the three services showing the most marked drop in the experimental districts

[b]All the data presented in this section, unless otherwise noted, are based on the 973 respondents who remained in the same dwelling unit over the two-year period between interviews.

Table 9-1

A Comparison of the Public's Rating of Local Municipal Services in 1972 and 1974, Experimental and Control Districts

Municipal Service Ratings	4 Experimental Districts					3 Control Districts				
	1972		1974		Change	1972		1974		Change
	(%)	(N)	(%)	(N)		(%)	(N)	(%)	(N)	
Respondents Rating Each Service Excellent or Good										
Sanitation	61	(560)	54	(552)	−7	59	(406)	57	(405)	−2
Fire Protection	84	(526)	80	(526)	−4	88	(395)	84	(384)	−4
Police Protection	57	(539)	43	(531)	−14	58	(392)	42	(395)	−16
Public Housing	40	(313)	27	(321)	−13	38	(231)	28	(231)	−10
Housing Inspection and Code Enforcement	38	(392)	32	(386)	−6	35	(269)	31	(265)	−4
Rent Control	42	(384)	30	(377)	−12	41	(258)	34	(250)	−7
Welfare	53	(254)	31	(273)	−22	42	(197)	33	(193)	−9
Parks	47	(502)	37	(486)	−10	37	(354)	37	(343)	0
Public Schools	46	(461)	37	(412)	−9	45	(317)	41	(307)	−4
Street Repairs	35	(535)	32	(540)	−3	29	(389)	26	(403)	−3
Subway and Bus Service	59	(547)	52	(524)	−7	62	(402)	58	(395)	−4
Services for Treating Drug Addicts	37	(199)	37	(170)	0	31	(147)	32	(117)	+1
Health Services	62	(424)	60	(444)	−2	67	(311)	58	(308)	−9
Recreation for Young People	35	(404)	26	(431)	−9	27	(298)	28	(321)	+1
Average change					−9					−5

when compared with control areas. In 1972, these three services were rated considerably higher in experimental than control districts, while two years later the ratings declined in the former areas to converge with those of the control districts. Parenthetically, police protection services suffered one of the sharpest drops in respondents' eyes—but about equally in ONG and non-ONG districts.

In Chapter 8, we noted that in 1972 many respondents were unable to evaluate a number of the services in their neighborhood. Pursuing this finding, we discovered that the proportion of "don't know" responses remained constant over the two years in both experimental and control districts. Apparently, the activities of ONG during this period did not affect the public's level of information about neighborhood services.

We should be clear about exactly what these findings of "no effect" mean. The experimental research tested whether the district manager-district cabinet program, as carried out in New York City, improved the public's rating of city services during its first two years of operation, and found that the program did not. The public survey (and other components of the research project) were not able to test whether the program would have such effects in the longer run, because the program was not pursued longer.[c] It can be argued that the full effects of such an administrative change—whether for better services or for worse—would take longer than two years to develop and become visible to the public. The first two years of the new administrative arrangement were clearly a period of developing new roles and relationships among officials and with community leaders. The survey data shows that the program did *not* effect the attitudes and perceptions of the general public in the short run; we can only speculate whether it would have had an effect, and in what direction, had it been pursued several years more.

Impact of ONG on Citizen Problems

It is possible that objectively improved service delivery, while not having an effect on service ratings, might have caused a reduction in the problems confronting residents, so that they would report fewer problems in 1974 than in 1972, at least in areas where the experiment was active. In fact, the public in experimental areas did not shift more favorably than that in control areas, in the kinds of problems they reported as affecting themselves and their families (Table 9-2). Virtually every problem was reported at a higher rate by our sample, and no systematic changes differentiate the responses in the experimental from those in the control districts.

[c]See Chapter 2 for a description of program changes effected by the Beame administration. The program was renamed the Office of Neighborhood *Services*; however, as our study was designed to evaluate the impact of Lindsay's Office of Neighborhood *Government*, we continue to refer to ONG in this chapter.

Table 9-2

A Comparison of the Public's Problems in 1972 and 1974, Experimental and Control Districts

Great Problems	Experimental Districts			Control Districts		
	1972 (N = 561)	1974 (N = 537)	Change	1972 (N = 413)	1974 (N = 392)	Change
Percent Rating the Following a Great Problem						
Fear of crime	35	46	+11	34	49	+15
Housing	17	33	+16	16	31	+15
Dirty streets and sidewalks	25	35	+10	24	35	+11
Low pay; not enough money to live on	18	40	+22	17	36	+19
Dirty air; pollution	29	34	+5	26	35	+9
Addicts in the neighborhood	18	28	+10	16	30	+14
Crime Victim in Household	18	14	−4	18	18	0

In 1972 fear of crime topped the list of great problems at a rate of about one in three. Two years later, this concern was still uppermost in people's minds, and the figure of those citing it as a great problem rose to almost one-half. More respondents feared crime in 1974 than in 1972 despite the fact that the reported victimization rate remained constant—indeed, dropped very slightly in the experimental districts. And so too with the crime-related problem of drug addicts in the neighborhood. In both ONG and non-ONG areas residents complained about addicts in the neighborhood at a substantially higher rate in 1974 than in 1972.

In 1972, environmental problems took second place only to fear of crime. Air pollution and dirty streets and sidewalks were great problems for about one in four respondents at that time. By 1974, over one-third of those in both experimental and control districts cited these as great problems.

Outranking these environmental concerns in 1974, however, was the problem of low pay or not enough money to live on. During the two-year period, inflation had taken its toll, and from fewer than one in five in 1972, about two in five in 1974 reported insufficient money to live on as a great problem. Perhaps as a corollary to the increase in economic concerns, the proportion citing housing as a great problem in 1974 doubled that in 1972—but again in both experimental and control districts. Indeed, while there is virtually no difference between experimental and control areas in problem ratings, the salient finding is that problem ratings rose considerably between 1972 and 1974: an average 12 percent in experimental and 14 percent in control districts.

The data presented thus far comparing service appraisals and problem ratings for those living in ONG and non-ONG areas have yielded no measurable impact of the program in either improving citizen perception of municipal services or in reducing citizen problems. However, it is always possible that the totals for each problem are obscuring *individual changes* in problem perception or service ratings over the two-year period. Panel analysis enables us to look at the problem and service ratings for each item in 1972 and then again in 1974 *for the same individual.* We can compare, for example, the number of respondents in the experimental and control districts who rated fear of crime "no problem at all" or "somewhat of a problem" in 1972 but a "great problem" in 1974, or the proportion who assigned the police a low rating at the first interview but a high one in 1974, and so forth. Table 9-3 presents these "change" data for problems and services, and again no significant differences between ONG and non-ONG districts are discernible. For almost every service, there is more of a tendency for ratings to have declined rather than to have improved. Similarly for every problem, things became *more* rather than less of a concern—about equally in experimental and control neighborhoods.

In sum, whether the problem and service ratings of the sample as a whole in the two interviews are used or whether individual changes on these items are assessed, the ONG program had no measurable impact on citizen evaluation of municipal services or on reduction of the problems of respondents.

Impact of ONG on Agency Contact and Satisfaction

Returning to our causal path, the next question is whether among those respondents with problems and complaints there were more attempts to contact city agencies about these problems in districts where the program operated and whether there were higher rates of satisfaction from such contact (Table 9-4). In fact, compared with 1972 *fewer* respondents in both the experimental and control districts contacted any agency about a top priority problem in 1974, despite the higher problem rate.

Why have contacts dropped? We think the answer lies beyond the confines of the study, although the data provide some leads. Between 1972 and 1974 the problem that rose most sharply was "low pay or not enough to live on." Inflation and recession were wreaking havoc with with ability of New Yorkers to stay on top of things, and while other problems remained, preoccupation with financial concerns may well have diminished the sense of urgency about such matters as dirty streets, insufficient heat or hot water, or lack of recreation facilities. The primary problem was stretching a salary or welfare check to cover the rising cost of living, and there was little that any city agency—even the welfare center—could do about such concerns.

The economic situation may have had a depressing effect on contact rates,

Table 9-3

Changes in the Public's Perceptions of Problems and Service Ratings in Experimental and Control Districts

Problems	4 Experimental Districts			3 Control Districts		
	More of a Problem	Less of a Problem	N	More of a Problem	Less of a Problem	N
Fear of crime	34	24	560	34	19	406
Housing	38	13	544	36	12	403
Dirty streets and sidewalks	33	19	559	34	21	410
Low pay or not enough money to live on	42	13	528	41	14	402
Air pollution	32	26	541	35	19	395
Addicts in the neighborhood	34	21	481	34	18	333
Service Ratings	Lower Rating	Higher Rating	N	Lower Rating	Higher Rating	N
Sanitation	33	24	549	27	25	399
Fire protection	22	25	496	23	23	368
Police protection	37	18	512	39	22	377
Public housing	33	26	202	31	26	158
Housing inspection	39	26	284	36	27	192
Rent control	38	29	287	31	29	179
Welfare	45	21	161	37	26	122
Parks	37	23	443	34	28	302
Public schools	33	27	364	36	33	257
Street repairs	35	32	513	33	34	380
Subway and bus service	32	24	514	31	28	385
Services for treating drug addicts	20	37	90	27	25	63
Health services	28	24	350	30	22	243
Recreation for young people	40	25	338	32	29	243

but why did the satisfaction rate with such contacts rise more sharply in ONG districts? The answer may, in fact, be a direct effect of the program, although we have no concrete evidence to buttress this suggestion. However, informal conversations with local service officials in ONG areas suggest several factors that may have increased the publics' satisfaction with the way in which their complaints were handled:

Table 9-4

Contacts and Satisfactions with Contacts in 1972 and 1974, Experimental and Control Districts

	4 Experimental Districts				3 Control Districts			
	1972		1974		Change	1972		1974		Change
	(%)	(N)	(%)	(N)		(%)	(N)	(%)	(N)	
Phoned, wrote, or visited place about most important problem[a]	32	(418)	21	(549)	−11[c]	32	(286)	22	(400)	−10[c]
Satisfied with contact about most important problem[b]	32	(131)	47	(107)	+15[c]	36	(86)	40	(78)	+4

[a]Percentages based on respondents reporting a most important problem.

[b]Percentages based on respondents reporting contact about a most important problem.

[c]Relationships significant at the .01 level.

1. Several district service chiefs felt that the implementation of ONG in their districts had placed them "in the limelight." Some, in fact, had been advised by their superiors in the central agencies of the importance of establishing good relations with the public. Adherence to this advice may have made a difference in the way citizens' requests for help were received or handled.

2. Analysis of local agency contacts with neighborhood community groups showed that these increased in ONG districts over the two-year period. Such contacts, in turn, may have increased agency sensitivity to citizen needs and enabled more effective handling of their complaints (see Chapter 7).

3. More concretely, some local officials in ONG areas noted that many citizen complaints that could not be handled by their agency (e.g., a sanitation problem that had been brought to a police precinct) were turned over to the ONG office for channeling to the appropriate agency. Thus, ONG may have helped reduce the need for a person with a problem to contact several agencies (or several sections of one agency) before finding someone responsible for handling a particular complaint. This reasoning may also explain the finding that knowledge of ONG was more than twice as high for respondents with an agency contact in the experimental districts than for a similar group of respondents in the control areas.

The very small number of respondents in both experimental and control districts who actually contacted an agency about top-priority problems places severe limits on the significance of any differences in satisfaction rates we may have found. Further, it is not possible, with so small a numerical base, to probe more in order to determine whether certain *kinds* of contacts were more satisfaction producing than others. While more than one in three contacts were with the police,[d] the remainder were scattered among at least a dozen different agencies with no more than three or four respondents accounting for any one source.[e]

The Impact of ONG on Attitudes toward City Government

By this time, it is clear that our respondents' problems and appraisals of city service agencies were unaffected by the presence or absence of the ONG program and that the program did not facilitate citizen contact with municipal agencies even though it may have affected the satisfaction of those who did have such contact. With this major link in the hypothesized causal chain all but eliminated, it almost seems fruitless to see whether citizen attitudes toward city government became more positive over the two-year period in ONG districts than in control areas.

However, following the problem through, we find that there has been no change in residents' attitudes toward government either in experimental or control districts (Table 9-5). Feelings of alienation or powerlessness still prevailed at a high rate, and the presence or absence of ONG made no difference at all.

Clearly, if ONG achieved significant results—and district managers, cabinet members, and many local community leaders attest that it did, as shown in Chapters 2, 6 and 7—these results were not evident to the general public. The analysis of changes in responses between Time 1 and Time 2 in the experimental and control areas has shown virtually no measurable impact of the ONG experiment on community residents. While changes in service ratings, problem incidence, and contacts with municipal agencies indeed occurred over the two years between interviews, no systematic changes differentiate the responses in the experimental from those in the control districts.

Citizen Knowledge of the ONG Program

The absence of ONG impact on citizen contacts and perceptions is not surprising, because ONG offices were not designed to be complaint processing

---

[d]We found that contacts with the police were associated with high satisfaction rates than were contacts with any other types of agencies.

[e]Depth studies of specific agencies, with adequate samples of both personnel and clients would be a more effective way of measuring and evaluating the differential success of local service agencies in handling citizen problems. For in this way, public responses could be related to the realities of administrative procedures. For a discussion of the advantages and limitations of large-scale surveys to evaluate the public's response to service delivery, see D. Katz, et al., *Bureaucratic Encounters: A Pilot Study in the Evaluation of Government Services*, Institute for Social Research, University of Michigan, 1975, pp. 3-5.

Table 9-5

A Comparison of the Public's Attitudes toward City Government in 1972 and 1974, Experimental and Control Districts

	4 Experimental Districts			3 Control Districts		
	1972	1974	Change	1972	1974	Change
	(%) (N)	(%) (N)		(%) (N)	(%) (N)	
Respondents who agree they could do little or nothing about an unfair law	69 (539)	68 (527)	−1	67 (391)	68 (366)	+1
Respondents who agree the people of New York City have little or no influence on city government	49 (525)	49 (527)	0	51 (378)	51 (381)	0
Respondents who agree people in neighborhood have little or no influence on how services in the area are run	66 (480)	62 (481)	−4	66 (356)	63 (345)	−3
Average change			−2			−1

centers. While local leaders were aware of the program and quite pleased with its operation (see Chapter 6), very little awareness of ONG trickled down to the public level, as pointed out in the administrative analysis of the program:

At the time of their appointments, the Managers were encouraged to meet with community groups in their districts but the goal of these meetings—from ONG's perspective—was to emphasize that the District Manager offices were not to become processing centers, but rather that their major concern would be with the coordination of the district-level representatives of the different agencies.[2]

There was some change, however, in the public's knowledge of the program and this change does differentiate respondents in the experimental from those in the control districts (Table 9-6). In ONG districts, knowledge of the program was professed by about one in seven respondents—an increase of 4 percent from 1972. In control districts, fewer than one in ten thought the program was operating—a drop of 1 percent over the two-year period.

A 5 percent difference in public awareness of the program is neither startling nor statistically significant, but several additional pieces of information combine to increase our confidence in the differences between ONG and non-ONG areas in public awareness of the program. First, we found that proximity to an ONG field office raised the level of visibility substantially. More than one in four (27 percent) of those living within a few blocks of an ONG district headquarters were aware of its existence, compared to just 9 percent of

Table 9-6

A Comparison of Knowledge of Neighborhood Institutions in 1972 and 1974, Experimental and Control Districts

	4 Experimental Districts			3 Control Districts		
	1972	1974	Change	1972	1974	Change
	(%) (N)	(%) (N)		(%) (N)	(%) (N)	
Knows of place in neighborhood that helps people deal with city agencies	23 (563)	32 (561)	+9	20 (413)	26 (412)	+6
"Knows" that neighborhood has:						
Community Planning Board	10 (554)	22 (561)	+12	10 (405)	24 (412)	+14
Community School Board	14	48	+34	14	47	+33
Office of Neighborhood Government	10	14	+4	8	7	−1

those living in other sections of an ONG district. Similarly, knowledge of "a place in the neighborhood where people could go for help in dealing with city offices and services" was considerably higher among respondents living near an ONG office (48 percent) compared with 30 percent of those living further away.

Digressing a moment, we find that the modest rise in the level of visibility of ONG in the experimental areas is in sharp contrast to the large increase in public awareness of two other community institutions—Community Planning Board and the community school boards. In 1972, among residents in the experimental districts, 10 percent knew of the Community Planning Board, and this figure increased to 22 percent by 1974. Knowledge of the community school board rose from 14 percent in 1972 to 48 percent in 1974. However, increases in knowledge of these community institutions occurred at about the same rate in the control districts—a finding that adds confidence to the 1 percent decrease in knowledge of ONG in these areas. It is interesting to note that the institution most closely embodying the concept of community control (the school board) had the highest visibility, followed by the Community Planning Board, which is a rung down the ladder of citizen participation, while the least visible institution is ONG—the administrative decentralization program.

That the small 5 percent difference between experimental and control districts in knowledge of ONG is more than coincidental is suggested in Figure 9-2, which shows that awareness of the program in 1974 was not randomly distributed. Respondents were asked a number of questions about their formal and informal participation in the political process: for example, whether they had voted in 1972 presidential or 1973 mayoral election; had participated in a

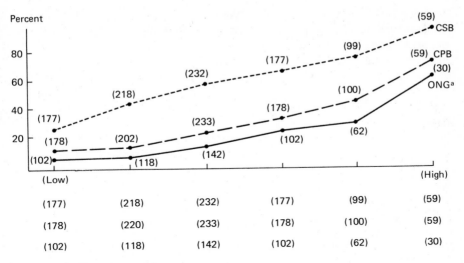

Note: N = figure in parentheses.

[a]Experimental districts only.

Figure 9-2. Knowledge of Community Institutions by Activity-Efficacy Scale.

protest, signed a petition, or spoken to a public official about a neighborhood problem; spoke often with neighbors about local or national affairs; were asked for ideas, information, or help in dealing with city agencies; belonged to a tenant or homeowners' group; would act (and be likely to succeed in such action) if the city government took action the respondent considered harmful to the neighborhood. Answers to these items were combined and scaled into an "activity-efficacy" scale and then related to respondents' awareness of the ONG program. Figure 9-2 shows a direct relationship between participation in the political process and knowledge of ONG, as well as knowledge of the school and planning boards.[f]

It is apparent that knowledge of the program existed among a small group of active citizens. Since these more knowledgeable residents were both formally and informally engaged in community activity, one would expect the public's awareness of the program to have increased over the next several years.

Moreover, residents of New York City appeared ready for change, because in November 1975 they approved six proposals for charter reform recommended by the New York State Commission for the Revision of the New York City

---

[f]The relationship between knowledge of ONG and each item in the scale was more than modest. In every instance a respondent who engaged in the particular behavior was two-and-a-half to three times as likely to know about ONG than were their inactive counterparts.

Charter. These proposals included establishing a citywide system of administrative decentralization along the lines of the ONG program.[3]

Many city officials, including the mayor, were openly opposed to these reform proposals, but undoubtedly to their dismay, the public voted for their enactment. As of January 1976, no steps had been taken to implement the public's mandate, ostensibly because of the city's fiscal crisis. Moreover, there appeared to be no sentiment at city hall to even develop plans for honoring the mandate.

The data we collected in 1974 suggest the kind of municipal reform New Yorkers support. In light of the 1976 citywide mandate, it would seem important to examine the study's data in some detail in order to understand better what public readiness for decentralization means and the role citizens see for themselves in local government.

Part Two: The Receptivity of the Public to Decentralization

Local self-rule has been a central value throughout American history, and this ideal of keeping government close to the people has taken many forms from that of the small town meeting to representation through elected officials.[4] The setting in which we examine citizen participation in the political process is that of a large city, and the specific question to be answered is how strong are the interest and readiness of local citizens for some kind of decentralization at the neighborhood level.

By virtue of living in the same neighborhood, it is said, people have common interests and concerns that should be reflected in government action. Citizens are to influence government, and government in turn is to be accountable to them. But citizen participation in the decision-making process at the neighborhood level in a city as large as New York and with such a multiplicity of interests is a sizeable undertaking. Although the ideal is of fundamental importance in the American value system, the implementation of it in this setting is highly complex and subject to many difficulties. Decisions must be made as to who shall represent the community, with what powers, and for what purposes, and these questions only begin to identify the many considerations that must accompany decentralization of authority. Of special concern to us is base-line information on the readiness and ability of the public to assume some responsibility in the decentralization process.

Although in theory propinquity leads to common views and interests, in fact people who live in the same neighborhood are not all alike; nor is their commitment to their neighborhood necessarily identical. Moreover, in a city such as New York, most people rent rather than own their homes and living, as they must, in close propinquity may or may not encourage a sense of community and desire for some kind of local control.

The data already presented make clear that residents of the seven districts were troubled about the problems of city living and the response of municipal services to their problems. Further, conditions got worse in the two years between interviews. The evidence is that citizens did not blame municipal services for their problems, but they were dissatisfied with the delivery of local services and large numbers either didn't know where to go for help or felt it's useless to seek help from city agencies.

Tightening the reins of authority at the center may be one answer to the problems of improving the delivery of services to New Yorkers. Large-scale use of the media might at least increase the visibility of city services and provide citizens with information about where to go for help for various kinds of problems. But the data point to the fact that problems and priorities differ from one kind of neighborhood to another. Low-income districts have large numbers of people who fall into the category of multiproblem families. In such districts, particularly heavy demands are placed on a service system—demands, as we have seen, that differ somewhat from those of a middle-class neighborhood. Similarly, areas with large numbers of minorities have different service requirements from neighborhoods with a mostly nonminority population. Both the number and kinds of problems, in other words, vary depending upon the mix of the population and the locality. These findings suggest that some kind of local control would make sense—whether it takes the form of administrative decentralization or actual community control.

Administrative Decentralization

Given our interest in the viability of decentralization in the minds of residents, we asked our sample several questions about their preferences for local control of municipal services. First, we asked about administrative decentralization—that is, whether they thought city services would be run better if local or central service officials made most of the decisions for their neighborhood.

Almost three out of five (57 percent) thought that municipal services would be run better if decisions were made at the local level. About one in five (22 percent) favored centralized decision making, and the same proportion thought it didn't matter one way or the other (Table 9-7).[g]

Ethnic groups varied somewhat in their endorsement of administrative decentralization. Whites were most likely to favor it (64 percent), then Hispanics

[g]In measuring the "impact" of ONG on the public, the analysis was restricted to the 973 respondents who remained in the same dwelling unit between 1972 and 1974. The analysis and all of the data presented in the remaining sections of this chapter, however, combine the responses of 973 "original respondents," 63 "substitute respondents" (a member of the household who was interviewed in cases where the original respondent had died, was ill, or otherwise unavailable for questioning), and 252 "inmovers" who were occupying dwelling units vacated by 1972 respondents. Together, this group of 1,288 respondents constitutes the 1974 neighborhood sample.

Table 9-7

Percent Who Prefer Decision Making by Local or Central Service Officials by Ethnicity and by Number of Bad/Very Bad Service Ratings, 1974

Ethnicity and Service Ratings	Prefer Local Officials to Make Decisions (Percent)	Prefer Central Officials to Make Decisions (Percent)	Doesn't Matter (Percent)	N
All respondents	57	22	20	1155
Ethnicity				
Black	49	19	31	396
Hispanic	59	30	11	300
White	64	22	15	411
Number of bad/very bad service ratings				
None	42	22	36	243
One	55	24	22	221
Two or three	63	21	16	358
Four or more	65	24	11	333

(59 percent), and lastly blacks (49 percent). The data show not that blacks prefer to have decisions about services made in a central office, but that they thought it simply didn't matter whether these decisions were made in the neighborhood or at headquarters. As Table 9-7 shows, blacks were twice as likely as whites and almost three times as likely as Hispanics to have responded, "it [where decisions are made] doesn't matter one way or the other." Blacks were not indifferent however, to political decentralization, as we will see shortly.

Table 9-7 also shows that endorsement of administrative decentralization is sharply related to citizens' attitudes toward service delivery itself. The more one sees service delivery as deficient, the readier he is to advocate administrative decentralization. Four out of ten who assigned no ratings of bad or very bad to the fourteen services, but 65 percent who gave these services four or more negative ratings, felt it would be better if decisions were made at the local rather than central level. Moreover, it is important to note that the proportion who said "it doesn't matter" decreases steadily with the harshness of service ratings. Apparently it *did* matter to those New Yorkers who had not found service agencies responsive to their problems, and their choice was administrative control at the local level.

Local Service Control

We also asked respondents whether they would favor electing a board of local residents to advise the city or to make decisions about the way city services should be run in their neighborhoods. Three out of four favored this for recreation facilities, slightly more than half for public schools, the police, and sanitation, and a little less than half for drug treatment programs (Table 9-8). This evidence, plus that on administrative decentralization presented in the previous table, points to receptivity among the public for a community role in service delivery.

Moreover, there was more agreement among blacks, Hispanics, and whites about the desirability of political decentralization than one might have expected given their responses to the idea of administrative decentralization. As may be recalled, blacks were the least enthusiastic about administrative decentralization and particularly likely to think it simply wouldn't have an impact on service delivery. By and large, however, this was not their sentiment on political decentralization. They held views similar to whites and Hispanics with respect to the local control of recreation, police, sanitation, and schools.

The absence of differences among the major ethnic groups of the city on

Table 9-8
Percent Favoring Local Control of Selected Municipal Services by Ethnicity, 1974

Local Control of:	Black (Percent)	Hispanic (Percent)	White (Percent)	All Respondents
Recreation				
Yes	72	69	73	72
No	16	21	13	16
Don't know	12	9	14	12
Police				
Yes	52	57	56	55
No	31	34	32	32
Don't know	17	8	12	13
Sanitation				
Yes	51	55	50	52
No	33	35	37	35
Don't know	15	10	13	13
Schools				
Yes	47	58	53	52
No	35	27	27	30
Don't know	18	15	20	18
Drug programs				
Yes	31	53	50	44
No	34	30	23	29
Don't know	35	17	27	27
Total Number	430	331	466	1227

local control of four major services is, in our view, an important finding.[h] It suggests that the city could move toward some kind of local control of these services and have the backing of a sizeable constituency of blacks, Hispanics, and whites. The data further suggest that the most favorable site would be recreation facilities.

Local control of drug treatment programs was less widely accepted, particularly by the blacks. They did not oppose the idea, but rather they just weren't sure how advisable such a plan would be. The basis for this statement is the finding in Table 9-8 that one out of three blacks answered "don't know" to this item. Although the proportion of Hispanics and whites who said "don't know" is lower than that of the blacks, of the five services considered, drug treatment was the one on which all three ethnic groups were least likely to have a crystallized opinion. In effect, the data suggest that any changes in how drug programs are administered ought to proceed with caution and with community preparation, because local citizens are divided about politically decentralizing them.

Just as with administrative decentralization, the desire for political decentralization correlates highly with the appraisal of service delivery so that the more services residents judge as bad, the more they endorse the idea of local control. Table 9-9 shows that among those who assigned a bad or very bad rating to even one of the fourteen municipal services evaluated, 39 percent would have liked to see local control of at least four of the services. The harsher critics of municipal services—those assigning three or more bad or very bad ratings—wanted local control of at least four services at a rate of 60 percent.

The relationship between the rating of a particular service and preference for local control of that service is also presented in Table 9-9. With the exception of addiction services, it is clear that the poorer the rating of a service, the larger the proportion opting for local control of that service.

As may be recalled, addiction services were rated by only 36 percent of the sample. Now we see in Table 9-9 that whether the service was considered good or bad, about the same proportion would have liked to see it administered by some form of local control. A combination of the fact that relatively few people rated the service and the fact that no relationship exists between the service rating and the endorsement of local control strengthens the conclusion that if local control is to be implemented, it would be better to start with any of the other services. For example, local control of recreation services has what might be considered a mandate from the public. Virtually, everyone rated this service, and even among those who rated it highly, three out of four (72 percent) favored local control of recreation.

The *personal* experience of residents is also reflected in their endorsement

[h]Attitudes of different ethnic groups toward decentralizing the schools parallel those reported in a survey conducted for *The New York Times.* See *The New York Times,* January 19, 1974, p. 64.

Table 9-9
Service Ratings and Attitudes toward Local Control, 1974

Assign ratings of bad/very bad to:	Favor local control of four or more services:	
	(%)	(N)
No services	39	(291)
One or two services	49	(460)
Three or more services	60	(532)
Service rating of:	Favor local control of:	
	(%)	(N)
Sanitation		
Excellent/good	46	(700)
Bad/very bad	60	(141)
Police		
Excellent/good	50	(521)
Bad/very bad	64	(227)
Recreation services		
Excellent/good	72	(259)
Bad/very bad	81	(413)
Public schools		
Excellent/good	53	(369)
Bad/very bad	64	(196)
Addiction services		
Excellent/good	60	(138)
Bad/very bad	56	(131)

of local control; the data on crime and schools are illustrations. Those who reported that fear of crime was a great problem were about as likely to favor local control of the police as were those for whom fear of crime was no problem at all. However, 69 percent of those who were *crime victims* in the previous year or two, compared to 53 percent who had not experienced a crime, favored local control of the police. Similarly, among those who had children in the public schools and felt their children were getting a good education, about half endorsed local control of the public schools, but three out of four wanted local control of the schools when they thought their children were not receiving a good education.

Political scientists and politicians have argued over the relative merits and dangers of administrative as compared with political decentralization. In light of the furor over school decentralization in the late sixties, Lindsay's advisors

... suggested that the whole issue of political decentralization be held in abeyance until the outlines of a public consensus became discernible, and that the Office [of Neighborhood Government] focus instead on creating the kind of administrative structure that would be compatible with a [future] political decentralization program.[5]

Such a public consensus may be more than a distant prospect, for among New Yorkers in our sample the readiness to endorse administrative decentralization goes hand in hand with support of local control of city services (Table 9-10).

And even among the 46 percent of the sample who either opposed administrative decentralization or thought it would make no difference in how municipal services were actually run, a sizeable proportion favored the political decentralization of two or more services. To be precise, 61 percent of those who thought administrative decentralization "doesn't matter" and 47 percent of those who were against it wanted local control of at least two of the five services about which they were queried.

Administrative decentralization is a less visible and more moderate change in the structure of service delivery than political decentralization. But what kind of political decentralization do residents want, especially those who see nothing to be gained from administrative decentralization? The options are essentially two: A local board either *advises* or *makes final decisions* about how services should be run. The former, of course, is the more conservative alternative, and the data show that this position was favored by a majority of respondents (61 percent). A total of 30 percent did advocate decision-making powers, and the remaining 9

Table 9-10
Administrative and Political Decentralization

Political Decentralization	Administrative Decentralization		
	Prefer Local Decision Making (Percent) (N = 662)	Prefer Central Decision Making (Percent) (N = 262)	Doesn't Matter (Percent) (N = 231)
Number of services for which local control is favored:			
None or one	8	53	39
Two or three	32	26	45
Four or five	60	21	16
A local elected board should:			
Give advice	54	75	69
Make decisions	42	18	19
Don't know	4	7	12

percent, "don't know." The fact that only 9 percent said "don't know" suggests that the public is decisive about the preferred structure for local control.

Those who said "yes" to administrative decentralization were more likely than those who did not to think a local board should act in a decision-making capacity, but the figure, 42 percent, is no resounding call for this kind of political decentralization (Table 9-10). In other words, respondents endorsed gradualism in the local control of major services such as sanitation, police, schools, and recreation. Thus, they are ready for partial, but not total change; they want to advise from the neighborhood about how services should be run, but are not as ready to assume the power to make the decisions. Their preference for an advisory role could be an expression of some confidence in the capability and good faith of the citywide service administrators; otherwise, residents might have expressed a stronger desire to wrest authority from these officials.

The public could also be fearful that particular groups in their neighborhood would exercise power in a detrimental way, if there were local control. And, if this situation were to happen, perhaps they would be better off with centralized authority over service delivery. Pursuing this line of reasoning, we asked respondents whether they thought particular groups in their neighborhood would end up running things under a system of local control. Only one in four anticipated that this would happen, and more than half of these thought the efforts of such groups would be beneficial to them.[i] In general, we should add that the strongest proponents of local control were the people who thought certain groups would end up running things and that this would be to their own advantage.

Returning to the discussion of what leads some residents to want a local board to make final decisions rather than to merely give advice, we begin to see a pattern in the data (Table 9-11). First, we find that the more critical respondents were of service delivery (as measured by the number of services rated "bad" or "very bad") the readier they were to favor a local board as final arbiter rather than advisor. And second, while in theory the public could prefer the more moderate advisory role but still favor some form of local control over a number of services, the data indicate that this was not the case. The fewer services that respondents would have liked to see locally controlled, the more they opted for local advisory rather than decision-making power.

Setting the Budget and Hiring and Firing

It is one thing to ask the public in general whether they favor some kind of local control but another to ask them specifically if their view of local control extends

---

[i]Respondents were asked: "If there were local control, do you think any particular groups in your neighborhood would end up running things?" Those who said "yes" were then asked: "Do you think their running things would benefit people like you?"

Table 9-11

Type of Political Decentralization Preferred by Number of Bad/Very Bad Service Ratings and by Number of Services for which Local Control Is Favored, 1974

	Advisory (Percent)	Decision Making (Percent)	(N)
Number of bad/very bad service ratings:			
None or one	72	28	474
Two or three	69	31	349
Four or more	58	42	333
Number of services for which local control is favored:			
None or one	83	17	280
Two or three	69	31	388
Four or five	56	44	488

to setting the budget and hiring and firing city employees. Of all the issues at stake in local control, the right to set the budget and to hire and fire in the local area are critical and controversial. These issues are critical because self-rule without authority over the budget or over who shall perform services is severely limited, and they are controversial because they require an agreed-upon plan as to who in the community shall exercise this authority and how it shall be done.

Thus far, our survey data indicate a qualified readiness for local control among residents (e.g., a preference for an advisory rather than a decision-making role), and the respondents' views on budget setting and hiring and firing are no departure from this position. As Table 9-12 shows, 48 percent endorsed budget setting at the local level, and fewer, 38 percent, endorsed the right to hire and fire city employees in the local area. And, at least one in six either hadn't made up their minds or chose not to be identified as for or against either issue. It is worth noting that the right to hire and to fire is the aspect of local control that was least likely to have the backing of our sample. In fact, more opposed the idea than supported it.

Supporters of these two components of local control, however, were the ones who decidedly wanted their neighborhood to have final decision-making power rather than simply an advisory voice. Specifically, 47 percent who endorsed local control over budget setting, but only 17 percent who did not, favored the decision-making role at the neighborhood level. The figures are similar for proponents of the right to hire and fire. It would seem, then, that satisfying residents who favor these two crucial components of local control requires giving them the right to make decisions.

Ethnicity differentiates respondents somewhat on the issues of local budget

Table 9-12
Should There Be Local Control over Setting the Budget and over Hiring and Firing of City Employees?

	Budget Setting (Percent) ($N = 1283$)	Hiring and Firing (Percent) ($N = 1282$)
Yes	48	38
No	35	44
Don't know	17	18

setting and hiring and firing. A comparison of blacks, whites, and Hispanics reveals that blacks were less interested in having these prerogatives than either whites or Hispanics (Table 9-13). Whites in particular seemed to recognize that budget-setting power at the local level was a prerequisite for effective local control.

Overall, we should add that poor neighborhoods were not where the major support was found for local control over the budget and over hiring and firing. Rather, it was in the working- and middle-class neighborhoods, especially those that are white (Table 9-14).

Commitment to Decentralization

A majority of the sample favored the decentralization of local services. Almost one-half (48 percent) also wanted some control over the local budget for services and about two out of five wanted authority to extend to the hiring and firing of city employees. By and large, respondents preferred an advisory rather than a decision-making role over how services should be run in their neighborhoods, but it should be remembered that some 30 percent wanted decision-making power, and these people are the strongest supporters of local control.

If neighborhood residents take on the responsibilities of local control, whether these are defined as giving advice or as making final decisions, they must be willing to extend themselves for their community. Mechanisms available to them include, for instance, attending meetings, working to elect representatives to a local board, or serving on such a board.[j]

The data indicate that almost three out of four were receptive to attending

[j]We queried residents about their willingness to attend local board meetings and to work to elect representatives to a local board, but we did not explore their willingness to serve on such a board. We reasoned that one question about readiness to serve could easily expand to several were we to try to understand why they took the position they did. Moreover, for our purposes, commitment to decentralization could be measured without trying to identify how much of a leadership role this might entail.

Table 9-13
Attitudes toward Local Control of Budget Setting and Hiring and Firing by Ethnicity, 1974

Local Control of:	Blacks (Percent) (N = 430)	Hispanics (Percent) (N = 330)	Whites (Percent) (N = 466)
Setting the budget for local services			
Yes	40	46	57
No	43	36	26
Don't know	17	17	16
Hiring and firing of city employees in the area			
Yes	28	43	42
No	51	40	41
Don't know	21	17	17

Table 9-14
Support for Local Control of Budget Setting and Hiring and Firing by Type of Neighborhood

Neighborhood Type	Prefer Local Control Over:		N^a
	Budget Setting (Percent)	Hiring-Firing (Percent)	
Minority poor	41	31	369
Mixed poor	46	34	135
Minority working class	44	33	162
Mixed working class	48	43	202
White working class	55	46	164
White middle class	59	41	251

[a]"Don't know" responses are included in the percentage base.

neighborhood meetings a few times a year. Fewer, but still more than one-half (55 percent) said that they would be willing to spend evenings or weekends working to elect board members whom they thought would be good representatives. And, as one would expect, citizens who favored decision making rather than advisory power at the neighborhood level were most likely to say they would give their time to these activities (Table 9-15).

In the first section of this chapter we saw that an active, efficacious segment of the public was most alert to the presence of ONG (Figure 9-2). Now we have

Table 9-15

Willingness to Attend Meetings or Work to Elect Representatives by Preference for Advisory or Decision-Making Role of Local Board

	Prefer Advisory		Prefer Decision Making	
	(%)	(N)	(%)	(N)
Would attend meetings	52	(735)	65	(368)
Would work to elect representatives	70	(751)	79	(375)

seen that the strongest proponents of decentralization (as indicated by a preference for the decision making over the advisory role of a local board) are those who express a willingness to participate in the decentralization process by attending meetings or working to elect good board members. Can we have any confidence that most or even just some of these avowals of readiness to become involved would be actualized if local control were to become a reality?

To answer this question, we grouped respondents on the same activism-efficacy index used in Figure 9-2 and also constructed a "local control" scale, comprised of eleven items:

Favor local versus central service officials making decisions about services (item 1);
Favor local control of each of five services (items 2-6);
Favor local control over budget setting and hiring and firing (items 7-8);
Favor decision making versus advisory role of local board (item 9);
Would attend meetings and work to elect board representatives (items 10-11).

Respondents were then grouped into a four-category index based on their total score on these items.

Table 9-16 points to a clear relationship between active participation in the political process and the local control score. Those ranking "high" on the activism-efficacy index were twice as likely to score high on the local control index as were their least active counterparts. Among the most active, 40 percent rank high on the local control index, compared to 21 percent of the inactive public. Conversely, just one in eight of the most active, but one in three of the least active, were only minimal advocates of any form of local control.

Clearly, a strong endorsement of local control was most evident among the highly active and efficacious segment of the public—a group that had been participating in the political process on both a formal and informal basis and that expressed a willingness to participate in the decentralization process. From such a group may well emerge the leadership at the grass roots level for the Charter Reform proposals approved by the electorate in November 1975.

Table 9-16
Position on the Local Control Index by Position on the Activism-Efficacy Index

Local Control Index	Activism-Efficacy Index				
	High (Percent) (N = 151)	Medium High (Percent) (N = 176)	Medium (Percent) (N = 230)	Medium Low (Percent) (N = 219)	Low (Percent) (N = 174)
High	40	30	24	22	21
Medium High	28	28	23	28	20
Medium Low	20	23	30	33	25
Low	12	19	24	17	34

Overall, our analysis of public receptivity to decentralization shows a convergence between the attitudes of our sample and the public's mandate for charter reform. New Yorkers are calling for change in the delivery of municipal services, and the term "local" strikes a sympathetic chord—particularly among those most dissatisfied with current service delivery and among those who have already been fairly active participants in the political process. This bodes well for the successful implementation of the charter revisions, if city officials begin to take the appropriate steps.

Notes

1. See, for example, "Refuse Collection: Department of Sanitation vs. Private Carting," by John F. McMahon and Herbert R. Gamache, under the director E.S. Savas, First Deputy City Administrator, Office of the Mayor, Office of Administration, City of New York, November 1970.

2. Stanley J. Heginbotham and Howard G. Katz, *Between Community and City Bureaucracy: Part III, Patterns of Community Involvement in the Experiment*, Bureau of Applied Social Research, Columbia University, New York, N.Y., 1973, p. 1.

3. See State Charter Revision Commission for New York City, "Proposed Amendments to the Charter for the City of New York," August 1975. Three additional propositions submitted without recommendation of the commission were rejected by the electorate.

4. For a concise discussion of this basic American value see Alan A. Altschuler, *Community Control* (New York: Western Publishing Co., 1970), esp. Ch. 2.

5. Stanley J. Heginbotham and Kenneth H. Andrews, *Between Community and City Bureaucracy: Part V, Problems and Prospects in Expanding to a City-Wide Program*, Bureau of Applied Social Research, Columbia University, Ithaca, N.Y., 1973, p. 2.

Appendix 9A
A Summary of Comparisons between Three Matched Experimental and Control Districts

Table 9A-1
Social Characteristics of Experimental and Control Districts, 1972

	3 Basic Experimental Districts (Percent) (N = 720)	3 Control Districts (Percent) (N = 725)	Difference	Crown Heights Experimental District (Percent) (N = 238)
Socioeconomic status				
Under $6000 family income	35	35	0	40
No high school education	29	23	+6	24
On welfare	16	16	0	17
On social security	27	22	+5	18
Ethnicity				
Black	21	23	−2	71
Puerto Rican	19	18	+1	4
Jewish	8	10	−2	10
Italian	16	8	+8	2
Irish	9	10	−1	3
Other	20	25	−5	11
Household characteristics				
Home owner	27	23	+4	20
Under 3 years in neighborhood	24	33	−9	24
Child under 18 in household	50	50	0	46
Divorced or separated	12	13	−1	16
Respondent aged 60 or older	23	20	+3	15
Social ties				
Belong to organization active in neighborhood problems	26	27	−1	38
Relatives within a few blocks	46	41	+5	45
Friends within a few blocks	61	55	+6	63
Belong to 2 or more organizations	18	19	−1	26

Table 9A-2
Perceived Problems in Experimental and Control Districts, 1972

	3 Basic Experimental Districts (Percent) (N = 720)	3 Control Districts (Percent) (N = 725)	Difference	Crown Heights Experimental District (Percent) (N = 238)
Great problem for Respondents				
Fear of crime	35	33	+2	39
Housing	18	18	0	22
Low pay	17	16	+1	22
Addicts in neighborhood	21	15	+6	19
Lack of teenage recreation	13	9	+4	13
Lack of good schools	7	7	0	8
Average	18	16	+2	20
Member of household victim of crime in last year	16	17	−1	22
Respondents rating Municipal Service "excellent" or "good":				
Fire protection	79	83	−4	77
Subway & Bus services	60	62	−2	57
Sanitation	60	59	+1	54
Police protection	57	54	+3	48
Traffic control	47	49	−2	49
Health services	47	49	−2	44
Parks	41	33	+8	46
Public schools	38	34	+4	33
Street repairs	34	28	+4	31
Rent control	29	26	+3	30
Housing inspection, etc.	28	23	+5	29
Welfare	25	22	+3	19
Public housing	24	22	+2	26
Recreation for young people	22	19	+3	27
Drug addiction services	12	12	0	11
Average	40	38	+2	39
Neighborhood a good or very good place to live	37	39	−2	35
Would like to stay in neighborhood	45	44	+1	48
People in neighborhood have little or no influence on city services in area	67	67	0	62

Table 9A-3

A Comparison of the Public's Service and Problem Ratings, Contacts and Satisfactions, Attitudes toward City Government, and Knowledge of Neighborhood Institutions, Experimental and Control Districts, 1972 and 1974

Items	3 Experimental Districts			3 Control Districts		
	1972	1974	Change	1972	1974	Change
Percent Rating municipal services excellent or good[a]	(N = 155-416)	(N = 133-409)		(N = 147-406)	(N = 117-405)	
Sanitation	63	56	-7	59	57	-2
Fire protection	85	81	-4	88	84	-4
Police protection	61	47	-14	58	42	-16
Public housing	41	31	-10	38	28	-10
Housing inspection and code enforcement	41	36	-5	35	31	-4
Rent control	45	34	-11	41	34	-7
Welfare	55	34	-21	42	33	-9
Parks	45	37	-8	37	37	0
Public schools	46	38	-8	45	41	-4
Street Repairs	36	31	-5	29	26	-3
Subway and bus service	60	50	-10	62	58	-4
Services for treating drug addicts	37	39	+2	31	32	+1
Health services	63	60	-3	67	58	-9
Recreation for young people	34	26	-8	27	28	+1
Average Change			-8			-5
Percent Rating the following a Great problem[b]	(N = 417)	(N = 417)		(N = 413)	(N = 392)	
Fear of crime	34	48	+14	34	49	+15

Table 9A-3 (cont.)

Items	3 Experimental Districts					3 Control Districts				
	1972		1974		Change	1972		1974		Change
	(%)	(N)	(%)	(N)		(%)	(N)	(%)	(N)	
Housing	17		35		+18	16		31		+15
Dirty streets and sidewalks	26		36		+10	24		35		+11
Low pay; not enough to live on	17		39		+22	17		36		+19
Dirty air; pollution	28		38		+10	26		35		+9
Addicts in the neighborhood	19		31		+12	16		30		+14
Average Change					+14					+14
Crime victim in Household^c	17	(416)	13	(411)	−4	18	(413)	18	(392)	0
Phoned, wrote or visited place about most important problem^c	34	(298)	22	(285)	−12	32	(286)	22	(400)	−10
Satisfaction with contact about most important problem^c	35	(100)	45	(85)	+10	36	(86)	40	(78)	+4
Attitudes toward city government^d										
Agree they could do nothing about an unfair law	69	(403)	66	(399)	−3	67	(391)	68	(366)	+1
Agree the people of New York City have little or no influence on city government	52	(391)	49	(395)	−3	51	(378)	51	(381)	0
Agree people in neighborhood have little or no influence on how services in the area are run	68	(361)	61	(371)	−7	66	(356)	63	(345)	−3

Average change

Knowledge of neighborhood institutions[e]			−4			
Knows of place in neighborhood that helps people deal with city agencies	22 (417)	35 (414)	+13	20 (413)	26 (412)	+6
Knows that neighborhood has:						
Community Planning Board	9 (410)	23 (416)	+14	10 (405)	24 (412)	+14
Community School Board	14 (410)	47 (416)	+33	14 (405)	47 (412)	+33
Office of Neighborhood Government	10 (410)	17 (416)	+7	8 (405)	7 (412)	−1

aSame as Table 9-1 excluding Crown Heights.
bSame as Table 9-2 excluding Crown Heights.
cSame as Table 9-4 excluding Crown Heights.
dSame as Table 9-5 excluding Crown Heights.
eSame as Table 9-6 excluding Crown Heights.

10

What Has Been Learned from the New York City Neighborhood Government Experiment?

Allen H. Barton

We have studied what happened when New York City tried out a program of district managers and district cabinets in selected areas of the city during 1972 and 1973. The research looked for evidence on two major questions.

First, does decentralization of big-city administration help solve urban problems by improving service delivery and citizen-government relations?

Second, if a city wants to decentralize, what forms and procedures of decentralization are workable?

Those who want simple and definite answers to these questions will not find them, because the real world is not organized like an experimental laboratory. The research describes what the city did and did not do: It shows that some good things happened, that some feared bad things did not happen, and that a lot of things never got far enough to have either good or bad effects. The New York experiment in administrative decentralization was not implemented strongly enough or for a long enough time to provide definite *proof* that this form of decentralization is either good, bad, or indifferent. What we have presented here is *evidence* concerning its potential effects, and those experienced in city government will have to interpret this evidence for themselves in order to draw conclusions for their own cities. New York City in 1972-73 tried out the only program of administrative decentralization and service coordination involving the full range of municipal departments to have been attempted in the United States; and this research describes what happened.

Summary of Findings

As a summary, we can report the following findings.

1. The program was drastically *changed in its planning phase*, from one emphasizing community representation by community boards and outreach to the citizens through little city halls for complaint handling, advice, and public information, to one emphasizing the strengthening of local administrative capacity and keeping out of the public eye (see the sections in Chapter 2 on program and goal definition). A district manager, without line authority but with mayoral backing, was to promote service coordination. There were to be

district cabinets of field administrators of city departments, to whom greater autonomy was to be delegated by their departments. Departmental service districts were to be redrawn to create common boundaries. The shift from political to administrative decentralization resulted from fears of raising public expectations without a local administrative mechanism to deal with these demands, from experience with racially toned conflicts in experiments with "community control" of schools, and the refusal of the City Council to permit little city halls, which they saw as mayoral competition in handling complaints and communicating with the residents of their districts.[1]

2. The program was further *modified in actual implementation*, when most city departments did not delegate additional authority to their field administrators and did not redraw service district boundaries to make them coterminous. The program did not get strong mayoral backing in dealing with the departments, and the City Council blocked allocation of small supplemental funds promised for locally initiated projects. District managers and cabinets were left to work with whatever local discretion and resources the field administrators already had. Managers had to turn to mobilizing community leaders and groups to pressure the departments and politicians to assist the local initiatives and to bring in outside funds for improvements (see the third and fourth sections in Chapter 2).[2]

3. Nevertheless, *local operating officials and community leaders responded actively to the managers and the cabinets* and worked together to initiate a wide range of interdepartmental projects to solve specific local problems (see Chapter 4; also the descriptions of the projects in Chapter 3). Most community leaders reported contact with the manager and his staff (see the first section in Chapter 6). Some managers emphasized "brokerage" activities of persuading different departments to work with one another and with community groups to improve services. Others emphasized the "entrepreneurial" role of mobilizing community groups to campaign for increased funds for local projects, while getting the city agencies to plan for cooperation in their use. The "entrepreneurial" role was emphasized in poor districts whose problems simply could not be dealt with with available resources (see the section in Chapter 2 on attempts to consolidate authority).

4. *Departments with clear line authority and district organization were able to cooperate most easily* with the managers and cabinets—for example, police and sanitation. Those with several independent functional components, organized on a centralized or boroughwide basis, like the human resources, health service, and housing and development administrations, had the most difficulty in cooperating. The attempt to create district-level "coordinators" for the several components of these administrations was ineffective since the coordinator's territorial authority was not accepted by the functional agency staffs. Eventually, most district cabinets arranged to include the local service managers of each specialized component of these superagencies, where they existed (see the

sections in Chapter 2 on mobilization of support and attempts to consolidate central authority).

5. Most projects initiated by the managers and cabinets *created procedures for local cooperation between field administrators of the several departments* that dealt with different aspects of the same situation, where no procedures or only very cumbersome ones had previously existed. Some projects identified strategic points at which small additional resources for services or equipment could eliminate recurring or major problems. A few projects organized local agencies and community groups to seek and to utilize large outside funds for community improvement (see the section in Chapter 4 on types of ONG activities, service delivery system deficiencies, and ONG roles in the projects).

6. *A little over one-third of the locally initiated projects were fully carried out*, with the rest only partially or not at all implemented. The obstacles were generally failure to obtain authority for changes from higher levels of departments, or failure to obtain City Council approval for minor discretionary funds. A few large projects depended on obtaining federal funds that were not forthcoming. Most of the obstacles reflected the failure of the city government to delegate authority to the district level (see the section in Chapter 4 on implementation problems).

7. After two years of operation, the field administrators of city agencies in experimental districts reported essentially the *same levels of interagency contact and cooperation* as did those in nonexperimental districts. A moderate level of cooperation existed with or without the manager and cabinet. With several specific agencies, there was *more reported conflict* in experimental than in nonexperimental districts. In "semi-experimental" districts that had a cabinet but no full-time district manager, significantly more conflict was reported as was less cooperation; the manager seems to have been important in avoiding difficulties raised by bringing local administrators together in the cabinet. It therefore does not appear that the experiment achieved a significant overall improvement in service integration, in spite of the success of a number of specific cooperative projects (see the sections in Chapter 7 on awareness of and perceived levels of service integration).

8. Nevertheless the field administrators of city agencies in experimental districts, after two years of experience, have *strongly favorable attitudes toward the District Manager and District Cabinet*. These administrators feel specifically that the program contributed to interdepartmental communications, cooperation, and conflict-resolution, and to agency-community relations. They favor continuation and extension of the program (see the sections in Chapter 7 on perceptions and attitudes toward ONG).

9. After two years of operation, the community leaders in experimental districts have the *same degree of overall dissatisfaction with city services* as do those in non-experimental districts. It therefore does not appear that the experiment achieved a significant overall improvement in service delivery, in spite of some specific project successes (see Chapter 6, Table 6-6).

10. Nevertheless, the great majority of community leaders after two years of experience, during which virtually all of them became familiar with and had direct contact with their local Offices of Neighborhood Government, had *strongly favorable attitudes toward the district manager and district cabinet* and wanted the program continued. There was some opposition among traditional political clubs, which became crucial in 1974 after a party regular was elected mayor (see the section in Chapter 6 on leadership attitudes).

11. The overwhelming majority of the general public *never became aware of the local Offices of Neighborhood Government*, which did not advertise themselves as public complaint or service centers. Many more were aware of the elected community school boards and the appointed Community Planning Boards, which provided community representation in these special fields. Those who were most active in community affairs were the most aware of the experiment (see the section in Chapter 9 on citizen knowledge).

12. After two years of the experiment, the public in experimental areas reported the *same degree of satisfaction or dissatisfaction with city services, and the same level of community problems*, as those in nonexperimental districts. In both types of districts, public discontent increased. The *sense of powerlessness and distrust of city government* was the same in both experimental and nonexperimental districts (see the four sections in Chapter 9 on the impact of ONG).

13. About the *same percentage of the public had contacts with city agencies* and knew of some local place to go for help in dealing with city agencies in the experimental as in the nonexperimental districts (see the section in Chapter 9 on agency contact and satisfaction). The program, therefore, did not increase access to government for the average citizen, although it had clearly done so for leaders of community organizations. However, among the one-fifth of the public who reported contacting a city agency about a major problem, there were *10 percent more who were satisfied with the city's response* in experimental districts than in nonexperimental districts after two years of the program, while no such difference existed before the program (see the section in Chapter 9 on agency contact and satisfaction). This finding suggests a modest success in efforts to improve the responsiveness of the departments—usually the manner in which the request was handled, rather than the substantive outcome.

14. The majority of the public in both experimental and nonexperimental districts said they *favored increased local decision making* both within city departments and through an elected community board that can influence city services (see Chapter 9, Part II).

15. The district manager and his staff of about half a dozen assistants and clerks *cost about $100,000 a year for a district of about 130,000 people*. Participation of departmental officials in the cabinet used about $12,000 worth of their time. Expenses for the Central Office of Neighborhood Government, when allocated among the few experimental districts, were about $80,000 a year

per district, but this figure would be cut drastically for a citywide program of fifty or sixty districts to an estimated $13,000 per district. The annual administrative cost of a full-scale program would thus be about $125,000 per district of 130,000 people—about $1 per inhabitant, or $8 million for the City of New York (see the first section in Chapter 5).

16. The experimental districts' allocations of departmental resources were also analyzed, in comparison to all other districts of the city, by taking into account (by regression analysis) characteristics of the population and the work load. *The experimental districts did not obtain more than their normal share of resources, except in two services*: parks maintenance and highways repair, presumably through the "entrepreneurial" activities of the managers and community leaders (see the second section in Chapter 5). The procedures used by the researchers to measure district-level allocations of departmental resources could also be used by the city government to provide local administrators and community boards with "district budgets" covering most of the city's operating budget.

Interpretations of the Findings: Pessimistic and Optimistic

These are the main findings of the research. What do they all add up to? How much weight should one give the "success stories" of the projects carried out, compared with the failure of many projects to be implemented? How much weight should one give the comparisons of experimental with nonexperimental districts that show no changes in overall perceptions of interagency cooperation, service delivery, or community problems, as reported by agency officials, community leaders, and the public, and how much weight should one give the highly favorable attitudes of these same people toward the program? What would be a reasonable expectation of changes in these perceptions, after two years of a program of these dimensions, even if fully implemented? To what extent should one take into account the fact that the program was much less than fully implemented?

It is plain that the program as actually carried out did not have effects on service delivery that were big enough to register in the overall service ratings of the public or even of the community organization leaders. What is harder to judge is whether it had the potential to eventually produce such effects had it been pursued longer and with more top-level support. We can bring to bear on this judgment the evidence of the projects initiated by district managers and cabinets, the attitudes of local administrators and community leaders, their perceptions of service delivery with and without the managers and cabinets, and the problems that the managers and cabinets encountered.

A pessimistic interpretation of the results would be as follows:

1. It is extremely difficult to get centralized departments to delegate more authority to their local administrators to permit them to coordinate their activities in dealing with local problems.

2. It is not possible to significantly improve service delivery by setting up a powerless district manager and cabinet. A few successful projects don't indicate an overall potential. (Indeed it is possible that a stronger district-level authority would have negative effects on the ability of centralized departments to rationally allocate resources, use expert knowledge, and function efficiently.)

3. The administrative decentralization did not improve the accessibility of city agencies to the public. The improved responsiveness of city agencies experienced by some of those who did make contact with them, reported by 10 percent of the 20 percent who made such contacts, involved only 2 percent of the adult population. (Indeed it is possible that if the experimental program had created a large increase in public contacts, the local administrators would have been unable to handle them that satisfactorily.)

4. The widespread involvement of community leaders and local administrative officials with the program, and the favorable attitudes expressed by them, are typical of the early period of new community programs. They would not endure in the long run if the program was unable to deliver substantial improvements in services, and it has not been demonstrated that the program could do this. The perception of increased conflict with some agencies by local administrators suggests that the effect was not all positive.

5. The problems of the poorer districts, and of areas into which large numbers of low-income people are moving, are so enormous that no reorganization of the existing city services can cope with them. This was suggested by the experience of the lowest-income experimental districts, which had to turn to seeking outside funds for their major problems.

6. Elective councilmen and local political clubs will try to monopolize the function of linking the public and local community groups with the city government and may succeed, as in the case of the Office of Neighborhood Government, in withholding resources and authority from district offices that they regard as competitors.

7. The program creates a new set of offices that cost money and the time of existing officials, when there is a need to reduce the costs of government.

An optimistic interpretation of the findings would be:

1. The field administrators of the departments want increased autonomy and are willing to work with other agencies locally to solve interdependent problems. The political circumstances of a lame-duck administration and a political feud between the mayor and City Council were unusually unfavorable; under better circumstances more delegation of authority, local budgetary discretion, and interagency cooperation could have been attained.

2. Even under the circumstances, useful projects involving interagency coordination were carried out. A strongly supported program, carried on for

more than two years, would have had more successes and significantly improved service integration and service delivery. Indeed, some major problems of urban communities cannot possibly be solved without such coordinated local action of many city departments and of community leaders and groups.

3. The program did not reach the general public because that was not its job, as finally formulated. The increased satisfaction of those citizens who did contact city agencies in experimental districts shows the potential of a district administrative center able to monitor local service agencies and get them together to deal with problems. *If* the program had moved on to increase public access, through storefront Citizens Advice Bureaus, for instance, the improved district administrative capacity could have handled the load.

4. The strongly favorable attitudes of those most directly involved in the program—community leaders and local service officials—suggest that they saw in the limited successes of the program evidence of greater long-term potential, even though their overall ratings of services were not affected. Certainly they demonstrated a cooperative local climate for attempts of this kind.

5. The integration of local services, and provision of orderly community representation, are essential to the productive use of outside funds for rehabilitation of housing, human services, and other efforts to fight poverty and neighborhood decay. District management by itself cannot solve these problems, but it is a necessary condition to successful outside programs of renewal.

6. The favorable attitudes of community leaders and the general public to the idea of administrative decentralization and community boards suggest that the politicians will eventually find it advantageous to support these mechanisms and to use them themselves.

7. The costs of the district manager's office were very modest, and it could have paid for itself by a relatively small improvement in service delivery. If it were more strongly supported for a longer period of time, it might achieve significant service improvements without additional costs, or in a budget-cutting period it could work out a distribution of cuts that would be least painful in terms of community priorities.

We are not in a position to prove that either the optimistic or the pessimistic interpretation is right. Most of the research team lean toward the optimistic interpretation, but with conservative estimates of how much overall improvement in services the program can produce under realistic circumstances. None of us believe that administrative decentralization will revolutionize the quality of services or the quality of city life. Some of the problems of the cities are deeply embedded in the class structure of society, the nature of a competitive market economy, and the nature of bureaucracy. Improving these things is a complex and long-term job. But that is no reason for not trying to do better than we are now doing in running our cities. In our opinion the program of district managers and district cabinets is one that other cities should seriously consider trying. In the charter revision referendum of 1975, New York City's voters decided to make the district manager-district cabinet program part of the city charter, so we will see at least one big city working with this system in the coming years.

The Future of Neighborhood Government

The program we studied in New York City did not experiment with community representation; it deliberately restricted itself to administrative decentralization. But we believe that the New York City experience with the district manager and district cabinet is important to cities considering political decentralization as well.

Our results suggest—although as indicated earlier they do not prove—that coordination of city agencies at the district level has a potential for improvement of services and the solution of some neighborhood problems, without requiring significant additional resources. The potential return from administrative decentralization is therefore a resource on which local community councils could draw to make their constituents better off without raising taxes or diverting resources from other districts. Indeed, without access to a district administrative office of some kind, a local council would find itself just another petitioner at the central administration of the city services. Some analysts fear that community representation would stimulate rising demands in the face of scarce resources, thereby leading to conflicts between communities, particularly along racial and class lines. But if each community has a *potential for improving services through better coordination of existing activities* at the community level, and is better adapting these activities to local priorities, then some at least of the community's demands could be met.

An additional resource, much used in middle-class communities, is voluntary local action of the citizens. The big cities, particularly their poorer neighborhoods, have been weak in voluntary organization for improvement. However, the experience of tenant control in troubled public housing projects, of housing cooperatives to manage and rehabilitate buildings that were not viable under private ownership, and some of the community action programs in poverty areas, are examples in the poorest neighborhoods of the benefits of voluntary, community-oriented action. The presence of a local government body, with access to the administrators of local public services, might help to bring out voluntary self-help activities in all types of communities.

Furthermore, organized "consumer" groups of local citizens acting under the aegis of a district government would be in a better position to *monitor the performance of public services* than either inspectors within the bureaucracy or citywide citizen groups. Park maintenance, street maintenance, housing code enforcement, drug law enforcement, and other local services are highly visible to the people in the neighborhood. If they could provide systematic feedback to local service managers and committees of a district government, the productivity of city services in the district might be much improved. This forms another resource on which a district council could draw, with the help of a manager and service cabinet.

Finally, there is the question of dealing with the massive problems that arise from poverty and its attendant social demoralization. The experience of community action programs in the 1960s certainly does not make for optimism that there are inexpensive (or even expensive) solutions to these problems. But the combination of legitimate community representation, local administrative coordination, and mobilization of community self-help groups is probably essential to the *productive use of large outside investments* in either physical rehabilitation or retraining and rehabilitation of people. Without local coordination of all government services and involvement of such community leadership as exists, the tendency is for buildings and facilities once rehabilitated to deteriorate again and for people to lose the benefits of training and rehabilitation programs.

The relationship between political and administrative decentralization of cities is necessarily speculative in the absence of a large-scale trial in this country. The decision of New York City's voters in 1975 was to give very modest authority to review and advise on city service delivery to appointive, rather than elective, community boards, working in collaboration with district managers and district cabinets. Since implementation of these changes is delayed by the city's financial crisis, it remains to be seen how this combination of reforms works out.

Notes

1. Susan and Norman Fainstein, "From the Folks Who Brought You Ocean Hill-Brownsville," *New York Affairs* 2, 1974, pp. 104-15.

2. See also R.K. Yin, R.W. Hearn, and P.M. Shapiro, "Administrative Decentralization of Municipal Services: Assessing the New York City Experience," *Policy Sciences* 5, 1974, pp. 57-70. Their study is based on judgmental coding of three interviews in each of five service agencies involved in the experiment.

Appendix

Program for the Decentralized Administration of Municipal Services in New York City Communities

Foreword

by Mayor John V. Lindsay

All cities today face a common problem—making government more responsive to the people. There have been many programs proposed that would restructure urban government in a new and significant way.

For the six years of my administration, I have been deeply involved in trying to make some of these proposals a reality. In 1967 we created ten Administrations, pulling together over fifty city departments to provide an effective mechanism for city-wide planning and ending much of the wasteful duplication that the former proliferation had caused.

In over 50 communities the Urban Action Task Force was established placing high ranking representatives of the Mayor in each one to help solve community problems.

Building upon these experiences, the time has come to take the very difficult and complex steps towards the decentralized administration of New York City government. Having created the ten Administrations to provide consistency and coordination on city-wide matters, it is now possible to extend this structure to the Community Planning District level to deal with neighborhood concerns.

This program will establish such a mechanism through a process of decentralizing the administration of city services and integrating the operations of city departments initially in five Community Planning Districts of New York City. It is, I believe, an extraordinary plan which moves New York City further in the direction of neighborhood government than any other city in the country. It has taken over eighteen months to develop, incorporating the lessons we have learned from our extensive experience with other programs in the past.

The eight major agencies involved in this program are: the Police Department; the Administrations for Environmental Protection; Housing and Development; Human Resources; Health Services; Parks, Recreation and Cultural Affairs; Transportation; and the Addiction Services Agency. These agencies will take the following steps:

This appendix contains the official text of the program for administrative decentralization in New York City, as published by the Office of the Mayor, City of New York, December 1971.

1. Each agency will grant increased authority to their district officers to deal locally with operational neighborhood problems, on the model of Police Commissioner Murphy's successful decentralization of command within the Police Department.
2. The present fragmented service area boundaries for all of these operating departments will be brought as closely as possible into conformity with each other and the Community Planning District lines so that coordinated planning and delivery of existing services can be improved.
3. The local commanding officers of each agency, like the Police Precinct Captain and the Sanitation District Superintendent, will join together in a District Service Cabinet so that they will have a formal mechanism to plan jointly for the most effective deployment of their men and equipment to meet the district's needs.
4. A District Manager with extensive experience in city administration has been appointed by the Mayor to chair the local Service Cabinet and to coordinate the operations of the various local departments in responding to the interagency problems that are most difficult to deal with effectively in the community.

This is not an "add-on" program. Unlike other efforts to improve the delivery of services in a given neighborhood by adding substantial new resources, this program is aimed at increasing the productivity of existing resources.

We plan to evaluate this program in the initial five communities carefully. The areas have been chosen to provide us with a representative cross section of our varied City. The program itself has been designed without requiring the expenditure of additional city resources. If successful in improving the municipal services delivered to the people of these five districts, we plan to extend this approach to the entire City. To assure an adequate evaluation of the results detailed planning has been carried out with a broad range of researchers, including the National Science Foundation, the Bureau of Applied Social Research at Columbia University, the City University, and the U.S. Department of Health, Education and Welfare, which granted essential funds to implement this overall project.

No program, of course, can be the ultimate panacea for urban ills. Government must be continually ready and able to adapt to new situations and new needs as they arise. I strongly believe that this program provides flexibility to New York City government and makes it more efficient and responsive to neighborhood concerns.

This program clearly marks a new dimension in the government of this City and moves government administration further into the communities where it belongs.

**Program for the Decentralized Administration
of Municipal Services in New York City
Communities**

New York City municipal services are presently implemented through ten major
Administrations, each of which has a central structure in the offices downtown
and a local command in the communities where services reach the people. Many
decisions that can and should be made locally to meet neighborhood problems
and needs have in the past been referred to the central command for final
approval. The program of administrative decentralization and coordination will
place the power and responsibility for local decisions with the district officers of
each agency who work in the communities they serve. It will also establish a
local cabinet of these officers to integrate the planning and operations of the
multiple city services in each of these areas.

There are eight key components which will be implemented as part of this
far-reaching change in the delivery of municipal services.

I. District Selection

Five Community Planning Districts have been chosen for the immediate
operation of this program: Crown Heights and Bushwick in Brooklyn, Wakefield-
Edenwald in the Bronx, Washington Heights-Inwood in Manhattan, and the
Rockaways in Queens. The communities vary in size, population, income levels,
historic sense of community, pattern of agency boundary line congruity, present
demographic composition, and municipal service needs. It is critically important
for purposes of comparison and evaluation that the five communities initially
chosen represent a cross section of New York City's communities with a full
range of the city's problems and conditions.

The pilot districts for this project do not include any of the three Model
Cities Neighborhoods, since the Model Cities Administration is the mechanism
for neighborhood development in these areas. However, the entire Model Cities
approach to decentralization is seen as complementary to this new approach
with many potentially significant lessons to be derived from both programs.
Both are aimed at increasing government responsiveness to community concerns
by improving city service delivery. For this reason, both approaches will be
jointly monitored and evaluated, so that the lessons learned from the experiences of one may be applied to further the development of the other. This gives
New York the unique advantage of being able to test and evaluate diversified
approaches to neighborhood development at the same time.

II. Redistricting

Few people who have been active in New York City's neighborhoods deny the need to redistrict agency service lines so as to conform them more closely to one another. The present crazy-quilt pattern of administrative districts prohibits effective coordination of services. For over twenty years, individuals, elected officials, government administrators, and civic groups have called attention to the difficulties and inefficiencies resulting from these confusing overlapping, and non-conforming lines. Despite the need, no comprehensive effort to move towards conformity has been undertaken until these experiments.

There are strong and sound objections to redistricting which must be borne in mind. First, the ideal service boundary may vary from agency to agency, based on the nature of the work performed by the agency. So, for example, a Parks maintenance district would reflect the amount of park land in a district, while the Department of Social Services area would be based upon the number of public assistance recipients, and the Police precinct boundary upon the intensity of criminal activity in the area.

Second, the location of existing capital facilities such as Police precinct houses, Sanitation garages, Welfare centers, Hospitals, and Department of Water Supply yards often reflect present service boundaries. Any change in agency lines may overload existing facilities, and leave others underutilized. Particularly in this time of budgetary pressures, we cannot lightly undertake a program of redistricting which would require new construction.

Third, even when facilities and functional needs permit the creation of common boundaries, the cost of actually changing the lines must not be ignored. For each agency, time, attention and energy must be diverted from the daily delivery of services to plan and manage this transition.

Fourth, both the State and Federal governments have established programs requiring some form of local districting, and have failed to consider preexisting local district lines in setting forth the new lines.

One of the most significant aspects of the experiments described here has been to develop a process to conform agency lines in the face of such objections, and to measure the advantages of conformity against the costs involved in making such changes. Until now we could only cite the arguments "pro" and "con," without being able to measure the actual costs and benefits.

With these experiments, we can substitute facts and experience for rhetoric.

Not surprisingly, no single set of city-wide administrative lines meet both city departmental and community criteria for a set of boundaries to which all other agency lines can be conformed. We have used the existing Community Planning District lines as our base since they come closest city-wide to combining an historic sense of community with a size consistent with the planning and operational needs of city service agencies.

The Community Planning District lines were adopted by the City Planning

Commission in 1968 after extensive public hearings. Procedures for altering these lines are broadly established, but have never been utilized. In several instances we are recommending changes in the Community Planning District lines.

Measures have been taken to conform the service area boundaries as closely as possible for the following Administrations:

(a) Environmental Protection Administration (Sanitation)
(b) Housing and Development Administration (Housing Maintenance Programs)
(c) Human Resources Administration (Department of Social Services, Youth Services Agency, Addiction Services Agency, Agency for Child Development, and Manpower and Career Development Agency). We will also strongly recommend that the Council Against Poverty use these lines as their base, when it redistricts the Community Corporations based on the 1970 census data.
(d) Health Services Administration (Department of Health, Department of Mental Health, Comprehensive Health Planning).
(e) Parks, Recreation, and Cultural Affairs Administration (Parks Department and Recreation Department).
(f) Police Department

III. Formal Delegation of Increased Powers to District Officers

Each community of this city has its own special needs. It is impossible to frame solutions to these individual issues from centralized offices downtown. The city agency officers closest to community problems are the men who work there— men such as the local Precinct Captain, the Sanitation Superintendent, and the Parks Department General Foreman. On a daily basis they are faced with the task of providing services to meet community needs.

Until now, local service chiefs have not had the discretionary authority to adapt their individual operations to meet specific community problems most effectively. Often they have been required to seek approval for any change in operating policy from a central office. This has resulted in frustrating delays in adapting service delivery to immediate neighborhood problems.

Even more detrimental to the functioning of effective government, local agency officers have been unable to work fully with each other at the district level. Each must seek approval for his individual actions from his own superiors in the chain of command before proceeding in joint action with other city agencies.

This program attempts to meet this problem directly by a process of administrative decentralization which will transfer specific powers and responsibilities now vested in central commands to the local agency officers. All local districts will be given greatly expanded responsibilities to vary the deployment of their resources to meet local needs more efficiently and effectively.

This proposal builds directly on the extremely successful command decentralization that has already been implemented by Police Commissioner Murphy over the past year. Precinct commanders have been made local "Police Commissioners," with greatly increased responsibility within their precincts to meet both day-to-day police operations and the development of long term police strategy to deal with particular community needs. Precinct commanders were assigned additional planning personnel, additional administrative staff from central Police headquarters, increased flexibility in the deployment of their resources, new measures of performance, and additional training.

This command decentralization is one of the most significant and complex components of the entire program. In some cases it has meant changing operating procedures that have existed for over fifty years.

In agencies such as Police, Parks, and Sanitation, identifiable district commanders who will exercise these increased powers presently are stationed in the community.

In other agencies such as the Human Resources Administration, Health Services Administration, and Housing and Development Administration we have refined the local structure to provide for each community the same broad, cross-cutting focus that the creation of the Administrations has given us on city-wide problems. For each Administration, we have created a local officer responsible for all the superagency's operations in the area.

Without having first grouped the over fifty independent, isolated departments into ten broad functional Administrations we could not have taken the steps specified in this program. It is only because we have achieved the Cabinet structure at a city-wide level that we can now make these advances locally. For each central Administration a single local officer has been designated who is responsible for the coordination of all operations in the Community Planning District.

For each community and its residents this improvement means increased responsiveness and flexibility. New programs may be developed and operating procedures altered by the local agency officers to increase agency effectiveness in their community. Operating procedures may then be more closely adapted at the discretion of the local agency officer rather than having constraints imposed from above that may not be relevant to the community's concerns.

This greatly increased flexibility to deploy men, equipment, and resources as the agency officer deems necessary will make it possible to adapt to the special concerns of each community more quickly and efficiently. For instance, under changes that the Police Commissioner has already put in effect, a Police Commander now has discretion over deploying a percentage of his men to plainclothes units. Comparably, the Sanitation Superintendent will have increased control over an entire range of sanitation services including collections, street sweeping and bulk pick-up. In each of the participating agencies similar kinds of powers will be transferred to local officers to tailor the agency's delivery of services to particular community needs.

These new powers and responsibilities are essential to achieving greater interagency cooperation. The local Police Commander will find it easier to work more closely with local officials from the Human Resources Administration on addiction problems. The Parks Foreman and Sanitation Superintendent can more easily develop a joint program to keep a park and the surrounding neighborhood clean. And the local Health Services Administrator could work with the Youth Services Director to develop health programs for youth.

IV. Creation of the District Service Cabinet

There does not exist in the city today a mechanism to bring local service chiefs together in each Community Planning District.

In each of the five communities there will be a District Service Cabinet composed of all the local agency chiefs participating in this experiment. This Service Cabinet will have direct power to take action on issues of interagency concern. Cabinet members will focus the combined resources of their departments on such multi-agency problems as methods to deal with addicts on the street; a community referral system to provide a central information pool on social services, housing, and welfare programs; or a joint Sanitation, Traffic, Water Supply, Highway, Police and Gas and Electricity program to deal with coordination of all street improvement.

By meeting together, the Cabinet members will be able to share their individual work experience and knowledge about how to get things done. They will review agency priorities and develop new programs for the community based upon these priorities. They will present an integrated approach to service delivery for individual communities.

At present, on too many problems and in too many communities, the most effective integration of service delivery between the different departments is carried out by elected officials or local groups, who are too often the only local 'bridge' between two or more operating city departments on a particular problem. The creation of District Service Cabinets establishes a governmental mechanism to fill this vacuum and will significantly ease this pressure on local groups.

In several communities in the city, Urban Action Task Force offices have conducted such local cabinets with remarkable impact, given the handicaps of non-conforming district lines, the absence of command responsibility on the part of many agency personnel, and the lack of any single district information system to provide the needed data and support. We have learned a great deal from these efforts and have tried to build on them in these pilot projects.

Significant increases in city agency productivity can result from the creation of a forum that brings agency officers together locally who can identify needed services for a community and eliminate unnecessary duplication, free up resources to provide more efficient service, and plan programs complementary to each other.

In each district, the Cabinet will have the following agency representatives:

Addiction Services Agency—District Director
Environmental Protection Agency—Sanitation District Superintendent; Water Resources "Desk Officer"
Housing and Development Administration—HDA Area Administrator
Human Resources Administration—HRA District Director
Health Services Administration—Neighborhood Health Services Manager or District Health Officer
Parks, Recreation, and Cultural Affairs—General Foreman for Maintenance; Assistant Supervisor of Recreation
Police Department—Precinct Commander
Transportation Administration—Highways Borough Foreman; Traffic "Desk Officer"

In addition, the Community Superintendent of Schools will be invited to become a member of the Cabinet in each district. Other agencies, such as the Fire Department, will be involved as their participation becomes essential to the development of locally responsive programs.

V. Appointment of a District Manager

For each district affected by this program, the Mayor has appointed a District Manager who will chair the Service Cabinet composed of the ranking district officers in each of the key decentralized agencies. This position is analogous to that of a professional City Manager found in many U.S. cities. The District Manager will bring to his position management expertise and extensive knowledge of city government operations. He will provide full-time support to the Service Cabinet on priority problems. Members of the Service Cabinet will continue to report to their present chain of command in their agencies.

The District Manager will be responsible for developing items of common concern in the community that require interagency action by the Cabinet. For instance, he might point out the need for coordinating the efforts of housing, fire, health and sanitation inspectors in a certain part of the community. The Parks and Sanitation Departments might work with a planner from the City Planning Commission to turn a rubbish strewn vacant lot into a small playground area or vest pocket park. The Police Department and the Traffic Department might combine with the Sanitation Department to ticket illegally parked cars that prevent effective street sweeping. The District Manager is aware of the need for these kinds of efforts and will work with Cabinet members to initiate programs for joint agency action.

VI. Decentralized Staff Assignments

Overhead agency staff from the Bureau of the Budget, and the City Planning Commission will be assigned to work under the District Manager to aid the Service Cabinet in resolving local problems and planning to meet district priorities. These staff will bring needed technical expertise into the Cabinet decision-making process. They will provide a direct line of communication from the Cabinet and District Manager to the Bureau of the Budget and City Planning Commission. They will also develop new procedures in coordination with agency personnel to make agency procedures more responsive to community needs.

Other technical assistance will be channeled to the District Manager and Cabinet through cooperating public and private institutions such as the City University of New York, the New York City Rand Institute, and Columbia University's Bureau of Applied Social Research.

VII. Development of a Single District-Wide Management Information System

At present, only a minimum of a required information from the many agencies serving a community is available on a basis that allows one agency to use another's data in addressing local problems. Without such a common information system there is no way that government or citizens can comprehensively address the complex, multi-agency problems that require action by several agencies. For example:

Fire Department data on false alarms is not correlated with Police data on arrests and complaints, with Housing data on the location of abandoned buildings, or with Youth Services Agency data on the residence and hangouts of youthful offenders who need counseling.

Similarly, outreach and community organization work is provided by all of the following agencies to some degree, with no Community Planning District-wide effort to identify either overlap or gaps in their coverage: the Department of Social Services, Community Development Agency, Department of Health, Department of Rent and Housing Maintenance, and Addiction Services Agency.

Nowhere is there in any Community Planning District a comprehensive, community-wide survey of the recreation resources and needs, as identified separately by the Department of Recreation, the Board of Education, the Housing Authority, the Youth Services Agency and the Police.

Under the program now being implemented, each community will have an information system that brings together both the *needs* and the *resources* identified by each agency. More important, the data collected by all city agencies will be developed in such a way that comparisons can be made, needs most clearly identified, and the resources of all agencies most effectively deployed.

The Management Information System in each of the target neighborhoods, when completed, will provide District Managers and the local Service Cabinets with full data on resources in the district, expense and capital budget break-outs for the district, service complaint analyses, and the status of on-going city construction projects in the neighborhood with completion dates and intermediary stages. The System will also include information prepared by the City Planning Commission on the target neighborhoods including physical and demographic characteristics from the 1970 census supplemented by Health, Housing, and Police data on local needs.

With this information system, members of each Service Cabinet will be able to weigh agency inputs against outputs, to measure the performance of most agency operations by standards which better reflect their real impact on a particular community, and to deploy their resources in a way which best supplements the resources of other City agencies.

VIII. Preparation of a Neighborhood Budget

The budget is the key policy-making tool in the city government. The shape and composition of the budget must ultimately be made subject to input from each community.

At present, the City issues a report on Capital projects either proposed or underway for each Community Planning District. This is a major step. However, it still does not identify any Community Planning District's share of such large "lump sum" items as major parks maintenance or highway strip paving.

Nor does the City have the capacity to identify the total amount of Expense Budget funds annually going to a given Community Planning District for the operating costs of city agencies.

Over the past year, the Bureau of the Budget has undertaken organizational changes to decentralize greater responsibility for budget administration to the major operating agencies. Parallel to these steps, an attempt will be made to assemble a community budget that identifies the dollar value of all services going into each of the Community Planning Districts. Because few city agencies gather their data on a Community Planning District basis and because the dollar value of overhead services used in any Community Planning District is very difficult to measure, the formulation of a community budget will not come quickly or easily. Nevertheless, the community budget is absolutely essential as a management tool to make the most sensitive resource deployment decisions for each community.

Conclusion

Our priority in this program is to provide an integrated agency structure at the district level to improve the efficiency and responsiveness of city services in meeting community needs. Without this administrative decentralization, it will be impossible to have both meaningful and realistic citizen participation in city government.

It is clear from our local consultations on earlier neighborhood proposals that the city government should not arbitrarily superimpose a new community structure onto the present network of active organizations such as Community Boards, Community School Boards, Community Corporations, Precinct Councils, or Block, Civic, and Tenant Associations that already exist. Moreover, government attempts in this city and elsewhere to open governmental processes further to community participation have too often generated expectations to which the government machinery was not organized to respond.

Implicit in proceeding with the present program is a major conclusion based upon past experiences: that a great deal must first be done in terms of reorganizing the city's own internal administrative mechanism, before developing any new system of local citizen participation.

There has been far too much rhetoric about the need for changes in the city's governmental structure without adequate attention to the extraordinarily complex management steps that must precede such changes. The proposals discussed here represent eighteen months of detailed work by key city agencies in the difficult, often tedious, and sometimes extremely sensitive process of changing the administration and its bureaucracy. Many of these steps have been taken for granted by proponents of further change.

We have learned how difficult it is to bring about such organization without disrupting the flow of government programs, and how critically important it is that such change be managed in the most professional way to assure successful implementation. Otherwise, we will have what we have seen so often before— sound, promising ideas that fall flat because of poor execution.

In our attempts to modify city government machinery in the delivery of services to each neighborhood, we have worked to assure that the quality of execution is on the same level as the soundness of this proposal.

For those who are disappointed with the process, or the scope, of these proposals—and there are always some—we would urge that they not let their enthusiasm for a government sensitive to each community's needs obscure the need to carry out the transition to such a system with deliberateness, skill, and thoroughness.

These are vital steps in making government more responsive to community needs and concerns. They represent a major experiment in restructuring of city government. What they will teach us and what we all may learn from them will be critically important in the further integration of government services at the neighborhood level.

Index

About the Authors

Allen H. Barton is director of the Bureau of Applied Social Research and a professor of sociology at Columbia University. He has studied the response of communities to disaster, decision-making behavior of juries, and the attitudes and behaviors of national leaders in the U.S. and Yugoslavia, and has written a number of articles on methods of research.

Norman I. Fainstein has the Ph.D. in Political Science from Massachusetts Institute of Technology and is an Associate Professor of Urban Affairs for the New School for Social Research in New York. Dr. Fainstein has published books and articles on urban social movements and politics.

Susan S. Fainstein has degrees from Radcliffe College and Boston University, and the Ph.D. from Massachusetts Institute of Technology. Dr. Fainstein is Associate Professor of Urban Planning at Livingston College, Rutgers University, New Jersey, and has published several books and a number of articles on urban social movements and urban politics.

Nathalie S. Friedman is an alumna of Barnard College and received the Ph.D. in Sociology from Columbia University. She has been chairman of the Sociology Department at Stern College for Women of Yeshiva University, and is currently a Senior Research Associate at the Bureau of Applied Social Research and Lecturer in sociology at Barnard College. Dr. Friedman has carried out several studies in the field of education, dealing with school-community relations and the impact of Federal programs in aid of low-income college students, and is working on a study of early retirement among printers displaced by computer technology.

Stanley J. Heginbotham received the Ph.D. in political science from the Massachusetts Institute of Technology. His previous research dealt with bureaucracy at the village level in India and resulted in the book, *Culture in Conflict: The Four Faces of Indian Bureaucracy*. He has been an Associate Professor of Political Science at Columbia, and is now Assistant Chief, Foreign Policy and National Defense Division, Congressional Research Service, Library of Congress.

Joel D. Koblenz received the Master of Business Administration and Master of Philosophy degrees at Columbia. He has taught in the Economics department at Columbia and is now the manager of financial services and controls on the corporate staff for W.R. Grace's chemical business.

Theresa F. Rogers received the Ph.D. from Columbia and has done research and teaching in the field of medical sociology. She is now a lecturer in sociology at Barnard College and a Senior Research Associate at the Bureau of Applied Social Research, working on a study of early retirement among printers.

John M. Boyle has degrees from the University of Notre Dame, George Washington University, and the Ph.D. from Columbia University. He has taught government at the City University of New York and St. John's University in New York, and is now a Staff Associate in the Division of Sociomedical Sciences, School of Public Health, Columbia University.

Ronald Brumback has Masters degrees in economics and business administration and is a candidate for the Ph.D. in economics at Columbia University. He is now a member of the Boston Consulting Group.